D1508109

LifeTraining²

LifeTraining²

by
Dr. Joe White

TYNDALE

Tyndale House Publishers, Wheaton, Illinois

LifeTraining 2
Copyright © 2000 by Joe White. All rights reserved. International
copyright secured.

Library of Congress Cataloging-in-Publication Data

White, Joe, 1948-
      p. cm.
   Includes bibliographical references.
   ISBN 1-56179-577-1
   1. Teenagers—Prayer books and devotions—English. 2.
Family—Prayer books and devotions—English. 3. Christian life—
Prayer books and devotions—English. I. Title.
BV4531.2.W477   1998
242'. 63—dc21

                           97-47626
                              CIP

A Focus on the Family book published by Tyndale House
Publishers, Wheaton, Illinois.

Unless otherwise noted, Scripture quotations are from the New
American Standard Bible, © 1960, 1963, 1968, 1971, 1973, 1975, 1977,
and 1995 by The Lockman Foundation. Used by permission.
Quotations identified NIV are from the HOLY BIBLE, NEW INTER-
NATIONAL VERSION ®. Copyright © 1973, 1978, 1984 by the
International Bible Society. Used by permission of Zondervan
Publishing House. All rights reserved. Quotations identified as KJV
are from the King James Version.

People's names and certain details of the case studies in this book
have been changed to protect the privacy of the individuals
involved. However, the facts of what happened and the underlying
principles have been conveyed as accurately as possible.

Front cover design: Image Studios

Printed in the United States of America

00 01 02 03 04 05/10 9 8 7 6 5 4 3 2 1

to my dad —
whose lifestyle and family devotionals at
the breakfast table during my growing-up
years inspired this book

Contents

AcKnowLedGmenTs

Like all authors, I could not have accomplished my work without significant help from others. In the case of this book, that's even more true than usual, as several people helped me to write the devotionals that appear here and that I pray will be a blessing to you and your family. I would like to acknowledge and thank those people here at the front of this book; they're also introduced more fully at the beginning of the sections to which they contributed.

These are the folks and the parts for which they wrote devotionals:

Will Cunningham (1 Corinthians)
Cooper White (Philippians; 1 & 2 Thessalonians; 1 & 2 Timothy)
Bob Waliszewski (Colossians)
Brett Causey (Titus; Philemon; 2 Peter; Epistles of John; Jude)
Jamie Jo Braner (1 Peter)
Debbi-Jo White (Digging Deeper)

My deep and sincere thanks to all these contributors, whose outstanding work made this book possible.

InTroduCTion

Today as I finish this love letter from my heart to yours, I'm sitting just inside a tall, picturesque window in our third-floor condominium in Breckenridge, Colorado.

It's the day after Easter. The weather outside is perfect: 38 degrees, no wind, and bright sun. Just beyond my window, six inches of fresh, powdery snow cover the ground.

The past three days I've been in paradise, snowboarding with my two sons and one of my daughters. We've raced down these gorgeous Colorado mountains until we fall into the hot tub in delightful exhaustion at night. Our boards have been our race cars. Our friendship and bond of love with one another have been our ultimate pleasures. As we've sprinkled the days with prayer, Bible study, and hilarious games around the fireplace, I can honestly tell you that "it just can't get any better than this" (this side of heaven, that is).

Last night, however, I didn't sleep well. I tossed and turned at midnight, 3:00 A.M., and 6:00 A.M. I was thinking of *you* and *your family*. I wanted to complete this book. I wanted you to find, own, and hold dear to your heart all the amazing truths that God's Word has brought to my family through the years. At the time I'm writing this, my kids are 23, 21, 20, and 17. They (and their mother) are my best friends. They all want to serve God with their lives.

The truths of Scripture have scraped them up off the floor when life in the public school, the pressure of high school sports, and thwarted relationships threatened to crush the life out of them. God's words have healed our broken relationships when my kids have wanted to tell me where to jump and how high! The truths from God's lips have taught us to forgive ourselves and one another so we could celebrate the next day together as if it were our last.

1

So today, as they're all back up in the mountains, snowboarding their legs off, my pleasure is to be here with you—praying and hoping that this book will help you to develop a personal walk with Christ that will cause you to smile from your heart when you lay your head on your pillow each night and when you wake up each morning. I also pray that you and your family can begin to celebrate friendships and bonding experiences like those which, by God's amazing grace, He has given to me and the ones who call me Daddy.

I'm not the least bit sad that I'm not on the mountains with my kids today, because I'm skiing the slopes of my dreams that in the next year, as you and your family use the devotionals in this book, your lives will be enriched. Together, let's enjoy the snowcapped trails of peace, love, and joy with the One who prepared our way.

MArK

Less than 40 years (and perhaps as few as 20) passed between the crucifixion of Jesus and when the Holy Spirit breathed words of truth into Mark's mind and inspired him to record his Gospel. It is the first known written record of Jesus' life, death, and resurrection. John Mark was a companion of both Paul and Peter. This "to the point" book provides a wonderful description of the activity of the Messiah.

Mark moves quickly through Jesus' amazing life with intense and captivating action. The word *immediately* is used over 40 times as Mark attempts to motivate the Gentiles in Rome and throughout the world to understand and to believe in Jesus. Mark will show us that Jesus is the Messiah, the Christ, the Savior, the One who came to save the world.

THE MESSENGER

"As it is written in Isaiah the prophet: 'Behold, I send My messenger ahead of You, who will prepare Your way; the voice of one crying in the wilderness, "Make ready the way of the Lord, make His paths straight."' John the Baptist appeared in the wilderness preaching a baptism of repentance for the forgiveness of sins."

↩ Mark 1:2-4

> Listen, my children, and you shall hear
> Of the midnight ride of Paul Revere,
> On the eighteenth of April, in Seventy-five;
> Hardly a man is now alive
> Who remembers that famous day and year.
>
> He said to his friend, "If the British march
> By land or sea from the town tonight,
> Hang a lantern aloft in the belfry arch
> Of the North Church tower as a signal light..."

This Henry Wadsworth Longfellow poem is one I still recall from my high school days. Paul Revere is an American hero who will never be forgotten—a chosen messenger who risked his own safety to warn his fellow colonists that the British were coming.

What an honor! I can almost hear the American officers speaking with words of faith and assurance: "We can depend on Paul Revere."

Musician Michael W. Smith, a longtime friend, used to be an opening act who "prepared the way" for Amy Grant and her electrifying concerts. When Smitty's own career took him to the top of the charts, he chose promising but unknown groups like dc Talk and Jars of Clay to lead the way and open for him. Before long, those groups were well known and on their way to their own individual successes.

But just imagine the honor of being chosen by God to "open" for Jesus. It was up to John the Baptist to prepare the people for what was to come. (And Paul Revere thought the British were big news!) John the Baptist was announcing news about God's only Son, who was coming to earth for a one-time appearance to live as a man and die for all our sins.

We need to heed John's message. The next time Jesus appears, there won't be any warning.

Discussion Starters:

1. In what ways are you as a Christian like John the Baptist?
2. What character qualities does God expect from Jesus' modern-day messengers?
3. As Paul Revere warned of the British attack on America, how can you warn your friends at school of Satan's attacks?

Lifeline:

Consider how you can be a "John the Baptist" in your own home.

EAGER FISHERMEN

"As [Jesus] was going along by the Sea of Galilee, He saw Simon and Andrew, the brother of Simon, casting a net in the sea; for they were fishermen. And Jesus said to them, 'Follow Me, and I will make you become fishers of men.' Immediately they left their nets and followed Him."

⌐ Mark 1:16-18

My next-door neighbor Gary Smalley told me a story about a guy who was ice fishing with his golden retriever. Scattered across the ice were many little huts, each containing a fisherman or two, a fire for warmth, and a hole drilled into the ice from which to catch the fish. The guy with the dog caught a huge fish, but as he pulled the "whopper" up to the surface, the line broke. He tried to grab the fish with his hands, but he missed. The dog then tried to grab the fish with his mouth, lost his balance, fell into the hole, and disappeared beneath the ice.

The fisherman was crushed. The dog had been his best fishing buddy. Now what would he do? But he only had to grieve for about 60 seconds. That's when he heard the guy in the next fishing hut screaming because a dog had popped up out of his hole in the ice and into his hut!

Gary tells me the story is true, but it sounds a little fishy to me! Anyway, I like eager fishermen because it's the guys who really work hard who have the most fun—and usually catch the most fish!

My teenage son Cooper and I pray for his seven best school friends every single night. Every Thursday morning, he brings them to our house for doughnuts and a Bible study. Some of them don't know Christ personally. But Cooper is a persistent fisherman, eager to "catch" his friends for God.

My 16-year-old friend Missy led three of her Iowa friends to Christ one day last fall. She would dive through the ice to catch more friends for God!

Eager fishermen can be found in all age groups, different churches, all 50 states, and most nations. If you enjoy a good challenge, why don't you join us today?

Discussion Starters:

1. What does "fishing for men" mean?
2. Do you think the "fishing for men" invitation was primarily for Peter and Andrew, who were fishermen? Or is it for everyone? Explain.
3. Sit down as a family. Focus on one person at a time as each of the other family members identifies a positive quality of the person and how Jesus might put it to good use as that person follows Him.

Lifeline:

Be an eager fisherman wherever God takes you today.

CARRYING FRIENDS TO JESUS

"And they came, bringing to [Jesus] a paralytic, carried by four men. Being unable to get to Him because of the crowd, they removed the roof above Him; and when they had dug an opening, they let down the pallet on which the paralytic was lying. And Jesus seeing their faith said to the paralytic, 'Son, your sins are forgiven.'"

↪ Mark 2:3-5

Larry is a helicopter mechanic for the Ohio Highway Patrol. He has been a Christian for many years and has walked with God with a peace in his heart that only a true Christian understands. He works on helicopters for a particular highway patrolman who didn't know Jesus . . . in the least. For over a year, Larry prayed for him and invited him to church—to no avail.

Finally, Larry invited the officer to a Promise Keepers event in Pittsburgh where I was speaking. During the event, the patrolman gave his heart to Christ, and he has never been the same. His "spiritual paralysis" was healed, and his sins were forgiven. He's now a happy man. (But watch out if you see a helicopter overhead; he *still* might give you a speeding ticket!)

Adam is 15 and is the best athlete in our school. Coming from the streets of New Orleans, he had a hard childhood. As a kid, he was kicked out of school more than once for his behavior. But every week his friends bring him to my house for a sophomore Bible study. I'm confident that he will meet Jesus soon. He, too, will never be the same.

Across America and around the world, caring friends still bring their spiritually paralyzed peers to Jesus the same way the guys in Capernaum lowered their friend through the roof when Jesus came to town.

By the way, Jesus is visiting your town today. Whom do you know who might need directions—or a personal escort—to see Him?

Discussion Starters:

1. Friends take friends to rock concerts. Friends take friends to football games. Why do relatively few friends bring friends to Jesus?
2. How many friends of yours can you think of who need to know Jesus today?
3. Over the next year, what steps can you take to help your friends see Jesus more clearly?

Lifeline:

When a friend is hurting, let him or her see Jesus in you.

FORGIVENESS—THE ULTIMATE FAMILY GIFT

"Immediately Jesus, aware in His spirit that they were reasoning that way within themselves, said to them, 'Why are you reasoning about these things in your hearts? Which is easier, to say to the paralytic, "Your sins are forgiven"; or to say, "Get up, and pick up your pallet and walk"?' "

↢ Mark 2:8-9

Bob is a flying ace. Twice he has been awarded the prestigious navy "Top Gun" distinction as the hottest F-16 pilot in the sky. His love for flying is surpassed only by his love for God and his endearment for his wife, Debbie, and their three precious children, who revere him not only as Dad, but as their hero and best friend as well.

Bob's quest to raise a model family underwent a foundation-shaking earthquake this year when his oldest daughter, Heather—unmarried and barely out of high school—brought a baby girl home from the hospital for Daddy to help her raise and support. Bob's emotional Richter scale catapulted to a record level.

Bob and Debbie had raised their girls with high morals and Christian convictions. They trained the girls in the way of the Lord, pouring their time, talents, and gifts into the girls' hearts. Heather was a wonderful child who loved to please her mom and dad. But she let herself fall into a relationship that culminated in sin which affected not only herself, but also her entire family.

Bob had a number of choices. He could kick his little girl out of the house; he could demand she get an abortion; or he could assure her that his love was unconditional and his forgiveness certain, in spite of the pain he felt.

The grace Bob has received from God not only saved his soul, but it also guides his lifestyle with the precision he uses to guide his F-16. Consequently, his choice was obvious. Any option but the last one would create a second mistake bigger than the first. Heather knows she will always be Daddy's little girl and has learned the value of her father's—and her Father's—love.

Discussion Starters:

1. Why do you think Bob's relationship with Jesus made his decision obvious?
2. How does Jesus' sacrifice on your behalf motivate you to serve your family members today?
3. Why do we hold grudges in the home? Is there anyone you need to forgive today?

Lifeline:

God gives us so much forgiveness that there's always enough to pass along to our friends and family members.

NEW WINE

"No one sews a patch of unshrunk cloth on an old garment; otherwise the patch pulls away from it, the new from the old, and a worse tear results. No one puts new wine into old wineskins; otherwise the wine will burst the skins, and the wine is lost and the skins as well; but one puts new wine into fresh wineskins."

↪ Mark 2:21-22

Larry King Live has become the most watched daily interview program in television history. Although Larry does not profess to be a Christian, he is very open to interviewing Christians in the public sector. One night Larry was in the Texas State Penitentiary on death row interviewing Karla Faye Tucker, a strikingly beautiful young lady in her mid-30s. She was awaiting execution for being an accomplice to a murder more than 14 years earlier. The murder was too gruesome for words, yet the mind-altering drugs she was on had left her in a state where, for a long time, she had felt no remorse. Indeed, her inner spirit was dead.

Then, with no explanation other than God's mercy, Karla Faye Tucker was completely transformed in that Houston prison by the Spirit of Christ. He came into her heart, granted her complete forgiveness, and gave her new life. Since that time, she had turned into an effective minister on death row, where she loved and served her fellow inmates each day. Her warmth, sincerity, and genuine love for Christ blew away Larry King and his viewing audience.

Karla Faye Tucker was not a *better* person after she accepted Jesus into her heart; she was a *new* person. She had a new mind and a new heart.

Becoming a Christian is not simply a matter of raising your hand, walking the aisle, getting baptized, or going to church (although those are all indications of a changed heart). Becoming a Christian is new wine in a new wineskin—everything old is left behind. When people see the new you, they see Jesus. You love Him, live for Him, and with time even become willing to die for Him. Without Christ, we're all on "death row." But with the pardon and release of Jesus, we are paroled from the prison of sin and find precious freedom—for eternity.

Discussion Starters:

1. What did Jesus mean when He said that new wine needs to be put in new wineskins?
2. What problems might you expect to encounter if you put your faith in Jesus yet continue to live like a non-Christian?
3. How does sinful living damage the cause of Christ when you call yourself a Christian?

Lifeline:

The acid test of true Christianity is how you treat the members of your family.

DIVIDED KINGDOM

"If a kingdom is divided against itself, that kingdom cannot stand. If a house is divided against itself, that house will not be able to stand."

⟿ Mark 3:24-25

It was extremely difficult to upset Jesus. He was the epitome of self-control, peace, and calmness under stress. This was a day, however, when the scribes (religious leaders) kicked over the beehive. In frustration and perhaps envy, they charged that His power came from Satan. Jesus boldly told them that a prolonged refusal to acknowledge the Holy Spirit would be something they would regret eternally (Mark 3:28-29). And as He pointed out their faulty logic, His defense was as true then as it is today: A house divided against itself can never stand.

In other words, Jesus wanted to know why Satan would be behind the casting out of demons (v. 22). That just wouldn't make sense. It would be like a general in a crucial battle suddenly turning around and shooting at his own men. Good always resists evil, and evil always resists good.

Satan will pull out all the stops in an attempt to divide your house. The most powerful institution that God has established on earth is the family, a home united in love and devoted to Christ. But if Satan divides your house, how long can it stand? So Satan whispers in your ear:

- "Your parents aren't being fair!"
- "Your little brother stole your flashlight. Get even."
- "Your big sister called you a liar behind your back."

And while he's working on you, he's also trying to get your parents to turn against each other. His list of accusations goes on and on for a lifetime. If you don't watch out, you begin to believe him. Then a wedge of strife forms between you and someone else. If allowed to remain, the wedge becomes bitterness, anger, fighting, and, eventually, a divided house.

The best way to keep this from happening is to stop listening to Satan and tune in to God's voice instead. God says to forgive, be patient, and stop judging one another. It's the voice of reason that will keep your house united forever.

Discussion Starters:

1. What are some recent temptations you've faced, threatening to create division between yourself and another family member? How did you respond in each instance?
2. As Christ forgave you, can you forgive others? Will you? How can you demonstrate your eagerness to forgive?
3. What are three things you can do this week to stop dividing and start uniting your family?

Lifeline:

Unite your family at all costs.

NOTHING LIKE REAL FAMILY

"Answering them, [Jesus] said, 'Who are My mother and My brothers?' Looking around at those who were sitting around Him, He said, 'Behold My mother and My brothers! For whoever does the will of God, he is My brother and sister and mother.'"

⌐ Mark 3:33-35

All we can see of the universe is that it contains millions of galaxies containing too many stars to count. They are all God's. He created them with a word . . . and that's just the known universe. The things beyond that we can't see are His as well.

All the people who ever lived on earth will one day bow down to God. He oversees the angels who joyfully give Him their worship. Everything that people consider important—such as gold, silver, and precious stones—is owned by God.

With all God has, what else could He ever want? God wants a family! He wants to bestow love and receive love. God wants sons and daughters to whom He can be a father. Each of His millions of children are even more special and unique to Him than you are to your parents. He knows about all your proudest moments in sports, music, and other achievements—as well as your innermost thoughts and fears. He rejoices when you do well. He hurts when you hurt. Jesus prays specifically for you, that you will find your way home to your heavenly Father.

Jesus came to earth to show us more about what God is like. Jesus' "family" consists of anyone willing to love Him, accept Him, and live for Him. He is eager for you to invite Him into your heart. And the second you do, welcome to the family!

Just remember that grateful kids honor and obey parents who give love so generously. Only fools take that kind of love for granted.

Discussion Starters:

1. How would you describe the fatherhood of God?
2. How does it make you feel when you think of yourself as an actual member of God's family?
3. Why should good kids want to honor and obey their parents?

Lifeline:

Gratitude is shown by obedience.

LITTLE BITTY SEEDS

"Behold, the sower went out to sow; as he was sowing, some seed fell beside the road, and the birds came and ate it up. Other seed fell on the rocky ground where it did not have much soil; and immediately it sprang up because it had no depth of soil. And after the sun had risen, it was scorched; and because it had no root, it withered away. Other seed fell among the thorns, and the thorns came up and choked it, and it yielded no crop. Other seeds fell into the good soil, and as they grew up and increased, they yielded a crop and produced thirty, sixty, and a hundredfold."

↪ Mark 4:3-8

Have you seen them? They're everywhere. There are more of them than people to count them, as many as snowflakes in a blizzard! What are they? God's "seeds."

Our nation is blessed with more "seeds" than any nation that ever existed. Almost every motel and hotel room in America has a Bible in a drawer. Thousands upon thousands of TV and radio stations across the country spread the seeds, around the clock, on invisible airwaves. Seeds are scattered throughout the Internet. Seeds are spread in churches on almost every street corner (in 453 denominations, by last count).

This is not to say that all the seeds are taking root. In Hollywood, for example, the seeds of God's Word seem to run up against a lot of rocky, shallow, and thorny soil. Studios create far more R-rated movies containing profanity and/or pornography than G-rated films, and you'll find more rated PG-13 than PG.

Seeds don't grow well in our public schools anymore. Public prayer was removed in 1962, the Ten Commandments in 1980, and Bibles in 1982.

Seeds don't produce well on primetime television either. Most of the time, the only mention of God you'll hear is as a profanity or oath when someone is angry, scared, or in trouble.

So where do God's seeds grow these days? They grow in hearts like yours. They grow in homes like yours. They grow whenever someone pushes the world aside and says, "God, You are my God. You're the God of my home. You're welcome here. You're in charge."

With that in mind, why not let some of God's seeds produce a harvest of fruit in your life today?

Discussion Starters:

1. Why does God compare His Word to seeds? (See Mark 4:13-20.)
2. How can your heart be like a garden that produces fruit for God?
3. How can you make your *home* such a garden?

Lifeline:

Let's make our homes the most fruitful gardens in all creation.

A SPECK OF FAITH

"How shall we picture the kingdom of God, or by what parable shall we present it? It is like a mustard seed, which, when sown upon the soil, though it is smaller than all the seeds that are upon the soil, yet when it is sown, it grows up and becomes larger than all the garden plants and forms large branches; so that the birds of the air can nest under its shade."

↶ Mark 4:30-32

My friend Neal Jeffery stuttered badly in high school. He was quarterback on his football team, but a receiver had to call the plays in the huddle. At the line of scrimmage, the fullback had to call the snap count for him. But Neal was a strong Christian with faith that God would bless him. Not only did he go on to play quarterback in college, but in the NFL as well. And not only did he learn to speak clearly, but he also became the most motivational Bible teacher that I know today. A high school kid who stutters may seem like an insignificant nobody to some people. But stir in a speck of faith and watch the mustard seed grow.

Debbie-Jo grew up without a father in her house. Although her mother struggled to hold the fragile family together, her brothers had numerous problems with the law. Drugs and alcohol were literally all around Debbie-Jo. Neither her family nor her friends read the Bible, prayed, or went to church. You can almost finish the story, can't you? A bad reputation in high school, perhaps? Rebellion against God? Broken home of her own?

Hardly, because she found a mustard seed of faith. She went to a Christian camp and accepted Jesus into her heart at age 15. The mustard seed grew. She now teaches a Bible study for 50 ladies, has raised four terrific Christian kids, and has been married for 25 wonderful years. I should know. She's married to me!

You may be the youngest, the smallest, the least popular, or the poorest. It makes no difference to God. Stir in a mustard seed of faith, and He'll bless you and use you beyond your wildest dreams.

Discussion Starters:

1. Why is a tiny speck of faith such a powerful thing?
2. Describe how your faith has been growing lately. Is it shooting up like a mustard seed, or does it need a bit of your personal attention to increase its growth?
3. How can you cultivate the mustard seed within you until it becomes a giant, productive tree for God?

Lifeline:

Home is a place where mustard seeds are planted and grow best.

FAITH DURING THE STORM

"And there arose a fierce gale of wind, and the waves were breaking over the boat so much that the boat was already filling up. Jesus Himself was in the stern, asleep on the cushion; and they woke Him and said to Him, 'Teacher, do You not care that we are perishing?' And He got up and rebuked the wind and said to the sea, 'Hush, be still.' And the wind died down and it became perfectly calm. And He said to them, 'Why are you afraid? How is it that you have no faith?' "

⮑ Mark 4:37-40

My young friend Jana is an inspiration to me. She has been sick for eight years and has had six major surgeries. Every two weeks, she spends six hours getting a transfusion that leaves her even more sick for a day or two. One such transfusion was improperly disinfected, leaving her with a gruesome two-year bout with hepatitis. And on top of her physical struggles, she underwent a horrendous personal trauma.

Yet through all her pain, Jana loves God and serves Him faithfully. She never blames Him or gripes about her circumstances.

One day, she told me the secret of her amazing faithfulness: "I see my life as a fight. I can either fight God, or I can fight to make good out of it. I have chosen the latter. I consider the pain I face very small in comparison to the great things God is going to do with my life. My emotions make me mad or sad or depressed, but I have to override my emotions and stop and think, 'What is truth?' The truth is that my life is His. He's a faithful Father, and I can always say, 'I love You, God.' "

The disciples in the boat with Jesus could have learned something from Jana. Storms don't destroy a Christian's faith; they test and strengthen it. Thank you, Jana, for showing us that no matter how big the storm we encounter, Jesus Himself is always in the boat with us.

Discussion Starters:

1. Recall a recent storm in your life. How did you react?
2. Why is having "faith during the storm" so important for us?
3. What storms are you facing now where you need Jesus' help to "be still" and find peace?

Lifeline:

Think of how a family member was faithful to God during a recent stormy period. Let the person know you noticed and that you appreciate his or her example.

A GENTLE TOUCH

"A woman who had had a hemorrhage for twelve years . . . came up in the crowd behind [Jesus] and touched His cloak. For she thought, 'If I just touch His garments, I will get well.' Immediately . . . she felt in her body that she was healed of her affliction. Immediately Jesus, perceiving in Himself that the power proceeding from Him had gone forth, turned around in the crowd and said, 'Who touched My garments?' . . . The woman fearing and trembling, aware of what had happened to her, came and fell down before Him and told Him the whole truth. And He said to her, 'Daughter, your faith has made you well; go in peace and be healed of your affliction.'"

↩ Mark 5:25, 27-30, 33-34

When I was little, my mom used to read me fascinating fairy tales about cows jumping over the moon, ladies cutting off the tails of blind mice, talking spiders, old women who lived in shoes, and other wild antics. When you think about them, it sort of makes you wonder what those guys were smoking down in Mother Goose land!

One fairy tale I'll never forget was about a princess who had such sensitive skin she could detect a pea underneath her—even when it was placed beneath 20 mattresses. *Wow, that's pretty sensitive,* I thought. *Oh well, it's just another fairy tale.*

But when I got older, I discovered a similar story in real life that pertained to the central figure of all human history, Jesus Christ. He was surrounded by a mob pressing in all around Him when one woman intentionally touched His garment with great faith. Instantly, Jesus sensed her touch and picked her out among all those who were frantically seeking His attention.

I'm impressed by people with sensitive spirits. I'm more amazed that God Himself listens and responds to a little pip-squeak like me whenever I approach Him with sincere faith.

"The Princess and the Pea" is a clever story, but it's a figment of someone's wild imagination. "The Savior and the Woman's Touch" is a true story that will bless us beyond our wildest dreams—if we just have enough faith to believe it.

Discussion Starters:

1. What made that one woman's touch different from that of all the other people who were jostling against Jesus that day?
2. How can you tell whether faith is sincere?
3. What hurts are you feeling today that need the sensitive attention of Jesus?

Lifeline:

Pray as a family every day for the needs and hurts that require a Savior's gentle touch.

ONLY BELIEVE

"While [Jesus] was still speaking, they came from the house of the synagogue official, saying, 'Your daughter has died; why trouble the Teacher anymore?' But Jesus, overhearing what was being spoken, said to the synagogue official, 'Do not be afraid any longer, only believe.' "

↪ Mark 5:35-36

Three best friends began gymnastics training at a very young age. All three succeeded in the sport, and the performance of their tiny bodies won them many medals at the meets they attended. In junior high, boys began to be attracted to these girls in their slim-fitting jeans and short cheerleader skirts. Life confirmed what gymnastics had taught them: "Skinny is better." After seeing the airbrushed models in their teen magazines, the three began to watch their diets carefully, eating only salads, fruits, and small portions of other foods. By the time they were in high school, they were bingeing, purging, and suffering the full effects of anorexia.

The disease came upon them like a whirlwind and left their emotions frazzled like a Florida hurricane. Depression and confusion became their daily companions.

But the three joined together and sought God's healing touch. They went to Christian counselors, prayed with their parents, and sought God diligently in Scripture and private prayer. As each entered college, God began the process of healing. They discovered a book titled *The Weigh Down Diet* that taught them how to seek God with all their hearts. They learned how to eat healthfully, and today all three are healing and finding the freedom that only the Savior can provide.

As these young women prepare their hearts for a lifetime of Christian ministry, they will tell you that Jesus is still the same miraculous healer He was 2,000 years ago. No disease is too much for His healing touch—not even death! (See Mark 5:35-43 for further proof.) Whenever you're facing a struggle beyond your control, remember His words of comfort: "Do not be afraid any longer, only believe."

Discussion Starters:

1. Do you have a need that enables you to relate to these three girls in any way? If so, what is it?
2. How can your family better support one another whenever one of you needs Jesus' healing touch?
3. "Do not be afraid any longer, only believe." How do those reassuring words speak to your heart today?

Lifeline:

Christ sometimes uses afflictions to bring us to our knees and united around the cross. When healing comes, remain there long enough to give Him the glory.

A CHRISTIAN AT HOME

"Jesus . . . came into His hometown; and His disciples followed Him. When the Sabbath came, He began to teach in the synagogue; and the many listeners were astonished, saying, 'Where did this man get these things, and what is this wisdom given to Him, and such miracles as these performed by His hands? Is not this the carpenter, the son of Mary . . . ?' And they took offense at Him. Jesus said to them, 'A prophet is not without honor except in his hometown and among his own relatives and in his own household.' "

⌐ Mark 6:1-4

The summer of my junior year in high school I became a Christian. It was the most wonderful night of my life! I couldn't wait to tell my best friend, Wade. Both of us needed the change Christ would make in our friendship and in our lives. Telling Wade couldn't have gone better! The real test was when I went home. It was difficult telling my older brother about my new relationship with Christ because he knew all my weaknesses. He knew my many failures. And I couldn't say much when he asked, "Who are you to tell me how to live?"

But I plugged along as best I could. My failures and inconsistencies continue to this day, but I continue to deal with them, thanks to the grace of God. And while it's hardest to be a witness at home, I've discovered it's well worth the effort! I'll never forget the night years later when that same brother's son was very sick. God allowed me to be with the brother I loved so much as he bowed his head and asked Jesus to come into his heart.

When you start looking closely, you see testimonies to God in unexpected ways, even at home. For example, my wife witnesses to me through her daily acts of kindness. My kids witness to me when they are obedient at times when they would rather do things their way. I witness to them whenever I serve them.

Home may be a difficult mission field, but it is the best place on earth to let your light shine for God.

Discussion Starters:

1. Why was it hard for Jesus to be effective in His hometown? Was it because of anything He did?
2. What is the biggest challenge you face in trying to live out the Christian life at home?
3. How can your family support you as you try to be a better witness at home?

Lifeline:

A family that is quick to forgive and slow to judge creates an atmosphere where witnessing is easy.

ABUNDANCE

"[Jesus] took the five loaves and the two fish, and looking up toward heaven, He blessed the food and broke the loaves and He kept giving them to the disciples to set before them; and He divided up the two fish among them all. They all ate and were satisfied, and they picked up twelve full baskets of the broken pieces, and also of the fish. There were five thousand men who ate the loaves."

↩ Mark 6:41-44

Each summer 15,000 kids from around the world come to our Christian sports camps (Kanakuk Kamps) in Missouri to have the time of their lives. Almost 2,000 more can't get in each year because the camps are full. Why the abundance? All I know is that we try to glorify God and His Word the best we know how.

I love my wife more than words can describe. I can't contain my love for her. My four kids and I share a mutual respect that is indescribable. Yes, we've had crazy conflicts and have even approached "gang warfare" at times, but our love saw us through. Why the abundance of good things in my life? Again, it is God's amazing provision.

When I think about God, I am overcome with gratitude. His love over-awes me. He not only puts up with me, but He also supports me as my dad, my best friend, and my guide. I can't comprehend the degree of His love. Why does He care so much? Same reason.

On days when I seek fulfillment on a worldly level, I find my plate half empty and become selfish, irritable, and impatient—with God, my family, and myself. But when I keep in touch with God, I always have much more than enough.

Jesus fed the 5,000 (plus women and children) and had baskets of left-overs. Similarly, He provides His children with confidence, peace, and ful-fillment in abundance. And as we reflect His love toward one other, we dis-cover an abundance of that as well.

Discussion Starters:

1. How do you tap into God's abundance for you each day?
2. Other than God, what sources have you tried in attempting to meet your needs? What happened in each case?
3. In 25 words or less, what would you say is the secret of an abundant life?

Lifeline:

If Christ can feed over 5,000 people with a few loaves of bread and a couple of fish, think what He can do with a family totally yielded to Him.

TRADITIONS OF MEN

"And [Jesus] said to them, 'Rightly did Isaiah prophesy of you hypocrites, as it is written: "This people honors Me with their lips, but their heart is far away from Me. But in vain do they worship Me, teaching as doctrines the precepts of men." Neglecting the commandment of God, you hold to the tradition of men.' "

↶ Mark 7:6-8

In the past 25 years, 35 million babies have been killed in America . . . legally, through abortion. If you and I oppose this practice, we are accused of being chauvinistic, old-fashioned, narrow-minded, and perhaps much worse.

According to recent statistics, the average homosexual male will have 300 sexual partners in his lifetime and will live to be only 41, due mostly to the proliferation of AIDS in the gay population. After celebrating her lesbian lifestyle on television, Ellen DeGeneres received the coveted Entertainer of the Year award. Those who despair at the growing gay movement or oppose gay marriages and parenthood have been labeled "homophobic hatemongers."

In Alabama it's illegal to pray in public schools . . . under any circumstances. You can read books that slander God. You can get a condom at the school health clinic. But you can't pray. To oppose this situation makes you an "ultra-right-wing fundamentalist."

You may be ridiculed in biology class as "unscientific" if you express the belief that God created the universe in six days.

Sometimes your high school friends can make you feel left out for not drinking at a party, for saying no to a joint, or for valuing your virginity. They support a more recent—and destructive—philosophy that says, "If it feels good, do it!"

All these things seem to be part of a new American tradition attempting to sweep God out of public life. The question to ask whenever you wonder what's right or wrong is this: "Is it tradition, or is it truth?" Popular, self-centered traditions won't get you to heaven—and they don't usually do you a lot of good here on earth, either.

But God has a tradition that's worth looking into. It's called truth. And it will set you free.

Discussion Starters:

1. What are some traditions that oppose your understanding of truth?
2. How do you respond when faced with a "new tradition" you don't agree with? Do you speak up and risk potential ridicule? Or do you tend to remain silent?
3. Since truth never changes, can it ever become old-fashioned? Or is it always new? Explain.

Lifeline:

How can you spread truth to the people around you this week?

THE PURE HEART

"For from within, out of the heart of men, proceed the evil thoughts, fornications, thefts, murders, adulteries, deeds of coveting and wickedness, as well as deceit, sensuality, envy, slander, pride and foolishness. All these evil things proceed from within and defile the man."
⬉ Mark 7:21-23

Forty-five years ago a single computer cost $3 million. Today, with a complete system at a couple thousand dollars, annual computer sales recently topped $90 billion. In 1969 the Internet had only four Web sites. A recent count estimated the number at close to 20 million.

Although the computer will never approach the capability of the human mind, the two share one thing in common. Just as a computer is programmed by an inserted disk or some other outside source, your "heart" (center of emotions) is similarly programmed from the things you see, touch, smell, hear, or taste. I know *many* teens and adults who are filled with lust accumulated from the things they've allowed themselves to see. They would give anything to reprogram their hearts. But when they open their mouths, foul language erupts. And when they think about a member of the opposite sex, foul thoughts come to mind.

Your heart is your first and most important personal computer. Even when you're not aware of it, your heart can pick up destructive influences more devastating than any computer virus. If you love yourself at all, you'll protect your heart in every way possible and never let a harmful movie, TV show, or CD touch it again. Why should we go to all that trouble? Jesus gives us the best possible answer: "Blessed are the pure in heart, for they shall see God" (Matthew 5:8).

Discussion Starters:

1. Have you heard people say, "I listen to raunchy music sometimes, but I don't pay any attention to the words"? Do you believe them? Why or why not?
2. How do you set limits on what movies to see (or not see)? If a film promises a great story and talented actors, but includes sex, nudity, or profanity, would you watch it? Might you feel as if you were harming yourself or sinning against God? Explain.
3. How can you work together as a family to help each other have pure hearts?

Lifeline:

As a potter molds clay into a work of art, so a godly home molds the heart into a masterpiece.

THE SIGN OF SIGNS

"The Pharisees came out and began to argue with [Jesus], seeking from Him a sign from heaven, to test Him. Sighing deeply in His spirit, He said, 'Why does this generation seek for a sign? Truly I say to you, no sign will be given to this generation.'"

↜ Mark 8:11-12

Dr. George Wald was a Harvard graduate, Nobel Prize winner in physics, and devout evolutionist. He once said: "There are only two possible explanations as to how life arose: Spontaneous generation arising to evolution or a supernatural creative act of God . . . there is no other possibility. Spontaneous generation was scientifically disproved 120 years ago by Louis Pasteur and others, but that just leaves us with only one other possibility . . . that life came as a supernatural act of creation by God, but I can't accept that philosophy because I do not want to believe in God. Therefore, I choose to believe in that which I know is scientifically impossible, spontaneous generation leading to evolution" ("Origin/Life and Evolution," *Scientific American*, 1978).

Although I applaud his honesty, I pity Dr. Wald's foolishness before an almighty, creative, loving God.

Every living cell is a miraculous sign from God. When I saw my precious wife give birth to the utter miracle of my youngest son, Cooper, indescribable awe came over me. I can't come close to comprehending how many miraculous events combined to give that baby life.

Every morning when I cook pancakes for my children, I thank God for the miracles that sit at our table. Every time a butterfly or bluebird flies past, I acknowledge yet another sign from God. The same is true when I speak to teenagers around the country and see their sadness turn to joy, their confusion turn to peace, and their guilt and shame washed away by God's forgiving grace.

But the ultimate sign, to me, is the one that was erected on Calvary, where "God's little boy" hung as a public human sacrifice to buy my redemption. That's the only sign I will ever need. That sign of signs was erected for the entire world to see, and it continues to direct sinful people to God.

Discussion Starters:

1. Why do people continue to demand signs from God?
2. What signs have you seen lately that have awed you?
3. If people see you as a sign of what God can do for a person, what impression will they have of God?

Lifeline:

If you wonder where God is, keep looking until you see how many miracles He has filled your home with. Then be sure to thank Him.

WHO DO YOU SAY THAT I AM?

"Jesus . . . questioned His disciples, saying to them, 'Who do people say that I am?' They told Him, saying, 'John the Baptist; and others say Elijah; but others, one of the prophets.' And He continued by questioning them, 'But who do you say that I am?' Peter answered and said to Him, 'You are the Christ.' "

⤙ Mark 8:27-29

As our family traveled from Denver to our much-anticipated ski and snowboard vacation in Steamboat Springs, Colorado, our last driving hurdle was Rabbit Ears Pass. At 9,425 feet, snow-covered Rabbit Ears is the site of the Continental Divide. Snow that melts on the east side of Rabbit Ears eventually winds up in the Atlantic Ocean. Snow that melts on the west side ends up in the Pacific Ocean.

Peter's statement to Jesus, "You are the Christ," is like a spiritual Continental Divide. People who agree with Peter that Jesus was divine, sent from God, the prophesied Messiah of Old Testament Scripture, the Savior of mankind, and the only way to heaven are in one group. All other people are in a different group.

The Muslims say Muhammad is the way to God. The Mormons say it's Joseph Smith's teaching. The Jehovah's Witnesses say that Jesus' sacrifice wasn't enough in itself to bring us to God for eternity. Each group's doctrinal beliefs differ at some point from what the Bible says about Jesus. So let's take a look at what the Bible *really* says:

- Jesus is the fulfillment of all Old Testament prophecy about the Messiah (Hebrews 1:1-4; 1 Peter 1:10-12).
- Jesus is the only way to God (John 14:6).
- Jesus is fully God (John 1:1; Colossians 2:9).
- Jesus is the complete atonement for our sin (Romans 5:11).
- The Bible is God's complete Word to us (2 Timothy 3:14-17).

Who do you say that Jesus is? Peter answered correctly, and upon that belief Jesus built His church and His eternal family. *Your* answer is equally important.

Discussion Starters:

1. How would you respond if your best friend asked, "Who do you think Jesus is?" What if a six-year-old asked? How about someone unaware of anything about Christianity?
2. What does "the Christ" mean? (If you don't know, look it up or ask around until you get an answer.)
3. When Jesus said, "No one comes to the Father but through Me," do you think He was trying to be exclusive? Explain.

Lifeline:

To believe Jesus is to love Him. To love Him is to follow Him. To follow Him is to obey Him. To obey Him is to walk with Him forever.

WHOM DO YOU LISTEN TO?

"Jesus took with Him Peter and James and John, and brought them up on a high mountain by themselves. And He was transfigured before them; and His garments became radiant and exceedingly white, as no launderer on earth can whiten them. . . . Then a cloud formed, overshadowing them, and a voice came out of the cloud, 'This is My beloved Son, listen to Him!' "

꩜ Mark 9:2-3, 7

"What's right for you may not be right for me."

"There are any number of ways to get to God."

"It may be pornography to you, but it's art to me."

"You may call it profanity, but I call it freedom of speech."

"It's not a moral issue; we simply have different opinions."

"C'mon, one little drink won't hurt you."

"Don't be so frigid. Sex is okay if it's safe."

Voices are all around us and give us a lot of mixed messages these days. It's easy to get confused and begin to question our beliefs. Who are you going to listen to?

Fortunately, God makes things clear for anyone who is willing to listen. He gave all authority to His Son. Jesus' message was very clear, and God made sure Jesus' words were written down. Practically everyone has a book containing Jesus' words (a Bible). And when the other voices start to get loud and confusing, those words are welcome and reassuring. Here are just a few statements (from Jesus and others) to help get us through difficult times.

- "You [Jesus] have words of eternal life" (John 6:68).
- "If you love Me, you will keep My commandments" (John 14:15).
- "He who overcomes will inherit these things, and I will be his God and he will be My son" (Revelation 21:7).
- "Do you not know that your body is a temple of the Holy Spirit . . . ? For you have been bought with a price: therefore glorify God in your body" (1 Corinthians 6:19-20).
- "If you ask the Father for anything in My name, He will give it to you. . . . Ask and you will receive, so that your joy may be made full" (John 16:23-24).

God's words come through today as powerfully as they did from the sky that glorious day on the mountain: "This is My beloved Son, listen to Him!"

Discussion Starters:

1. What "voices of the world" have you heard lately that contradict what Jesus has said?
2. When you receive conflicting messages, how do you determine what is the truth?
3. How can your family help each other listen to the right voices?

Lifeline:

Hold each other accountable to keep ungodly voices out of the home.

FROM THE BEGINNING

"But from the beginning of creation, God made them male and female. For this reason a man shall leave his father and mother, and the two shall become one flesh; so they are no longer two, but one flesh."

⮑ Mark 10:6-8

How long have people been on the earth?
Who or what caused us to be here?
Whose idea is marriage anyway?
What are the rules for sex and marriage?

You have questions? Jesus has answers! Take a look at today's passage, straight from the mouth of the One who was there to witness the beginning of creation—unlike the secular scientists and psychologists.

How long have people been on the earth? "From the beginning." (The difference between this concept and Darwin's theory is vast.)

Who or what caused us to be here? "God made them male and female." Humankind was created by a supernatural God. Even Darwin conceded in *Origin of the Species*, "To suppose that the human eye...could have been formed by natural selection seems, I freely confess, absurd in the highest degree."

Whose idea is marriage? God ordained it. It was His institution and He stands squarely behind it with as much intimate love and authority for us as for Adam and Eve. Evolutionary psychologists try to make us believe that because the monkeys we evolved from were unfaithful to their mates, it's understandable if we are, too. To quote my friends from Indiana, "Hogwash."

What are the rules for sex and marriage? A quick look at Washington, D.C., Hollywood, and ESPN may suggest there aren't any rules. But while the rule book for sex, marriage, and gender orientation may be ignored, it hasn't been tossed out completely. I met a Green Bay Packer lineman this fall whom a beautiful, young, married lady had attempted to seduce. I like his response: "Ma'am, you're a snake out of the Garden of Eden. Go home where you belong." When two people commit their marriage to the parameters God ordained, it gets better as the years go by. It's pure, it's holy, and it's definitely worth waiting for!

Discussion Starters:

1. Which of these four questions would be of most interest to your closest friends? Why?
2. What does "from the beginning" mean in terms of Genesis 1 and the creation account?
3. If you were putting a price tag on marriage, what would it be? What, if anything, is more important? To what extent will you go to protect it?

Lifeline:

Only a creative God could build something as priceless and unique as a marriage relationship.

THE EYE OF THE NEEDLE

"Jesus . . . said to them, 'Children, how hard it is to enter the kingdom of God! It is easier for a camel to go through the eye of a needle than for a rich man to enter the kingdom of God.' They were even more astonished and said to Him, 'Then who can be saved?' Looking at them, Jesus said, 'With people it is impossible, but not with God; for all things are possible with God.' "

↩ Mark 10:24-27

I belong to an organization that helps support thousands of poverty-stricken children in Haiti. When I visit to personally hug our many "adopted" kids there, I'm amazed at their smiles! I'm blown away by their sense of appreciation! I'm taken aback by their pure love for Jesus! He's just about all they've got. They get one shirt to wear to school (every day for a whole year)! They wash it and wear it with pride. Even the poorest of Americans are rich by Haiti's standards.

We are so abundantly blessed in America. One of our fastest-growing industries is the rental of mini-storage buildings. Our houses can't hold all we possess. Yet Jesus makes it clear that money and things in excess can hinder a person from coming to God. Rather than putting our faith in possessions, we must be willing to hunger for Him like the Haitian kids do. We must be willing to make Him number one, *numero uno* in everything.

Ancient Middle Eastern villages had giant wooden gates that welcomed guests during the day but could be closed at night for protection. Beside the large gate in the huge stone wall was a smaller entrance called "The Needle's Eye" because only one person at a time could pass through. For a camel to enter, it had to first be unloaded and then squeeze through on its knees.

One camel, on his knees, unloaded. No excess baggage could get through the wall.

Our Haitian kids and others like them have a single bowl of beans and rice to eat each day. I'm guessing you have more. If so, are you hoarding your possessions or counting your blessings?

Discussion Starters:

1. What point do you think Jesus was trying to make with His illustration of the camel and the eye of the needle?
2. Why do excessive wealth and possessions keep people from God?
3. What actions can your family take to be more aware of what Jesus is trying to teach in this passage?

Lifeline:

Families that give together, stay together.

HUMILITY IN THE HIGHEST

"They brought the colt to Jesus and put their coats on it; and He sat on it. And many spread their coats in the road, and others spread leafy branches which they had cut from the fields. Those who went in front and those who followed were shouting: 'Hosanna! Blessed is He who comes in the name of the Lord; blessed is the coming kingdom of our father David; hosanna in the highest!' "

↜ Mark 11:7-10

Never has there been, nor will there ever be, a parade as significant as when Jesus rode into Jerusalem on a donkey across the garments and branches scattered by thrilled people. Daniel had designated the time for this event 600 years earlier (Daniel 9:24-27). Zechariah had foretold that the Messiah would ride in on the colt of a donkey (Zechariah 9:9). All the Macy's Christmas parades and Tournament of Roses New Year's parades and Mardi Gras parades combined can't approach the historical magnitude of this parade we now call Palm Sunday.

It was a day when Jesus was publicly acknowledged as the king of all mankind, the Messiah and Savior of the world. The example He set on that day, however, drops me to my knees. God rode in His "Parade of Roses" on a donkey. The humility astounds me. He had led a life of humility, of course, but even His "big day" was low-key in light of how other human leaders would have chosen to celebrate. The apostle Paul explains the mind-set of Jesus in Philippians 2:6-7: "Although He existed in the form of God, [Jesus] did not regard equality with God a thing to be grasped, but emptied Himself, taking the form of a bond-servant."

This story makes me want to pick up the dish towel and dry the dishes for my wife tonight. It makes me want to write my mom and dad a thank-you note, then get a broom and sweep out their carport. It makes me want to apologize for all I've done wrong and let other people have their way a *lot* more often.

Someday the humble will be exalted and the proud will be brought down. And as we begin to understand and apply this valuable lesson, there's no place like home.

Discussion Starters:

1. What do you imagine Jesus was thinking as He rode into Jerusalem on the donkey, knowing that many of the people who were praising Him would soon turn against Him?
2. How can you lay *your* coat before Jesus (symbolically)?
3. How does Jesus' life of exemplary humility affect the way you will live this week?

Lifeline:

From now on, let us mount our pride on the seat of a donkey.

THE ROOT OF BITTERNESS

"Whenever you stand praying, forgive, if you have anything against anyone, so that your Father who is in heaven will also forgive you your transgressions. But if you do not forgive, neither will your Father who is in heaven forgive your transgressions."

⟿ Mark 11:25-26

A first-grade teacher read her students many old sayings we've all heard. But she would stop each phrase just before the conclusion and ask her five- and six-year-old students to fill in the rest. Their answers (taken from *Priceless Proverbs*, Price Stern Sloan Publishers) have made me laugh out loud over and over again. Here are a few:

"Better be safe than . . . punch a fifth grader."

"Never underestimate the power of . . . termites."

"Don't bite the hand that . . . looks dirty."

"You can't teach an old dog new . . . math."

"A penny saved is . . . not much."

"Two's company, three's . . . the Musketeers."

"Children should be seen and not . . . spanked or grounded."

"If at first you don't succeed . . . get new batteries."

No proverb or word of wisdom is more reliable and profoundly life-shaping than Jesus' statement "Forgive . . . so that your Father who is in heaven will also forgive you." Have you ever wondered why He spoke so frankly on this subject? It's because forgiveness is much more important than we may realize.

Forgiveness heals! Forgiveness is the glue that will restore broken relationships with parents, brothers, sisters, and friends. It restores joy and peace stolen by your personal vendettas. It heals your relationship with God. No pharmacy, hospital, or doctor can provide a bottle of medicine as powerful as the healing power of forgiveness.

Bitterness kills! If you don't forgive when someone offends you, you're left with the bitterness, and it's a killer. It kills your relationship with the ones in your home who should mean the most to you throughout your life. It kills all remnants of inner joy and peace. Worst of all, it kills your daily fellowship with God.

Forgiveness or bitterness? The choice shouldn't be that hard to make.

Discussion Starters:

1. Why does God put so much emphasis on forgiveness?
2. What should you do if you try to forgive someone but find it hard to do so?
3. Whom do you need to forgive today? Are you willing to do so before the sun goes down? (See Ephesians 4:26-27.)

Lifeline:

Forgiving hearts create happy homes.

RENDER TO CAESAR

"They came and said to [Jesus], 'Teacher, . . . is it lawful to pay a poll-tax to Caesar, or not? Shall we pay or shall we not pay?' But He, knowing their hypocrisy, said to them, 'Why are you testing Me? Bring Me a denarius to look at.' They brought one. And He said to them, 'Whose likeness and inscription is this?' And they said to Him, 'Caesar's.' And Jesus said to them, 'Render to Caesar the things that are Caesar's, and to God the things that are God's.' And they were amazed at Him."

⟿ Mark 12:14-17

As I sped down Interstate 70 (doing 70 MPH) one beautiful November morning, a speed zone sign swept by me in a blur. It was a 40 MPH construction zone with no workers around. Well, almost no workers. The one guy there had a white car with flashing lights on top. His job was simple: catch nuts like me who don't pay attention to warning signs. Within seconds those irritating little lights were flashing in my rearview mirror. I think I'd rather see a dentist approaching with a drill in his hand than a highway patrolman in hot pursuit of my billfold. "Render to Caesar."

The law says you must be 17 to attend an R-rated movie and 21 to buy a drink of alcohol. "Render to Caesar."

Each April 15, the IRS looks to take a chunk of our yearly incomes. "Render to Caesar."

In spite of my complaining, I don't mind paying taxes. We live in the best country in the world, and I'm glad our highways have good men patrolling them. The blessings we have are worth every dime I chip in. "Rendering to Caesar" is an important part of making it happen. And every time I begin to gripe, I am reminded of the even more important part of the command: "Render to God the things that are God's." When I do that, I find I have little, if anything, to complain about.

Discussion Starters:

1. What, if anything, are you expected to "render" to the government? What should you render to your father? Your mother? Your teachers?
2. Why is it important to render to others with a positive attitude?
3. Which forms of giving/spending do you suppose give the most joy to God?

Lifeline:

Mom and Dad have God-given authority. Kids will receive theirs in due time.

FALSE CHRISTS

"See to it that no one misleads you. Many will come in My name, saying, 'I am He!' and will mislead many. . . . If anyone says to you, 'Behold, here is the Christ'; or, 'Behold, He is there'; do not believe him; for false Christs and false prophets will arise, and will show signs and wonders, in order to lead astray, if possible, the elect."

↪ Mark 13:5-6, 21-22

You're headed for Fun City when you reach a fork in the road. You know one road goes to Fun City, the other to Liarsville, but you don't know which is which. Two men are standing at the fork. One man *always* tells the truth and the other one *always* lies, but again, you don't know which is which. Both know the way to Fun City. You can ask either man *one* question. What question would you ask? Ponder this a while before checking the answer at the bottom of the page.

It is easy to be misled. Sometimes we may even begin to believe that drinking is as cool as the beer commercials make it seem. Maybe the right perfume *will* make me irresistible. Maybe I should overlook moral character if I can date the popular person. Maybe I'll be the exception to those who face horrible consequences from doing drugs, having premarital sex, and so forth.

Most of us must deal with temptations to indulge in momentary sin. But when deception takes on a spiritual aspect, the dangers can be even worse. I have seen many high school and college students—even entire families—get wooed into cults. Many appear harmless and even loving. But some teach that you have to *work* your way to heaven since Jesus didn't completely pay for your sins. Others say that Jesus wasn't truly God. Still others believe God is in everything, both good and evil. These teachings are not only inaccurate, but they are also *dead* wrong.

It is one thing to get caught up in a sin that can cost you your life yet is covered by the forgiveness of Christ. It is far worse to be misled in a way that will cost you your eternal life.

Discussion Starters:

1. What has been the most deceptive thing you've heard or seen lately?
2. How would you define a "false Christ"?
3. How can you differentiate truth from clever lies?

Lifeline:

Strong families discern truth together.

[The answer to the opening question: Ask either man, "What will this other guy say is the way to Fun City?" and then go the *opposite* way!]

THE WINNING TEAM

"For nation will rise up against nation, and kingdom against kingdom; there will be earth-quakes in various places; there will also be famines. These things are merely the beginning of birth pangs. . . . You will be hated by all because of My name, but the one who endures to the end, he will be saved. . . . Take heed, keep on the alert; for you do not know when the appointed time will come."

         Mark 13:8, 13, 33

It will be years before sports fans forget the upset win of the young Arizona Wildcats over the number-one University of North Carolina Tarheels in the 1997 college basketball national championship. Or how about the USA ice hockey team upset of the mighty Russians in the 1980 winter Olympics? And who can forget 16-year-old Kerri Strug vaulting to a gold medal for the 1996 USA gymnastic team in spite of a badly sprained ankle? These heroes all had one thing in common: They really wanted to win.

According to today's passage, Jesus is coming back—perhaps very soon. He said He would come back during a time of war. More people died in wars during the twentieth century than in all the previous centuries combined.

Jesus said the gospel of the kingdom would be preached to the whole world (Mark 13:10). Each day approximately 186,000 people around the world come to Christ. I sat beside evangelist Franklin Graham recently and asked him when he thought this prophecy would be fulfilled. He said, "It has been done."

Jesus said that false Christs would arise (Mark 13:22). Today there are 1,800 cults in America with over 20 million followers.

Jesus said there would be a push toward supernatural phenomena. Ouija boards, Dungeons and Dragons, séances, witchcraft, psychics, and so on have worldwide followings.

Jesus said Christians would be persecuted for their faith. If you think it's bad bringing up Jesus, the Bible, or other Christian teachings in class, there are places on earth where you might be *killed* for it.

But Jesus also said that if you want with your whole heart to overcome and be on His winning side, you *will!* And the rewards will be beyond belief.

Discussion Starters:

1. Which of Jesus' "signs of His coming" have you observed recently?
2. What did Jesus mean when He said to "keep on the alert"?
3. How can your family better pull together as a team to defeat the enemy of this world?

Lifeline:

Individuals often lose tough contests. But a team—united, focused, and full of heart—is almost impossible to defeat.

THE LESSON OF THE FIG TREE

"Now learn the parable from the fig tree: when its branch has already become tender and puts forth its leaves, you know that summer is near. Even so, you too, when you see these things happening, recognize that He is near, right at the door."

~ Mark 13:28-29

The last "whipping" I received from my dad was when I was in seventh grade. My dad is a good man with a keen sense of humor and a raging love affair with life, yet his discipline, when needed, was firm and fair. He would quietly remove his leather cowboy belt from his jeans and use it to strike the seat of my pants three or four times with sufficient force to make sure I got the message.

My last "message" was a reminder that I shouldn't lie to my mom. When Dad was told of my offense on Friday night, he simply told me, "Bring me my belt on Sunday afternoon."

I had two long days to think about my crime and the impending punishment. Waiting was by far the worst part of the retribution. Not much is worse than the anticipation of judgment.

On the other hand, I've discovered there is not much better than anticipating something *good* about to happen. After a long trip, all I can think about is coming home to see my wife and kids. When my youngest son, Cooper, was in his delightful preschool stage, he would always meet me at the door, throw his arms around my legs, and say, "Welcome home, Daddy. What did you bwing me?"

I'd laugh and say, "I brought you me!" With eyes full of excitement, he would respond to the little game as if we'd never played it before. "I know that, but what *else* did you bwing me?"

To truly know God is to look forward to His return with awe and anticipation. To reject God's Son is to anticipate impending punishment for our sins that would gladly have been forgiven and forgotten.

What are you anticipating today: God's judgment . . . or His embrace?

Discussion Starters:

1. What is a recent event you have anticipated with excitement? What's one you have anticipated with fear?
2. How do you, personally, feel about the imminent return of Christ?
3. What can you do to feel more secure and find peace of mind during these days of anticipation?

Lifeline:

"Daddy's coming home" can be the three sweetest words in the English language.

FUAGNEM

"While [Jesus] was in Bethany at the home of Simon the leper, and reclining at the table, there came a woman with an alabaster vial of very costly perfume of pure nard; and she broke the vial and poured it over His head."

↜ Mark 14:3

FUAGNEM isn't a word you'll find in Webster's unabridged dictionary or read about in *USA Today*. It's a word we use at Kanakuk Kamps that stands for "Fired Up And Going Nuts Every Minute." In other words, it means, "giving it everything you've got all the time."

The woman with the perfume was definitely a FUAGNEM girl. Chances are, she had been saving that expensive perfume her whole life. Maybe she was expecting to use it as a dowry for her husband. Perhaps she was adding a few drops with each passing birthday. For a poor Bethany peasant girl, the perfume was no doubt her most valuable possession. Yet without hesitating, she gave it all to the one she had trusted for her salvation.

Before John Elway led the Denver Broncos to the historic upset of the world champion Green Bay Packers in Super Bowl XXXII, he told an ESPN commentator that he would give every penny he'd ever made in the NFL (certainly millions of dollars) for just one Super Bowl ring. His team got fired up by Elway's FUAGNEM commitment, and Green Bay didn't know what hit them.

Prior to his sophomore high school football season, I asked my son Cooper if he thought he would start on the varsity team (a rare feat in our tough 3A-4A league). He responded with utter conviction, "Either I'm going to get a concussion or blood clot and die, or I'm going to start on defense this year."

The lady with the perfume went down in biblical history the day she gave it all to Jesus. John Elway won his Super Bowl ring. And yes, my sophomore son made the starting team and was even named Defensive Player of the Week in the second round of the state playoffs.

Don't you think it's about time *you* went a little FUAGNEM?

Discussion Starters:

1. Why are so few people unwilling to "give it all" to Jesus?
2. What do *you* tend to hold back from being a "give it all" Christian?
3. Why is it so hard to have a FUAGNEM attitude when it comes to faith in Christ?

Lifeline:

If Jesus were visiting your house today, what prized possession would you give Him?

BETRAYAL

"As they were reclining at the table and eating, Jesus said, 'Truly I say to you that one of you will betray Me—one who is eating with Me.' They began to be grieved and to say to Him one by one, 'Surely not I?' And He said to them, 'It is one of the twelve, one who dips with Me in the bowl. For the Son of Man is to go just as it is written of Him; but woe to that man by whom the Son of Man is betrayed! It would have been good for that man if he had not been born.' "

↪ Mark 14:18-21

It's easy to point an accusing finger at Judas, that betrayer, liar, and thief. We would never do anything to betray our Lord and Savior. Or would we?

Maybe you're a senior at a party with a cross around your neck and a can of beer in your hand. A ninth grader thinks you look cool and takes his first drink. Three years later he's a full-blown alcoholic.

Maybe you have a date with Sally, whose character is as beautiful as her physical features. You take her to the hottest movie in town—R-rated but not supposed to be "that bad." To your shock, various actors take God's name in vain, undress, and have sex. You're aroused and Sally is embarrassed.

Maybe other girls are trashing a new girl because the guys have been noticing her. Without thinking, you join in and land a couple of terrific insults that get a good response from the group.

Maybe crude jokes and four-letter words are flying around school like sand in a desert windstorm. Before long it seems natural for them to come from *your* mouth as well.

Maybe you forget to study for a big test, but you just happen to sit next to straight-A Debbie, whose answers are as plain as day. Isn't it better to sneak a peek than go home and face your parents with an F?

I have to confess, I've betrayed Jesus too many times to count. I'm humbled beyond words that, when I ask, He forgives me and forgets about it. It's a humbling experience to confess your sins, but not nearly as bad as not confessing. If you don't believe me, just ask Judas.

Discussion Starters:

1. Why is it so easy to judge *other* people's sins?
2. In what ways do people your age betray Jesus?
3. Can you think of a time when *you* betrayed Jesus and found forgiveness? If so, share it with someone who might need to hear.

Lifeline:

Following Jesus will get you to heaven. Following Judas will get you to the end of your rope.

DON'T LEAVE ME, DADDY

"[Jesus] went a little beyond them, and fell to the ground and began to pray that if it were possible, the hour might pass Him by. And He was saying, 'Abba! Father! All things are possible for You; remove this cup from Me; yet not what I will, but what You will.' "

⌒ Mark 14:35-36

Any time one of my four kids asks me to do something with him or her, the event goes on my "top 10" list of that day or week.

"Hey, Dad, let's go get an ice cream cone at Baskin Robbins." That's a top 10.

"Hey, Dad, let's go throw the football together." That's a top 10.

"Hey, Dad, will you take me shopping? I need a new dress for the sorority dance." I received this top 10 call when Courtney was a sophomore in college. I was ecstatic. We met in Dallas at the Galleria Mall, where I looked for dresses with her for five straight hours. It was fantastic! And in addition, I saw a picture that day in the men's waiting area that would become one of the most cherished pictures of my life.

I was looking through *Sports Illustrated's* "Pictures of the Year" edition and found a photo of "Mr. Basketball," Michael Jordan. He wasn't shooting a three-pointer or dunking the ball with the graceful acrobatics that set him apart as the greatest player in NBA history. He was lying on the floor, clutching a basketball in his arms and bawling his eyes out.

M. J. had just won his fourth NBA championship with the Bulls. So why the tears and utter despair? It was Father's Day and his daddy wasn't around to see the game. His father had been tragically murdered three years before.

Jesus was grieved beyond imagination in the Garden of Gethsemane. He could hardly bear the thought of going through the excruciating torment of death by crucifixion without His Daddy beside Him. The worst part of any sin is that it separates us from God. When Christ bore our sins on the cross, it separated Him from His Father for the first and last time in all eternity. But Jesus made that sacrifice so that we, too, could come to the Father. After what He did for us, is anything He expects of us too great a sacrifice to make in return?

Discussion Starters:

1. Why did God have to turn His head when Jesus died?
2. Why did God create the parent-child bond to be so strong?
3. What can you do to become closer to your parents (or children)?

Lifeline:

Parents and their children have a bond that should never be broken.

IS JESUS THE CHRIST?

"Again the high priest was questioning [Jesus], and saying to Him, 'Are You the Christ, the Son of the Blessed One?' And Jesus said, 'I am; and you shall see the Son of Man sitting at the right hand of Power, and coming with the clouds of heaven.'"

↩ Mark 14:61-62

"I am the way, and the truth, and the life; no one comes to the Father but through Me" (John 14:6).

"I am the vine, you are the branches; . . . apart from Me you can do nothing" (John 15:5).

"He who has seen Me has seen the Father" (John 14:9).

"I and the Father are one" (John 10:30).

Make no mistake about it, Jesus was very sure about who He was. He was in no way insecure about His identity. "I am the Christ." "I am the only way to God." "I am God in the flesh."

Some people attempt to limit His significance by calling Him "a great moral teacher," "a very good man," "one of many prophets," or "a special messenger from heaven." But such claims are inaccurate and/or incomplete in light of biblical eyewitness accounts of Jesus and the claims He made about Himself.

Jesus knew He was God and said so. For that, the Jews accused Him of blasphemy, and He was willing to die for His claim.

The apostle Paul clearly confirms Jesus' claim to deity throughout the epistles. Here are just a couple of examples:

- "He is the image of the invisible God, the firstborn of all creation" (Colossians 1:15).
- "For in Him all the fullness of Deity dwells in bodily form" (Colossians 2:9).

God created heaven and hell. He created the world we live in and the universe around us. He created you in His likeness. Only someone with that kind of power has the credentials to become sin on your behalf so that you can face Him some day without shame, without guilt, and wholly adequate to spend eternity in His kingdom.

Is Jesus the Christ? I think you have your answer.

Discussion Starters:

1. How can you be sure that Jesus was actually God in the flesh?
2. Why is this significant to you as you face eternity?
3. What are some other Bible verses you can think of that emphasize the importance of Jesus?

Lifeline:

"He is no fool who gives what he cannot keep to gain what he cannot lose" (Jim Elliot).

BARABBAS AND TELEMACHUS

"But the chief priests stirred up the crowd to ask [Pilate] to release Barabbas for them instead. Answering again, Pilate was saying to them, 'Then what shall I do with Him whom you call the King of the Jews?' They shouted back, 'Crucify Him!' But Pilate said to them, 'Why, what evil has He done?' But they shouted all the more, 'Crucify Him!' Wishing to satisfy the crowd, Pilate released Barabbas for them, and after having Jesus scourged, he handed Him over to be crucified."

↩ Mark 15:11-15

In his wonderful book *Loving God*, Chuck Colson tells of a monk named Telemachus who lived faithfully and reverently during the final years of the tyrannical Roman Empire. One day he unexpectedly heard the voice of God within his spirit telling him to go to Rome.

As Telemachus strolled into the huge city, a strange inner directive guided him into the Roman Colosseum. He could hear the cheers of the people and the roaring of animals as the Romans, thirsty for thrills, pitted gladiators against one another or against wild beasts. The fighting was bitter and bloody. All encounters ended in death. Telemachus couldn't believe what he saw! Spontaneously he stood up and screamed, "In the name of Christ, forbear!"

No one heard. He ran to the barrier, jumped across it onto the sandy Colosseum floor, and again addressed the Roman leaders at the top of his lungs, "In the name of Christ, forbear!" The crowd began to laugh and jeer at this puny figure who seemed so out of place among the warriors around him. One of the gladiators knocked Telemachus to the dirt. He again stood to his feet and cried, "In the name of Christ, forbear!" Another huge gladiator turned to the monk and slashed him across the chest with a fatal blow of his sword. With his last breath, Telemachus cried, "In the name of Christ, forbear."

The crowd became silent. One by one they filed from the stadium. Never again would the Colosseum host Rome's deadliest games. Telemachus's unwarranted death unified the people in opposition to this ruthless practice. Thousands of gladiators were spared by the courage of one simple man.

Discussion Starters:

1. How does Telemachus remind you of Jesus?
2. How does Barabbas's unexpected good fortune remind you of what Christ did for you?
3. What did Jesus mean when He said, "Greater love has no one than this, that one lay down his life for his friends" (John 15:13)?

Lifeline:

Love is truly genuine when it's strong enough to die for.

REVERENCE

"Those passing by were hurling abuse at [Jesus]. . . . In the same way the chief priests also, along with the scribes, were mocking Him among themselves. . . . Those who were crucified with Him were also insulting Him."

⌐ Mark 15:29-32

I recently heard a terrific story from my friend Coach Bill McCartney. In 1994 Coach planned to take his Colorado Buffaloes football team to the national championship. The only thing that stood in the way was the perennially tough team at the University of Michigan (the Wolverines). Coach had been studying Haggai 2 and, believe it or not, he sensed God saying that He would do two things. First, He would use Coach to "shake the nations" (v. 7). Second, He would bless Coach on the 24th day of the ninth month (vv. 10, 18)—and the upcoming game just happened to be on September 24.

McCartney had previously coached at Michigan for 13 years and had made many friends there. The night before the game, he was praying with 10 couples, all devout Christian friends who happened to be Michigan fans. Coach felt led to tell them that he believed he would win the next day, based on what God had told him in Scripture. (I'm sure that as good Michigan fans, they were praying for the opposite!)

The next day, Michigan led the whole game. In the final minute they were up 26 to 20. The crowd of 100,000 was going wild. Colorado finally got the ball on their own 30 but had only six seconds left and 70 yards to go. In the hushed silence, someone screamed from the grandstand, "Hey, McCartney, where's your God now?"

Down! Set! Hike! Quarterback Kordell Stewart dropped back and threw the ball as far as his arm could heave it. A Michigan defender tipped it . . . right into the hands of Colorado receiver Mike Westbrook, standing in the end zone. Final score: Colorado 27, Michigan 26! God would not be mocked!

When the players accepted the ESPY Award for Play of the Year, they held the trophy above their heads and said, "We give the glory for this to Jesus Christ!"

We can mock God, but our empty words do not diminish His glory in the least. How much better it is for us to offer God our reverence, and to receive His love, mercy, forgiveness, and peace in return.

Discussion Starters:

1. What is the difference between reverence and ridicule?
2. How do you feel when people ridicule you? How do you suppose a perfect, all-powerful God feels when people ridicule Him?
3. What are some ways that people mock God today?

Lifeline:

When you say "Jesus," you've said it all!

WHO TORE THE VEIL?

"Jesus uttered a loud cry, and breathed His last. And the veil of the temple was torn in two from top to bottom. When the centurion, who was standing right in front of Him, saw the way He breathed His last, he said, 'Truly this man was the Son of God!' "

↫ Mark 15:37-39

A group of scholars has calculated that it would have taken numerous teams of horses pulling in opposite directions to tear the veil of the temple in half. The purpose of the veil was to keep everyone out of the Holy of Holies, a small room containing the Ark of the Covenant (which held the tablets with the Ten Commandments, a jar of manna, and Aaron's staff that had miraculously budded and produced ripe almonds [Numbers 17]). Only the high priest could enter the Holy of Holies, and then only once a year to offer a blood sacrifice for the sins of the people. It would be immediate death for anyone else who attempted to see what was behind the veil.

But the moment Jesus died, in an instant, the separating veil was torn in two. If you and I had ripped it, the tear would have gone from the bottom to the top. But this rip was "from top to bottom"—God's work.

God was now approachable. The Holy of Holies was open for business, accepting all comers. No more sacrifices were required. The high priest was no longer needed to access God's presence. At that very moment in history, we received a permanent invitation to come to God for rest, advice, mercy, grace, or anything else we need from a loving Father. (See Hebrews 10:19-22.)

As an earthquake shook the ground beneath the Roman centurion, so his proclamation shakes my occasionally hard heart into a state of tenderness. I can echo his statement made almost 2,000 years ago: "Truly this man [is] the Son of God!" And thanks to what Jesus did for me, now I'm a child of God as well.

Discussion Starters:

1. How do you feel, way down inside, about what Jesus did for you on the cross?
2. How well do you think you could communicate with God if the veil had not been torn and the Holy of Holies were still a place for yearly sacrifices? Explain.
3. Now that you can come to God with confidence through personal prayer, do you make the most of the opportunities you have? Why or why not?

Lifeline:

A family that prays together stays together.

JESUS REALLY DID DIE

"Joseph [of Arimathea] bought a linen cloth, took [Jesus] down, wrapped Him in the linen cloth and laid Him in a tomb which had been hewn out in the rock; and he rolled a stone against the entrance of the tomb."

↩ Mark 15:46

We love to talk about the resurrection of Jesus and the new life it makes possible for us. It's a glorious story with angels, the rolled-away stone, fresh hopes, and new beginnings. Yet what makes the Resurrection so significant is that Jesus had been executed by crucifixion—the most painful and humiliating way the Roman Empire knew how to kill a person.

Make no mistake: The cross was a punishment that led to certain death. The victim remained hanging until his lungs collapsed and he slumped lifelessly. To ensure the death of Jesus, a Roman soldier thrust a spear into His side. The separated blood and water which poured from His wound is a medical sign of death.

According to Roman custom, two coroners would confirm the death of a crucified victim before signing the death certificate. A mistake could result in their own deaths. The same was true of the centurion who reported Jesus' death to Pilate. And you can bet that Jesus' Jewish opponents were going to make sure He was out of the way for good.

Numerous doubters have proposed theories to explain away history's greatest miracle. One example is the "swoon theory," suggesting that Jesus really didn't die, but just lost a lot of blood, swooned (fainted), and was revived in the coolness of the tomb. The proponents of this theory want us to believe that after Jesus was beaten numerous times, nailed to a cross, speared, and deprived of food and water for three days, He recovered. In that condition He was able to unwrap His grave clothes, push a two-ton stone away from the entrance to the tomb, and escape the Roman guards. He then appeared to His disciples for 40 days and they actually believed Him to be the risen Lord of life. Could anything be more preposterous?

It's much easier for me to believe that Jesus died, rose again, and will live forever as a loving and merciful Lord and Savior. After all, it's true.

Discussion Starters:

1. Why did Jesus have to die?
2. Why do so many critics try to explain away Jesus' resurrection?
3. The degree of Jesus' love for us is reflected in His willingness to die for us. How does that make you feel?

Lifeline:

Jesus wore the crown of thorns so that you and I can wear the crown of life.

20/20 VISION

"Entering the tomb, [the women] saw a young man sitting at the right, wearing a white robe; and they were amazed. And he said to them, 'Do not be amazed; you are looking for Jesus the Nazarene, who has been crucified. He has risen; He is not here; behold, here is the place where they laid Him. But go, tell His disciples and Peter, "He is going ahead of you to Galilee; there you will see Him, just as He told you." ' "

⇐ Mark 16:5-7

A recent Easter edition of *Time* magazine ran a cover story entitled "Rethinking the Resurrection." The story reported on an assortment of liberal theologians and other current "experts" who expressed their doubts concerning the plausibility of Jesus' resurrection.

As I put down the magazine with tremendous disappointment, I shook my head and thought, *Any reasonable attorney in a court of law would first interview eyewitnesses of the event and let them testify*. But *Time* magazine quoted none of them.

Did the resurrection of Christ really occur? Let's see what the eyewitnesses said and did after the event.

On the day of the Crucifixion, Jesus' disciples had been utter cowards, literally running for their lives (Matthew 26:56). When they thought Jesus was dead, they weren't eager to line up and face the same punishment He had received. But after they saw Jesus alive, they were infused with new hope and strength. They committed to Him with tremendous courage—so much that 10 of them eventually died martyrs' deaths for what they believed. Peter wrote, "We were eyewitnesses of His majesty" (2 Peter 1:16). And John confirmed that after the resurrected Jesus had spoken with the disciples and shown them His hands and His side, they rejoiced (John 20:20).

The next time someone questions Jesus' resurrection, get a Bible and turn to the book of John. Think about the people who were closest to Jesus and died for what they saw as eyewitnesses to the event. You'll see a lot clearer with John 20:20 vision.

Discussion Starters:

1. Why do unbelievers continue to scoff at Jesus' resurrection—even after 2,000 years?
2. It has been said that many a man has died for a lie when he thought it was the truth, but only a crazy man would die for a lie when he *knows* it's a lie. How does the to-the-death commitment of the disciples give credence to the Resurrection account?
3. What does Jesus' resurrection mean to you on a personal level?

Lifeline:

Jesus is alive, and so are you! Live the life He makes possible for you today.

RoMans

"The just shall live by faith" (Romans 1:17, KJV).

The entire Protestant Reformation took place largely because Martin Luther spent a lot of time thinking about this single verse. John Wesley pioneered the Methodist movement in England (which led to much of the evangelism of America) because of his understanding of that same verse.

And that's just one verse from a magnificent book of the Bible. The book of Romans is a masterpiece in the way it helps us understand the concept of grace. As a new Christian at age 17, I read it like there was no tomorrow. It laid the foundation for my faith. This is a book that stands staunchly and sternly, directing us away from the gates of hell. The book of Romans is where millions and millions of people have discovered the love and the salvation of God. As you read it, may you do the same.

NOT ASHAMED

"For I am not ashamed of the gospel, for it is the power of God for salvation to everyone who believes, to the Jew first and also to the Greek. For in it the righteousness of God is revealed from faith to faith; as it is written, 'But the righteous man shall live by faith.' "

↩ Romans 1:16-17

Karen McGregor had wanted a horse since she was three years old. She had spent so many nights falling asleep thinking about horses that she began to dream about them. Alas, to a rural girl in Calgary, Alberta, money didn't come easy. The $1,500 price might as well have been a million dollars. She had never seen that kind of money. But her desire grew even stronger as she worked and saved every penny she could.

Just as Karen finally scraped together enough money to buy her dream horse, she happened to hear about a mission trip to San Jose, Bolivia. The only thing stronger than the desire to own her first horse was her desire to tell others about her tremendous love for Jesus, who had died to set her free from the penalty of her sins. But the mission trip had a hefty price tag.

Karen's dilemma became painfully apparent. She couldn't have both of the things she wanted; one of the two had to go. After some time devoted to intense prayer, she made her decision. The horse had to wait (maybe forever). The needs of the mission kids in Bolivia outweighed Karen's personal dreams. And as a result, Bolivia will never be the same. Neither will Karen. She will have all the days of eternity to claim her highest prize.

Discussion Starters:

1. Because Karen was not ashamed of the gospel, other people's lives were changed for the better. Can you envision potential life changes if you were to take a bolder stand for what you believe? Explain.
2. Have you ever felt ashamed or embarrassed to share your faith? Why? How did you deal with your feelings?
3. What personal desire would be hardest for you to sacrifice in order to share your love for Jesus? (Your boyfriend or girlfriend? Your group of friends? Your car?)

Lifeline:

Shame results in timidity. Love produces bold sacrifice.

MICHELANGELO OF THE SKY

"For since the creation of the world [God's] invisible attributes, His eternal power and divine nature, have been clearly seen, being understood through what has been made, so that [unrighteous people] are without excuse."

☞ Romans 1:20

"Been there, done that." That was Rob's motto.

Drugs? He'd done them all. Assault? He had beaten numerous of his fellow teens in fits of rage. Lockup? Though only 17, he had heard many jail gates and doors close in cold finality behind him. Gang life? He was one of his neighborhood's most notorious members.

Rob's parents were 15 and 16 at the time of his out-of-wedlock birth. Eight years later, a disastrous car accident left Rob an orphan with more psychological baggage to haul than a cargo jet could carry. To put it mildly, Rob was mad. The chip on his shoulder left no room for trusting relationships. And God was definitely at the bottom of his list of priorities.

Rob attended our summer camp in Missouri, where he and I became close friends. We spent hours talking about God . . . about forgiveness . . . about a person's ability to receive supernatural help to dispel guilt, anger, and rage. Rob asked a lot of questions, but his heart remained cold and hard toward God.

Mysteriously, he sought me out one night just after sunset. He wrapped his arms around my neck and hugged me for 10 long minutes as he sobbed a river of tears onto my shoulder. He was finally able to explain that he had been watching the majestic sunset. It was as if he had seen a painting, a masterpiece like he'd never seen before. He told me, "I knew a painting that spectacular *had* to have a painter, so I asked that 'Master painter' to reside in my heart and to forgive me for all the wrongs that I had done."

When God makes Himself evident to us, even the most resistant among us will eventually sit up and take notice.

Discussion Starters:

1. What are some ways that God reveals Himself to you through the wonders of His creation?
2. Why do you think some people choose to reject God even after they witness His many wondrous expressions in nature?
3. What are the short-term results of a person's refusal to acknowledge God's existence? What are the long-term results?

Lifeline:

Take note of God's many "paintings" today. Stand in awe of them and watch your affection for Him grow.

THE BALANCE BEAM

"Therefore you have no excuse, everyone of you who passes judgment, for in that which you judge another, you condemn yourself; for you who judge practice the same things."

↪ Romans 2:1

My palms still threaten to break out in a nervous sweat when my mind recalls the years my two girls competed in gymnastics. No event was as grueling for the young athletes, nor as gut-wrenching for their dads, as the balance beam. The beam requires a series of death-defying feats on a surface no more than four inches wide, spanning a length of 16 feet, and perched more than four feet off the floor. Watching my little girls do hand-springs on the floor was one thing. But peeking through my tightly squinting eyes at their tiny bodies contorting over a four-inch beam was much, much worse.

The plank between being overly tolerant and being judgmental is the balance beam of the Christian life. Perhaps you've heard condemning statements where the gavel falls with resounding finality as the speaker piously declares:
- "You're going to hell for that."
- "Do that one more time and God will get His due revenge."
- "That politician is a pervert."
- "You'll never get to heaven if you . . ."

Yet just as we can be too judgmental, we can also be too tolerant:
- "To each his own."
- "Your rules are fine for you, but they don't apply to me."
- "If it feels good, do it."
- "Truth is relative."

A careless gymnast is penalized for falling off either side of the balance beam. Similarly, a careless Christian can experience distress from harsh judgmentalism as well as excessive tolerance. It isn't easy, but we must strive to remain upright and on the beam. Whenever we feel ourselves beginning to tumble off, we can always count on God being there to help us keep our balance.

Discussion Starters:

1. In what ways have you seen tolerance for the behavior of others taken too far?
2. What judgmental statements have you heard directed at others lately?
3. Do you tend to be too judgmental or too tolerant? How can you maintain a healthy balance between the two? (Be specific.)

Lifeline:

Referring to a down-and-out person, Albert Camus said, "There, but by the grace of God, go I." What do you think he meant?

THE WALKING SERMON

"You, therefore, who teach another, do you not teach yourself? You who preach that one shall not steal, do you steal? You who say that one should not commit adultery, do you commit adultery? You who abhor idols, do you rob temples? You who boast in the Law, through your breaking the Law, do you dishonor God?"

↬ Romans 2:21-23

Rather than reading something from me today, here are some words of wisdom by an unknown author from a poem called "I'd Rather See a Sermon."

I'd rather see a sermon than hear one any day;
I'd rather one should walk with me than merely show the way.
The eye's a better pupil and more willing than the ear;
Fine counsel is confusing, but example's always clear.
And the best of all the preachers are the ones who live their creed;
For to see good put in action is what everybody needs.
I soon can learn to do it if you let me see it done;
I can watch your hands in action, but your tongue too fast may run.
And the sermon you deliver may be very wise and true;
But I'd rather get my lesson by observing what to do.
For I might misunderstand you and the high advice you give;
But there's no misunderstanding in how you act and how you live.

Discussion Starters:

1. Describe a family member who has "walked his talk," or point out a "walking sermon" quality in each family member.
2. Why do you think it is so difficult for nonbelievers to believe in Jesus when they observe a Christian who doesn't practice on Saturday night what he or she sings about in church on Sunday morning?
3. What is an area you've identified lately where you could stand to do a better job of "walking" more like you "talk"?

Lifeline:

The next time you take a walk, look for some "sermons" of your own.

POP QUIZ

"There is none righteous, not even one; there is none who understands, there is none who seeks for God; all have turned aside, together they have become useless; there is none who does good, there is not even one."

⌒ Romans 3:10-12

The students have just zipped up their backpacks to dash home from school after a hard day of classes. But the principal's bizarre announcement over the P.A. system stops them in their tracks: "Students, we have an unexpected guest visiting us today, and I want everyone to immediately proceed to the auditorium for an assembly."

Some people grumble as they head for the auditorium. Others are curious and wonder, *Who is this guy who thinks he's important enough to extend an already long day? He'd better be good.*

The auditorium fills with whispers of complaint and speculation. Soon the guest walks onto the stage. He has a wise face with a long white beard. He wears a flowing white robe. His voice resonates throughout the assembly as the crowd becomes silent.

"Hello, students. I am God. Some of you don't recognize Me, and I'm concerned that many of you are going to flunk My final exam. Therefore, I've come to give you a little pop quiz." He begins to pass out copies of the Ten Commandments. His voice is deep and solemn as He continues. "You may score yourselves. If you have kept a commandment perfectly, give yourself a 10 for that one. Otherwise, give yourself a zero. Do that for each of the commandments. A perfect score is 100. That's the only passing grade. Any score less than 100 means complete failure."

Everyone is finished in 15 minutes. No one passes.

Attempting to achieve righteousness on our own would require that we score 100 on the Ten Commandments as well as the hundreds of other laws in the Bible. Only one person has ever achieved that feat—Jesus. He doesn't expect the same of us. That's why He provided a better way to "pass the test." All we have to do is put our faith in Him, and He covers our sins, shortcomings, and failures with His love, mercy, and forgiveness. If you believe in Him, congratulations! You've passed!

Discussion Starters:

1. If you would like to see how well you would have done on the pop quiz, turn to Exodus 20:1-17. (But also read Matthew 5:21-30 to see that murder = name-calling, and adultery = lust.) What's your score?
2. Why does everyone fail the test?
3. How can a holy God allow unholy people into heaven? What is His remedy for this eternal dilemma?

Lifeline:

Without the cross, heaven would be an empty dream.

THE GIFT

"For all have sinned and fall short of the glory of God, being justified as a gift by His grace through the redemption which is in Christ Jesus; whom God displayed publicly as a propitiation in His blood through faith."

⇝ Romans 3:23-25

How would you like a brand-new Porsche, Lamborghini, or Lexus—for free? How about a MasterCard with unlimited spending and no bills to pay . . . ever?

God has an even better offer. Today's passage gets to the very heart of Scripture. It tells us that we all have sinned. The wages of sin is death. The horror of death is separation from God in hell. That's where we're headed and what we deserve. But wait! God is offering us a gift—an amazing, overwhelming, unparalleled, unmatchable gift.

Step forward and receive your gift of being justified. (Say what?)

Justification is a big word that means your glob of accumulated sins has been totally forgiven and you have been declared righteous. How do you become justified? It's a gift from God—no charge. What did you do to deserve this life-saving gift? Not a thing! That's the definition of *grace*, bestowing something that is completely undeserved. *Redemption* is the process by which all this happens—Jesus' blood being shed for you on the cross. And the last big word in today's passage is *propitiation*, which is a sacrifice that appeases the wrath of God toward our sin and prevents us from receiving the brunt of His judgment.

Recently a college athlete came to my office to talk about God. He had caused two abortions. His wife had left him. His drinking was out of control. In his search for meaning in life, he scoffed at the idea of a personal, loving God.

At the very moment I began to explain the Bible's description of the love of a heavenly Father for His Son, my daughter brought my 12-day-old grandson to see me. He was dressed in a tiny hat and pajamas. As she placed the precious package in my arms, my daughter spoke for him: "Granddad, I want to go hunting with you."

I was overcome with a dad's love too powerful for words. The athlete saw the picture of God's redemption unfold before his eyes. That night he gave his life to Christ and has since dedicated his life to purity so others might see the truth as well.

Discussion Starters:

1. How can you explain God's amazing grace?
2. How should His grace motivate you?
3. Why is grace so hard to comprehend?

Lifeline:

Grace is getting good things we don't deserve. Mercy is not getting bad things we do deserve.

MEET THE TWINS

"For what does the Scripture say? 'Abraham believed God, and it was credited to him as righteousness.' Now to the one who works, his wage is not credited as a favor, but as what is due. But to the one who does not work, but believes in Him who justifies the ungodly, his faith is credited as righteousness."

↩ Romans 4:3-5

In Genesis 25 we read about a pair of remarkable twins born to the Jewish patriarch Isaac and his wife, Rebekah. The amazing account includes a play-by-play description of the birth of Jacob and Esau. Esau actually was born first, with Jacob close behind, grasping Esau's heel. In their culture, the first-born son—even the firstborn of a set of twins—was traditionally given a special blessing. But through a long and complicated chain of events, Jacob was the one who ended up with the majority of the birthright, blessings, and rewards. Romans 9 refers to this pair of twins to illustrate how the Gentiles came to receive God's blessings even though they weren't "firstborn."

But today I'm more interested in another set of twins whose importance is emphasized in Romans. As significant as birth order was in the Old Testament, it was no more important than understanding the birth order of the twins we're going to call "Faith" and "Works." Many Christians get confused about the birth order of this pair. But today's passage is clear: As it was with Abraham, so it is with us.

Faith is the firstborn and therefore should come first in our lives. We are saved by faith. Through faith we are able to trust Christ and give our lives to Him (Ephesians 2:8-9). Faith is necessary for joining God's family (John 1:12) and being declared righteous before God (James 2:23). Nothing else can get you to heaven—no good deed, church ritual, sacrifice for another, or life of absolute piety.

If the second twin, Works, tries to come before Faith or stand apart from him, there will always be problems. But when he comes second in the birth order, things go as God planned. In fact, if Faith is genuine, he will always have Works along with him (James 2:17-18). And they make a dynamic duo you don't want to miss out on.

Discussion Starters:

1. Why don't works play any part in saving you?
2. Why can't faith be genuine if not accompanied by good works?
3. Can you think of any church rituals that may be good but can never take the place of faith? What are they?

Lifeline:

Are the Faith and Works twins alive and well in your life today?

WHAT A TEAM!

"For this reason it is by faith, in order that it may be in accordance with grace, so that the promise will be guaranteed to all the descendants, not only to those who are of the Law, but also to those who are of the faith of Abraham, who is the father of us all."

↪ Romans 4:16

When I first walked onto the field as a member of the Southern Methodist University football team, I found myself surrounded by large, fast, confident athletes who towered over my six-foot, 195-pound frame. They had the moves, the biceps, and the scholarships!

Hayden Fry was the head coach of the Mustangs in those days. Although I was a seventh-team defensive noseguard as a freshman, he took a special liking to me. (Who knows why?) He "adopted" me during my sophomore year, maybe because I was too stupid to give up. The first game of my junior year, he started me—and he never put me on the bench again. He played me at Ohio State, Michigan State, Tennessee, Texas, and Arkansas. He even tried to send me to the Hula Bowl, but the regulating committee found out I wasn't the superstar he had made me out to be.

He took me off the bench and put me in the game, and for that I'll be forever grateful. As a result, I played my guts out for him. I'll love him until I die.

It wasn't too hard to figure out that playing on Astroturf in Dallas on Saturday afternoons with a free college education was better than paying hundreds of thousands of dollars to get educated and then sitting on the sidelines.

Paul makes a similar point in Romans. Instead of attempting to pay for my own sins and ending up in hell for all eternity, my faith in Jesus is like a "scholarship" that entitles me to full tuition in heaven forever and allows me to see some terrific action in the game of life in the meantime. The deal gets even better when I realize that God becomes not only my Coach, but also my Father.

And as good as that sounds, the final bonus is that this "team" has no cutoff. I hope you've already joined. If so, there's still room for all your friends. Why not let them know about it?

Discussion Starters:

1. What does it mean that Abraham is "the father of us all"?
2. Becoming a Christian is like being adopted by God (Romans 8:23). How can an adopted orphan show gratitude to his or her new family?
3. How can you do more for our "team"? Who else can you recruit?

Lifeline:

Gratitude builds commitment. Commitment builds obedience. Obedience builds countless blessings.

PAIN AND PROMISE

"We also exult in our tribulations, knowing that tribulation brings about perseverance; and perseverance, proven character; and proven character, hope; and hope does not disappoint, because the love of God has been poured out within our hearts through the Holy Spirit who was given to us."

↩ Romans 5:3-5

My first girlfriend left me for my best friend in junior high. That was puppy love, but it still left a pain in my gut.

My first wife left me for my best friend in college. That was true love which left a pain in my heart that lasted for many months. It almost killed me.

Both my first wife and my college friend are wonderful people. Although there's little doubt that initiating divorce is wrong in most circumstances, I've never blamed them, nor have I ever been bitter. I cried my eyes out for a few months. Yet during that horrible time I fell completely in love with God for the first time. I learned to give Him my todays as well as my tomorrows.

God not only healed my broken heart, but He also brought Debbie-Jo to me. (In case I haven't told you, she is the greatest woman alive and the mom of my four kids.) God also gave me a passion for people who, like myself, find themselves in the bottom of an emotional canyon with no apparent way out.

I learned a lot in my brokenness before God. I can see Him at His best when I am at my worst. He is never closer than the day I fall on my face. Pain gives me a choice. When I choose to run to God, I get *better*. If I choose to rely on my own answers, I get *bitter*.

I discovered that my pain is like a golf tee. I can use it to be "teed off" or "teed up." Pain either makes me mad and useless or else it helps me go a lot farther than I might have otherwise.

God is never more ready to fill our hearts than when we're deep in the canyon of despair. As we learn to rely on His Holy Spirit, our tribulations turn to perseverance, then to proven character, and finally to hope. Our painful times will come and go, but God's promises remain available to us all the time.

Discussion Starters:

1. How do trials build character when God is in charge?
2. What has been the greatest time of brokenness you've ever faced? Did it eventually result in stronger character and/or hope? Explain.
3. How can you prepare yourself to endure painful trials that lie ahead?

Lifeline:

Bitter or better? It's your choice when the painful ball of failure lands in your court.

DYING FOR AN ENEMY

"For while we were still helpless, at the right time Christ died for the ungodly. For one will hardly die for a righteous man; though perhaps for the good man someone would dare even to die. But God demonstrates His own love toward us, in that while we were yet sinners, Christ died for us."

Romans 5:6-8

It was Christmas Day in the cold, damp foxholes on a European battlefield during World War I. The details of the story remain foggy, but I remember reading long ago of an unprecedented event that took place on this particular day set aside to honor the Christ Child's birth.

A platoon of Germans had made a run across the coiled barbed wire barrier to ambush their American enemies, but the raid was called off when heavy gunfire stopped them in their tracks. Several Germans died on the spot. But one German soldier took a hit in the shoulder, became tangled in the barbed wire, and lay there helpless and screaming.

His painful wails persisted until one brave young American soldier stood and ran to the German's rescue. As he removed his enemy from the entanglement, all gunfire stopped in grateful astonishment. The heroic American freed the wounded warrior and carried him to his friends. Without fear, he then turned and walked gallantly back to his foxhole. Eventually the battle resumed. But on one Christmas Day, for a brief shining moment, two groups of soldiers saw what it meant to be willing to die for one's enemy.

What the American soldier did for his German foe is a picture of what Jesus has done for each of us. We're tangled in sin, writhing in emotional and spiritual pain, and vulnerable to attack. Nobody said Jesus *had* to come and die for us. It was His idea. He volunteered for the mission and carried it out to the end. In doing so, we all learn that "the end" is not death but resurrection and eternal life.

In response, perhaps more of us can begin to bravely reach across barriers to show love and compassion to others we usually don't care much about. It's a risky mission that will require faith and courage. Are you up to it?

Discussion Starters:

1. How does this story remind you of Jesus and His heroic death on the cross?
2. Why were we considered enemies of God before we surrendered our lives to His leadership?
3. Who are a few "enemies" whom you would eventually like to see put their faith in Jesus?

Lifeline:

Since Jesus was willing to die for us as His enemies, think how much He will love us as His friends!

A GRACE TRIP

"What shall we say then? Are we to continue in sin so that grace may increase? May it never be! How shall we who died to sin still live in it? Or do you not know that all of us who have been baptized into Christ Jesus have been baptized into His death? Therefore we have been buried with Him through baptism into death, so that as Christ was raised from the dead through the glory of the Father, so we too might walk in newness of life."

⏤ Romans 6:1-4

"What's the big deal? Jesus will forgive me anyway!"

Married businesspeople sometimes use this phrase when they're traveling alone and have the opportunity to spend the night with a lovely young stranger. College students sometimes say it when they're at a party where everyone else is getting drunk. High school kids may think it when a joint is passed around or when a make-out session starts to get out of control.

We read that twice as many "Christian" kids watch MTV as non-Christian kids. We read that "Christian" teens have sex almost as often as non-Christian kids. "Christian" adults in Hollywood, in the NBA and NFL, in the White House, in Congress, on Wall Street, and elsewhere in the country rationalize alcohol abuse, cheating in business, pornography, and sexual promiscuity. "It's okay. Jesus will forgive me."

Paul states in no uncertain terms how God feels about our naïve rationalizations. "May it never be!" In the original Greek language, he uses the most forceful negative statement available.

If you truly become a follower of Christ, your old "self" who tends to commit such acts of lawlessness *dies*. That's not you anymore; that's the *old* you. That person is dead. Gone. Kaput. The *new* you exists only because Christ brought you to life. You should, therefore, be attuned to His desires rather than your old, sinful ones. The new and improved you says, "If it pleases God, I do it. If it doesn't please God and conform to His Word, I say no."

God's grace doesn't cost you a cent, but it cost Jesus His life. Overlooking it or trying to abuse it is just about the worst insult we can direct at God.

Discussion Starters:

1. What does living on a "grace trip" mean to you?
2. Why do some people treat grace like a disposable toy?
3. After studying today's passage, what do you plan to do in response?

Lifeline:

True grace produces true obedience.

DEAD TO SIN

"Now if we have died with Christ, we believe that we shall also live with Him, knowing that Christ, having been raised from the dead, is never to die again; death no longer is master over Him. For the death that He died, He died to sin once for all; but the life that He lives, He lives to God. Even so consider yourselves to be dead to sin, but alive to God in Christ Jesus."

⮑ Romans 6:8-11

My son Cooper, now 17, plays football like there's no tomorrow. Some of the fans call him "Missile Man." Though only 5' 10" tall and 160 pounds, the way he runs down the field on a kickoff, blasting defenders off their feet, reminds me of a bowling ball rocketing down the alley, spreading pins everywhere.

But recently the Missile Man was temporarily knocked out of commission. A series of concussions put Cooper on the sidelines.

After a hard game, Cooper had been warned by his doctor how concussions have a "mounting effect" as each one makes the brain more susceptible to the next, opening the door to brain damage and severe postconcussion syndrome. But Cooper had begged to play in one more game, and the doctor reluctantly granted his wish.

Early in the second half Cooper tackled a runner with a hard hit. The ball carrier was knocked to the ground and jumped back up; Cooper's body went completely limp. For many weeks after that game, Cooper experienced painful headaches, insomnia, and dizziness.

Sin works much the same way as a series of concussions. The first blow doesn't seem so bad, maybe even harmless. We can't detect any damage. We don't change our behavior even when the second sin adds to the effects of the first, as do the third, fourth, and fifth. By then a caring "doctor" has issued the warning, "You're going to hurt yourself." If we don't heed His wise advice, we may experience a knockout blow that sidelines us longer than we might wish.

Is it time for a spiritual CAT scan to ensure that sin is not accumulating in your life and threatening serious damage? Listen to the Great Physician. Take care of yourself. We need you in this game!

Discussion Starters:
1. What does it mean to consider yourself "dead to sin"?
2. How does a healthy relationship with Jesus enable you to stop sinning willfully?
3. What can you do if you discover apparent sin in your life today?

Lifeline:
To be alive to God is to be dead to sin.

I CAN'T STOP SINNING

"For what I am doing, I do not understand; for I am not practicing what I would like to do, but I am doing the very thing I hate. But if I do the very thing I do not want to do, I agree with the Law, confessing that the Law is good. So now, no longer am I the one doing it, but sin which dwells in me."

⟿ Romans 7:15-17

On Saturday nights I cohost Focus on the Family's *Life on the Edge Live!* teen call-in radio show. It provides me with endless opportunities (which I cherish) to reach across the national airwaves and hug America's hurting kids.

Many calls are encouraging! A girl in New York gets a thousand friends in her public high school to wear Christian T-shirts. A guy in Las Vegas witnesses to his unsaved friends daily. A Christian in Florida tells his girlfriend that all forms of sex are for marriage only. A Dallas girl sets strong moral standards that exclude drinking, tobacco, drugs, and petting.

Some calls, however, are painful to hear. Recently a 15-year-old girl from California pleaded for help. Her involvement in drinking, drugs, and sex was out of control and affecting her physically and emotionally. She told me, "I want to stop but I just can't." I encouraged her to put an end to her sexual involvements and save herself for her true love who would someday seal his commitment to her with a wedding ring. She wasn't convinced: "I can't quit. I just can't do it."

So many of us understand her desperation. Guilt and failure are two of Satan's favorite tools to eliminate any motivation to repent and turn to God in obedience. They speak to our inner spirit and incapacitate us.

You've blown it in the past? Join the club! Jesus knows you're not perfect. That's why He came to earth in the first place. But He wants us to trust Him and keep trying. Every day is a brand-new opportunity to say, "I might have failed yesterday, but today is the first day of the rest of my life. Christ can give me the grace to never sin like that again!"

Discussion Starters:

1. Why is it impossible to do all the right things in our own power?
2. How do guilt and failure work together to defeat us? Do you have any personal examples?
3. How does Christ help us break free from the cycles of guilt and failure that try to keep us down?

Lifeline:

Pointing out someone's failures spells failure. Pointing out someone's successes spells success.

FREE AT LAST

"But if I am doing the very thing I do not want, I am no longer the one doing it, but sin which dwells in me. . . . Wretched man that I am! Who will set me free from the body of this death? Thanks be to God through Jesus Christ our Lord! So then, on the one hand I myself with my mind am serving the law of God, but on the other, with my flesh the law of sin."

↵ Romans 7:20, 24-25

I saw a television interview with a 65-year-old man who spent four years in a Nazi slave camp. He was part of a group forced to burrow a huge tunnel through a mountain of rock to conceal German covert bombing and missile operations. Many of his friends died in that tunnel. They all were starved beyond belief and beaten unmercifully.

When the Allied soldiers defeated Germany and arrived at the tunnel to free the slaves, the men literally clasped their hands together in prayerful celebration. They were finally free to eat, free to laugh, free to cry, free to go home to their families. They probably had a better understanding of freedom than most people ever will because they were deprived of it for so long.

It's a terrible thing when we *choose* slavery. Yet all of us occasionally choose to be slaves to sin—alcohol, tobacco, drugs, pornography, sex, or any number of other "masters." In most cases, we start out with willful participation but find ourselves enslaved and miserable before we know it. And we discover we aren't able to break free on our own power.

But when we turn to Jesus, He forgives us and frees us. He lifts us from our sin and severs our chains with His chisel of grace. I know this is true because people tell me.

That's how Diane stopped smoking.

That's how Wes stopped having sex with his girlfriend.

That's how Lori stopped using drugs.

That's how Bill stopped cheating his customers.

That's how Bryce stopped looking at nude pictures in magazines.

No chain around your heart is too powerful for Jesus to break. He can free you whenever you are ready.

Discussion Starters:

1. Why do so many people allow sin to enslave them?
2. What kinds of "slavery" do you see among other people your age?
3. If someone asked you how to break free from some sin that was enslaving him or her, what would you say?

Lifeline:

When we agree to let God be our Master, nothing else has the power to make us slaves.

THE LAW OF THE SPIRIT

"Therefore there is now no condemnation for those who are in Christ Jesus. For the law of the Spirit of life in Christ Jesus has set you free from the law of sin and of death. For what the Law could not do, weak as it was through the flesh, God did: sending His own Son in the likeness of sinful flesh and as an offering for sin."

↪ Romans 8:1-3

The following declaration of freedom is true and was candidly expressed by a 16-year-old friend of mine.

Joe,

Thanks for your letter and the book. It is very good and has helped me greatly with some problems I have been facing lately. I can feel myself changing greatly every day since I decided to let God run my life. It is truly amazing. I get so excited about life now, it is just unbelievable. Before I accepted Jesus Christ into my heart, I had a problem with drinking.

At first, I thought drinking was all right since I grew up around it. How terribly wrong I was! I tried to stop drinking after realizing I was putting myself in bodily harm. The first night of that month was one of the toughest struggles I've been through. I felt that I needed to drink more than anything else. But I didn't. The second night of that month, I gave in. My strength was not strong enough to overcome my dependency. I felt like a failure. I knew I could not do it alone.

Now, as a true Christian, I've tried to stop again. This time it was different! I asked Jesus to help me with my problem and to show me the way to a happy life, and that is exactly what He did. When I tried to stop drinking for the second time, it was one of the easiest things I have ever done. I felt no need whatsoever to have alcohol in my system. It was amazing how much easier it was that second time. But we both know why it was so easy. It was because Jesus was in the driver's seat.

I have never been so happy, and this happiness will be growing more and more every day! I know there will be trials, but I also know that whatever comes my way, with the Lord's help, I will be able to handle anything!

Discussion Starters:

1. What was the secret of the 16-year-old's success?
2. Why did he fail the first time he tried to stop drinking?
3. How can the Romans 8:1-3 passage help you with your own struggles to overcome a problem you are facing?

Lifeline:

When I try, I fail. When I trust, Jesus succeeds.

A WINNER EVERY TIME

"Who will separate us from the love of Christ? Will tribulation, or distress, or persecution, or famine, or nakedness, or peril, or sword? . . . But in all these things we overwhelmingly conquer through Him who loved us. For I am convinced that neither death, nor life, nor angels, nor principalities, nor things present, nor things to come, nor powers, nor height, nor depth, nor any other created thing, will be able to separate us from the love of God, which is in Christ Jesus our Lord."

↪ Romans 8:35, 37-39

Every day countless millions of dollars are literally thrown away. They are thrown into slot machines, onto blackjack tables, beneath rolling dice, and in various other games of chance in the alluring casinos that sparkle like diamond-studded earrings across our country.

When you walk in the door of a casino, your odds of walking out a winner are usually less than 40 percent. In addition, income from many such establishments supports organized crime. Still, there is no shortage of people who continue to dream big and "lose their shirts" night after disappointing night.

Even worse than losing money is losing someone close to you, especially if you have invested your heart in the other person. It may be that *you* do everything possible to salvage the relationship, but the other person simply decides to walk away. My mom lost her father that way. I lost a girl that way—one I loved very much. Your heart breaks in two as the door slams shut. The pain is indescribable.

Losing makes you cautious. It makes you wonder about commitments. It makes you doubt the sincerity of others.

Well, there's one person on whom I would bet my entire savings—and even my life. I know for a fact that Jesus already laid His life on the line for me. He has promised never to leave me, and I believe Him. Why? Because "while we were yet sinners, Christ died for us" (Romans 5:8).

Christian faith rarely involves bright neon lights, clanging slot machine bells, or glitzy entertainers. But it's a sure thing that never stops paying off. You'll be counting your winnings for eternity. You can bet on it.

Discussion Starters:

1. Why might you be cautious about believing someone will never leave you?
2. Why is God's Word believable? What portion of it do you really need to believe right now?
3. How does it make you feel knowing for sure that God will love you forever?

Lifeline:

Memorizing today's passage is like having a priceless gold coin in your pocket.

OH, THOSE NAMES!

"As He says also in Hosea, 'I will call those who were not My people, "My people," and her who was not beloved "beloved." And it shall be that in the place where it was said to them, "You are not My people," there they shall be called sons of the living God.' "

✎ Romans 9:25-26

As I think back over my growing-up days in grade school, junior high, and high school, I still grieve a little over the names that people called me: Wimp! Loser! Quitter! Jerk! Two-faced! Punk! Shorty! Fatty! Chicken!

Ouch! Those names (and you may have been called worse ones) cut like a knife, don't they! But I've also found that other names have just the opposite effect: Teammate! Coach! Leader! Friend! Lover! Sweetheart! Honey!

It doesn't take long to forget petty, negative names slipping off someone's loose tongue when I dwell on the names used by people I truly care about (who also care about me). Of all the names I've ever been called, two will be my favorites for all time. I never cease to appreciate when my mom and dad smile and call me "son." And I don't think any name will ever compare to the title my kids give me: "Daddy."

God could have called you and me "slaves." He could have called us "losers." He could have called us "unlovable." He could have called us "strangers."

But the moment we put our faith in Jesus, He calls us "sons" and "daughters." God has big plans for us as His children—plans more grandiose than the very creation of the universe. His plans unfold continually as He looks into our hearts, where His Holy Spirit is at work. With God as our Father, every day is a new adventure.

Discussion Starters:

1. What are the most positive associations you have with being called "son" or "daughter"?
2. God could have kept us at arm's length. Why do you think He chooses such endearing names for us and invites us to get closer to Him?
3. What are some of the names for God that mean the most to you? (Father? Shepherd? Counselor? King? Others?)

Lifeline:

Prayer is participation in a Father/son or Father/daughter banquet.

YOUNG HEROES

"If you confess with your mouth Jesus as Lord, and believe in your heart that God raised Him from the dead, you will be saved; for with the heart a person believes, resulting in righteousness, and with the mouth he confesses, resulting in salvation."

⤳ Romans 10:9-10

Kathy D.'s father was an alcoholic who darkened his daughter's junior year in high school by committing suicide and leaving his family in utter dismay. Kathy soon turned to drugs in her desperate attempt to numb the pain and escape a cruel reality that left her hopeless.

Then, like a laser light from heaven, a bright-eyed, 17-year-old named Kathy Adams showed up and invited her to the Young Life club my wife and I led in our small Ozark mountain community. Kathy A. took Kathy D. under her wing like a mother eagle covering her nesting chicks, providing warmth and protection. Kathy D. soon allowed Christ to fill the void in her heart left by her disturbed father. The two Kathys lit up the local high school with their warmth, and soon they had many of their friends coming to Young Life club. One night 30 students gave their hearts to Christ. Over the years, more than 500 others have asked Jesus into their hearts in that little three-room house.

If you look for them, I think you'll find modern-day heroes in every high school in America. They are the valiant teenagers who not only believe that Jesus died and rose from the grave, but also are eager to tell their friends about Him. They guide a searching generation of their peers to Bible studies, prayer groups, and youth meetings so as many as possible will find purpose, meaning, and eternal life in heaven.

Discussion Starters:

1. Do you know any modern-day heroes in your school? How can you be supportive of the stand they are taking for Jesus?
2. What does it mean to "confess with your mouth that Jesus is Lord" in practical ways? Is it enough to "believe in your heart" if you never get around to telling people about it? Explain.
3. Who are three people you can invite to a church activity before the week is over?

Lifeline:

Believing in your heart and confessing with your mouth are the "heads" and "tails" of the same coin.

AMAZING FAITH

"So faith comes from hearing, and hearing by the word of Christ."

⤴ Romans 10:17

It's not hard to be amazed at God's design for the world when we take a close look at nature. Who would ever believe that a tiny little acorn could get covered with a little dirt and, in time, become a mammoth tree capable of providing shade to a country home, supporting a swing from an upper limb, and cradling a tree house for dozens of neighborhood kids? Yet we've all seen enormous oak trees, so we can marvel at God's design.

Who would ever believe that a Canadian goose would sense a change in the weather, lift off from the shores of Alaska, and migrate all the way to the Gulf of Mexico? Yet we know that's what happens, and we see God's plan for the goose quite clearly.

The great thing about faith is that people, too, can tap into God's plan for them and find inner peace and satisfaction in an otherwise hectic world. The Word of God says to guard your heart (Proverbs 4:23), and my beautiful 19-year-old friend Kalene has the faith to hear and respond. She "saves her kisses" for her future husband, and him alone. She passes up other would-be suitors most Saturday nights, believing that some day she will find "Mr. Right" and will be able to offer him the virgin soil of her heart that has never been tampered with.

The Word of Christ says that no one can serve two masters (Matthew 6:24). So with great faith, Jason, Jarred, Jill, Erin, and others avoid the potential masters of drugs, alcohol, sex, pornography, blasphemous music, and wild weekend parties. They remain faithful to their pure Christian convictions.

Faith is belief accompanied by commitment. The words of Christ through Scripture fill our minds with His precious promises, and our hearts turn those words into a lifestyle that sets us free. Faith comes from hearing, and hearing by the Word of Christ. Most of us have heard. But do we have the faith to act?

Discussion Starters:

1. How does the Word of Christ eventually become a living and active faith?
2. What portion of Scripture did you hear recently that you responded to in faith? What was your response?
3. How does someone's inner faith manifest itself for others to see?

Lifeline:

Hearing with your ears produces interest. Hearing with your heart produces faith.

A SECOND-ROUND GRAFT PICK

"But if some of the branches were broken off, and you, being a wild olive, were grafted in among them and became partaker with them of the rich root of the olive tree, do not be arrogant toward the branches; but if you are arrogant, remember that it is not you who supports the root, but the root supports you. You will say then, 'Branches were broken off so that I might be grafted in.' "

⌐ Romans 11:17-19

A recent season of professional football featured a Cinderella story that surprised the critics and amazed the analysts. The Randy Moss story was everywhere. Though his speed, size, and vertical jump had tantalized every scout in the NFL, he was also well known for his explosive behavior on and off the field. He was considered an undisciplined street fighter and therefore not much of a draft choice. Sixteen teams passed over him in the draft.

Then came the Minnesota Vikings and a veteran all-pro receiver named Cris Carter, who is a Christian. Cris Carter agreed to "adopt" Randy Moss and pour his life into the young rookie. The covers of *ESPN Magazine, Sports Illustrated,* and *USA Today* told us the rest of the story. The young rookie was nothing less than sensational. The throwaway became a star. The long shot became a sure shot. The team who adopted him became division champions! A "wild branch" was grafted in and became a part of a team— a team that went to the Super Bowl.

Likewise, the Jews were (and always will be) God's chosen people. For years the Gentiles were "out of the loop" when it came to getting to God. But Jesus' death changed all that. God "so loved the *world*," not just the Jewish people. With incredible genius and love beyond belief, God reached down to a wild and unattached branch and grafted us into a nurturing and growing tree. We didn't really belong there, but God made it happen.

Randy Moss joined Cris Carter and the Vikings in the streets of Minneapolis for a night of celebration. The believing Gentiles will someday join the Hebrew children of God in the golden streets of heaven for a celebration that will never end!

Discussion Starters:

1. Has anyone ever stood up for you, allowing you to be accepted by a group who might have otherwise rejected you? Give some specific examples.
2. How does it feel to realize that God personally reaches out to include you in His great love?
3. Since God has grafted you into His family, what are some victories you hope to achieve for Him someday?

Lifeline:

Amazing demonstrations of love deserve equally amazing responses of obedience.

FASCINATION

"Oh, the depth of the riches both of the wisdom and knowledge of God! How unsearchable are His judgments and unfathomable His ways!"

Romans 11:33

Are you ready to be fascinated? Consider with me for a moment some awesome facts that reflect the wisdom of our Creator expressed through His creation.

The human body has 100 trillion cells. A single cell contains enough information to fill 10 million volumes of literature.

The human eye can handle 1.5 million simultaneous messages. One hundred thirty-seven million nerve endings pick up every message that the eye sends to the brain. Even Darwin wrote in his book *Origin of the Species*, "To suppose that the eye with all of its inimitable contrivances for adjusting focus to different distances, for emitting different amounts of light, and for the correction of spherical and chromatic aberration could have been formed by natural selection seems, I freely confess, absurd in the highest degree."

The inner ear contains as many circuits as the telephone system of most cities.

The information in the brain could fill approximately 20 million books. The brain has 10 billion circuits, each five to 10 times more complex than any computer ever built.

The universe has millions of galaxies. The Milky Way galaxy alone has over 100 billion stars. If our universe were on a scale where the earth and moon were only one inch apart, you would still have to travel 10 million miles just to reach the center of our galaxy. (And after 4,000 years of scientific effort, our greatest space accomplishment has been to successfully transport a person to and from the moon.)

Some people say all these amazingly intricate designs and massively expansive spaces happened by chance. They theorize that the creation of the universe and of human beings is nothing more than a lucky accident. But it doesn't require much of an IQ to see the wishful thinking in modern science. Likewise, it doesn't take much faith to believe in an intentional and loving Creator, and to stand in awe of His work all around us.

Discussion Starters:

1. Do you believe you were designed by a divine Creator, or are you the result of a lucky accident? Why?
2. How does the awesome complexity of God's world affect your faith?
3. Why do so many men and women try to refute God and His majestic power?

Lifeline:

George Beverly Shea says it best when he sings, "My God, how great Thou art."

CONFORMED OR TRANSFORMED?

"Therefore I urge you, brethren, by the mercies of God, to present your bodies a living and holy sacrifice, acceptable to God, which is your spiritual service of worship. And do not be conformed to this world, but be transformed by the renewing of your mind, so that you may prove what the will of God is, that which is good and acceptable and perfect."

⮌ Romans 12:1-2

The Japanese kamikaze pilots of World War II flew their fighter bombers directly into the decks of American aircraft carriers, giving their lives for the country they loved. An American soldier dives on a live hand grenade in a German foxhole to shield four buddies from the explosion. Sacrificial deaths. We are amazed by them. They inspire us with undaunted courage and valor. My 17-year-old friend George lunged in front of his girlfriend during a drive-by shooting in Boston. The shooter unloaded his pistol into George's neck and back. His girlfriend was unharmed. George also miraculously survived, but his act was no less a sacrifice.

Living sacrifices don't get as much press coverage, but they can be equally courageous. Some kids abstain from drinking at parties, for which they are ridiculed and never asked to return. Some teenage guys protect their dates' purity at all costs, fighting off peer pressure, raging hormones, and cultural acceptance of "safe sex." Some Christian teens go to Bible studies and youth groups, and then live out their faith the other six days of the week.

These people all make sacrifices for God. They are on the altar, offering their very bodies and souls to Him and showing others what Christian faith is all about. I admire girls like Jill and Johnia, who date the two best football players in our school. The guys didn't have a lot of Christian background when they met Jill and Johnia, but they're catching up quickly. Not only do both of them now know Christ as their Lord and Savior, so do many other guys on the team who have seen a difference in them—all a result of what God did in response to Jill's and Johnia's unwavering stand for Christ.

When God is at work you can "get a life" *and* be a holy sacrifice. Being a living sacrifice is the best of both worlds!

Discussion Starters:

1. What happens to someone who becomes conformed to this world? Why do so many people tend to conform?
2. How does a person become *transformed* rather than *conformed* to the world around him or her?
3. What makes a living sacrifice "holy and acceptable to God"?

Lifeline:

Conforming or transforming? You're always doing one or the other.

OVERCOMING BITTERNESS

"Never pay back evil for evil to anyone. Respect what is right in the sight of all men. If possible, so far as it depends on you, be at peace with all men. Never take your own revenge, beloved, but leave room for the wrath of God, for it is written, 'Vengeance is Mine, I will repay,' says the Lord. 'But if your enemy is hungry, feed him, and if he is thirsty, give him a drink; for in so doing you will heap burning coals on his head.' Do not be overcome by evil, but overcome evil with good."

↫ Romans 12:17-21

"I pledge allegiance to the flag of the United States of America and to the republic for which it stands, one nation, under God, indivisible, with liberty and justice for all."

The pledge of allegiance was written by Francis Bellamy in 1892. I like to connect the concepts of "freedom" and "under God." We may tend to think of freedom in terms of winning wars. Our soldiers from the Revolutionary War to Desert Storm have fought for freedom. Yet "freedom under God" is even more significant. God frees us from inner voices that threaten to enslave us in sin or trap us in mental instability, envy, anger, jealousy, or hatred.

The Civil War divided our nation, yet it brought to an end the insidious practice of slavery in America. Freedom under God promotes liberty and justice *for all*. Yet slavery in another form continues to rage in America. I see it in teenagers who want to kill themselves and couples who want to divorce. It's a slavery that cannot be ended with weapons or eloquently phrased proclamations. This freedom *does* require bloodshed—the blood of Christ applied for our sins.

Otherwise we all remain slaves to bitterness, which makes us hold grudges like a three-year-old holds a Butterfinger bar. Maybe your boyfriend was cruel to you. Your dad called you names. Your sister wore your favorite shirt and tore it. Your football coach kept you on the bench. The bitterness we harbor from such offenses burns like a hot coal inside of us.

We need freedom . . . under God. And we can receive it the moment we pledge Him our allegiance.

Discussion Starters:

1. Why is bitterness such a powerful slave master?
2. How does today's passage relate to the "freedom under God" concept?
3. Whom do you need to forgive today? How can Jesus' death on the cross help you?

Lifeline:

"Father, forgive them; for they do not know what they are doing" (Luke 23:34).

A HIGHER LAW

"Every person is to be in subjection to the governing authorities. For there is no authority except from God, and those which exist are established by God. Therefore whoever resists authority has opposed the ordinance of God."

⤳ Romans 13:1-2

As a high school student, Brandon had the good looks that could have taken him to Hollywood. His speed and strength could have taken him to all-star status in Division I football. His personality could have taken him on a date with almost any girl in Houston. But at 16 Brandon began to drink beer on Saturday nights, and within two years he was an alcoholic. His alcohol and drug habits led to failure in his high school football career, many broken relationships, two car wrecks, and even some prison time.

Alcohol is responsible for more automobile deaths, fire deaths, broken homes, wife abuse, child abuse, murders, and burglaries than any other single factor. Our government says it's illegal to drink alcohol if you're under 21. While that should be enough of a deterrent for Christian teenagers, God's law also says "strong drink" is wrong at *any* age.

The Bible refers to two kinds of alcoholic beverages. The first is *oinos*, a fermented grape juice purified by a small alcohol content. Historical research suggests that *oinos* had a maximum content of 2 percent alcohol. Jesus turned water into this kind of wine (John 2:1-11). The other biblical word for an alcoholic beverage is *yayin*, which refers to strong drink and is condemned many times in Scripture (Proverbs 23:29-35, for example).

Alcoholic consumption by teenagers is a case where our national laws confirm what the Bible teaches. But what if the law of the land contradicts God's law? For example, our government allows abortion, pornography, adultery, and homosexual sex, yet such practices remain in direct opposition to God's law. Even though they are legal, our Christian convictions should prevent our involvement in such things.

God has established governments, and we are to support them as much as we can with a clear conscience. But governments won't be standing before Him on judgment day. We remain responsible for our actions *as individuals*. And there's no better time to begin than during your teenage years.

Discussion Starters:

1. When civil law and God's law don't agree, which should you obey? Why?
2. Scripture doesn't address certain governmental laws (such as speed limits). How should we respond to such laws? Why?
3. Which current laws do you most tend to resist? Why?

Lifeline:

God's law always has a purpose: to protect us and provide for our well-being, happiness, and peace.

LUST KILLS

"Let us behave properly as in the day, not in carousing and drunkenness, not in sexual promiscuity and sensuality, not in strife and jealousy."

⌐ Romans 13:13

Recently I received yet another letter that tells the tragic story of what happens when someone mistakes lust for love.

> I just want to tell you I've made a terrible mistake. I had been dating a Christian guy for 11 months, [and] we both told each other our physical limit was kissing. A few months ago we began to go further than that. We never went all the way, though. I felt terrible every time we went further. My relationship with God was almost nonexistent. I still feel guilty. Please tell other teens how they should totally wait for their future spouse. I wish more than anything that I would've completely waited. Tell them to make a physical limit and stay behind that line. Tell them that no matter how much the temptation is to go further, don't give in. It will be worth the wait. Just to top things off, we broke up yesterday.

There's a huge difference between love and lust, but lust is such a chameleon that it's often hard to tell the two apart. I do know that most of the "I love you's" exchanged between guys and girls in high school and college are actually "I want you's." Otherwise, why do so many people break up when things don't go exactly as they had hoped?

If you're ever confused between love and lust, turn to the reassuring words of 1 Corinthians 13. You'll find no better definition of love. Here are just a few verses, but read the whole chapter: "Love is patient, love is kind and is not jealous; love does not brag and is not arrogant, does not act unbecomingly; it does not seek its own, is not provoked, does not take into account a wrong suffered, does not rejoice in unrighteousness, but rejoices with the truth" (vv. 4-6).

If this isn't your working definition, you don't yet know genuine love. And in this case, what you don't know *can* hurt you.

Discussion Starters:

1. How would you explain the difference between love and lust in your own words?
2. What people do you know who seem to be struggling most with lust issues? How can you help?
3. How can you keep your core values strong throughout your teenage years?

Lifeline:

"Lust can't wait to get. Love can't wait to give" (Josh McDowell).

PUT ON JESUS

"But put on the Lord Jesus Christ, and make no provision for the flesh in regard to its lusts."

~ Romans 13:14

My Labrador retriever seldom leaves my side. His shiny black coat glistens in the sunlight as he gallantly retrieves the doves, ducks, pheasants, and quail we hunt together each winter. He will chew on a sorry little gnawed-up chicken bone for hours, and you might lose a hand if you try to take it away from him. But if you lay a piece of freshly cooked sirloin steak on the sidewalk beside him, he'll drop that old bone in a split second!

Sin is *so* much like Ol' Brave's chewed-up chicken bone. It may satisfy your craving for a while, but only because you don't realize you could have something much better.

Take a look at these quotes from letters I received from high school friends:

- "I knew it was wrong, but I did it anyway."
- "I felt like I had 600 knives go through me. I was crushed."
- "I feel so used and ashamed."

Drinking *looks* fun. Sex *looks* fun. Sin *looks* cool. But when we get drawn into sinful activities, they all seem so meaningless, don't they?

God, as usual, is way ahead of us. He doesn't only tell us not to sin, but He also provides us with a much better option. Paul says to "put on the Lord Jesus Christ." In other words, we can access Jesus' continual companionship, friendship, and unconditional love. Anything else we pursue to fulfill our needs is a lame substitute.

Now take a look at these quotes from some of my other high school friends:

- "I have fallen in love with Jesus this year. God has blessed me with the strength to stay free from drugs, alcohol, and sex."
- "I have acquired this sense of peace that only He could bring."
- "While doing my Bible study this year my relationship with the Lord has grown greatly. . . . I used to rely on drugs and sex for fun, but now I know that God has forgiven me and loves me like none of that ever happened."

Discussion Starters:

1. What are some enticing sins you've encountered lately?
2. How can "putting on the Lord Jesus Christ" actually replace our desire to sin?
3. How can Jesus truly become a friend and source of fulfillment?

Lifeline:

When something you love is removed and you feel a void in your life, you can successfully replace it with something you love more.

JUDGE NOT

"But you, why do you judge your brother? Or you again, why do you regard your brother with contempt? For we will all stand before the judgment seat of God. . . . So then each one of us will give an account of himself to God. Therefore let us not judge one another anymore, but rather determine this—not to put an obstacle or a stumbling block in a brother's way."
⎈ Romans 14:10, 12-13

No one knew why the beautiful blonde drove her baby blue BMW convertible to the school principal's house each evening at 6:30 and stayed until 10:00. The principal was 35; the blonde was barely 22, fresh out of college and a new resident in the small community.

The community *did* know that the principal had lost his wife to cancer only a year before. Now rumors of his new "affair" spread across town like wildfire. What must the principal's 12-year-old daughter be witnessing? How could the principal appear so pious each Sunday morning in his Baptist church, nodding his head in response to the preacher's comments?

To add fuel to the fire, the blonde became obviously pregnant after a few months. She looked like she had swallowed a basketball. It was clear to everyone at school that she had also swallowed "a line" from the suave principal.

Tempers raged at the next school board meeting. A unanimous vote of the board expressed the town's judgment in a firm and final manner. The principal was asked to resign.

Forced to look for work in another town, the principal sorrowfully began to pack his 12-year-old daughter's clothes, dolls, and priceless books—books which happened to be in Braille. His daughter would have to look for another teacher who was specially trained to teach blind kids to read—just as she was finally finding hope after living in darkness since birth.

The blonde woman's grief at losing a client was minor compared to the pain she felt over the recent loss of her husband—the father of her new baby—a casualty of the war in the Persian Gulf. The sorrow of three people was intensified by the harsh judgment of a town that all too quickly formed erroneous opinions and spread false rumors.

Discussion Starters:

1. Why does today's passage come down so strongly against judging others?
2. Have you struggled with this problem in your own life? In what ways?
3. What steps can you begin to take in order to leave all matters of judgment in God's hands?

Lifeline:

It has been said that God hates the sin but loves the sinner. We should learn to do the same.

STUMBLING BLOCKS

"So then let us pursue the things which make for peace and the building up of one another. Do not tear down the work of God for the sake of food. All things indeed are clean, but they are evil for the man who eats and gives offense. It is good not to eat meat or to drink wine, or to do anything by which your brother stumbles."

⌒ Romans 14:19-21

Is it wrong to wear a low-cut dress?

Is it wrong to wear tight pants?

Is it wrong to French-kiss passionately and then make the other person stop before petting begins?

Is it wrong to drink a beer at a party?

Is it wrong to say you love someone so he or she will go further with you on a date?

Is it wrong to let a seductive undergarment show through a light-colored blouse or pants?

Is it wrong to wear powerful perfumes, hoping to arouse men's sexual fantasies?

To answer these all-important questions, define the word *enticement* in your mind. Then look closely at how the models are dressed in car ads and beer commercials. Ask a boy what he was thinking about when you wore those tight shorts to the Fourth of July picnic. Ask a younger friend what that can of beer in your hand does to your Christian witness.

Not everyone is necessarily pulled into sin by each of these things, but some people *are*. It's not enough to simply think about ourselves; it's just as important to consider our weaker Christian brothers and sisters, as well as those who haven't yet become Christians. Satan is a master at causing people to stumble. He knows our weaknesses like he knew Eve's craving for the forbidden fruit in the Garden of Eden. And if we're not careful, he uses *us* to initiate sin in other people's lives.

Some of our choices are obviously right or wrong. Others are less clear. But anything that threatens to trip up a fellow follower of Jesus should be avoided—because we *want* to, not because we *have* to. Our call is simple. Let's leave the blocks in the toy box and stop using them to make our brothers and sisters fall.

Discussion Starters:

1. What are some stumbling blocks that have been placed in your path? Did you get tripped up?
2. Can you recall causing anyone to "stumble" in the past?
3. Even if you're convinced that you're doing nothing wrong, is it possible that any of your behaviors might cause problems for someone else? If so, what do you think you should do?

Lifeline:

When we're free to do something, we're usually just as free *not* to.

THREE LITTLE WORDS

"Now we who are strong ought to bear the weaknesses of those without strength and not just please ourselves. Each of us is to please his neighbor for his good, to his edification. For even Christ did not please Himself. . . . Therefore, accept one another, just as Christ also accepted us to the glory of God."

↩ Romans 15:1-3, 7

One of my sons gets his feelings hurt far too easily. The other one shoots his mouth off too much. One of my daughters has a hard time saying she's sorry. The other one demands too much attention. My wife can't remember my favorite recipe and keeps adding onions to the meatloaf.

I used to fuss about their inconsistencies. Now, by God's grace, I hardly notice. In return they don't seem to mind my oversized feet and nose—not to mention my thousands of other faults too numerous to list in this book.

"Accept one another" is a simple three-word phrase that is the best possible prescription for holding a family together. Acceptance is the strongest glue for relationships. No earthquake or tornado can compare to its power.

My wife had a rocky childhood from contending with generations of family idiosyncrasies. At first her emotional wounds didn't fit into my pious formula for "the perfect wife." Yet we have a blast together these days because I've learned to accept her just as she is and thank God for giving me far more than I deserve!

My good buddy Lee Eaton raises horses in the bluegrass hills of Kentucky. A few years ago he bought a young colt that turned out to be crippled. The previous owner offered to refund Lee's money, but Lee had grown to love the young horse and accepted her as if she were perfect. A couple of years passed and the filly gave birth to a beautiful little foal . . . that grew up and won the Kentucky Derby! Lee has given away a good share of the $35 million that little crippled horse made for him. More important to him is his priceless family, who have learned from Lee that good things happen when we "accept one another."

Discussion Starters:

1. What does it mean to "accept one another"? Think of some specific examples.
2. What "faults" have you noticed in those you love? How can acceptance help you downplay those faults and see more clearly the worth of each person?
3. What changes would you expect to see if everyone in your family began to accept one another completely?

Lifeline:

Acceptance prevents any shortcoming from diminishing a person's sense of worth.

SPEAK UP!

"For I will not presume to speak of anything except what Christ has accomplished through me, resulting in the obedience of the Gentiles by word and deed, in the power of signs and wonders, in the power of the Spirit; so that . . . I have fully preached the gospel of Christ."

↩ Romans 15:18-19

Jill Brawner was recently crowned homecoming queen at my son's public high school. Early in the football season, Jill began to date the all-state running back on the team, a handsome senior named Matt Fisher. They've dated for a whole year, and everyone thinks Matt is the luckiest guy alive.

You say you've heard this story? Small town. Homecoming queen dates the football star. Nothing to do on Saturday night but drink _____ and have _____. But before you fill in the blanks too hastily, let me set you straight about Jill. She's a virgin who has never tasted alcohol or been touched sexually by a guy. Her consistent Christian witness has led Matt to a closer walk with Christ. Within the last two years, many other guys on the football team have chosen to become Christians as well.

No one in the locker room dares to ask Matt, "How far did you get on your last date with Jill?" It's not that they fear his crushing right fist. Instead, their respect for his southern Missouri girlfriend won't even allow them to think such things.

Jill's best friend is Erin Teeter. Hardly a day goes by that Erin doesn't have her arm and her huge heart around some new girl in town or a freshman searching for God's answers to a lifetime of hurt. While small-minded gossipmongers gather in cliques and spread rumors about girls with problems, Erin is busy getting those girls to church, to small-group Bible studies, or to hook up with Christian teens who can give them a "light" to find their way out of the darkness.

The apostle Paul enjoyed any opportunity to preach, but he especially liked to talk about Jesus to people who had never heard before (Romans 15:20-21). Jill and Erin are fellow apostles on the mission field of their campus. Can you identify anyone in that role at your school? If not, that means the job is still open . . . maybe for you.

Discussion Starters:

1. What can we learn from Paul about speaking up for Jesus?
2. What are some ways to "preach the gospel" without using words?
3. Where is a mission field you can get involved with today?

Lifeline:

"Witness always. Use words when necessary" (St. Francis of Assisi).

HONEST TO GOD?

"I urge you, brethren, keep your eye on those who cause dissensions and hindrances contrary to the teaching which you learned, and turn away from them. . . . By their smooth and flattering speech they deceive the hearts of the unsuspecting."

↩ Romans 16:17-18

It seems that I have a problem with integrity. Those who know me will probably say I'm committed to telling the truth, but a closer look at my heart reveals that I have often erred in this area of life. But before you shake your finger at me, see if you might need to join me in my quest for a higher level of integrity and honesty.

Take a look at these potential verbal problems, nicely summarized by Nancy Leigh DeMoss ("Making It Personal," *Spirit of Revival*, September 1995:24-29). First look up the verse(s) provided, then read the short explanation of each specific problem. Which ones are true of you?

Exaggeration (Proverbs 8:8; 30:5-6)
• Overstating the truth by using words like "always" or "never."
• Making sweeping generalizations about people or situations.

Flattery (Psalm 12:2)
• Giving insincere praise.

Misleading Others (2 Corinthians 8:21)
• Leaving a false impression (though my own spoken words may be true).

Inaccuracy (Hebrews 13:18)
• Carelessness with regard to factual details of stories.

Deception (Psalm 120:2)
• Attempting to create a better impression of myself than is honestly true.

Hypocrisy (Psalm 62:4b; Proverbs 26:23)
• Speaking kindly to another while harboring bitterness in my heart.

Inconsistency (Malachi 3:6; James 1:17)
• Flip-flopping on issues as my "audience" changes.

Guile (Psalm 32:2)
• Maintaining hidden agendas and ulterior motives when dealing with people.

Broken Promises (Psalm 15:1, 4)
• Agreeing to be somewhere at a certain time or to meet a need, and failing to do so.

Discussion Starters:

1. In what areas do you want to improve your integrity before God?
2. What is the difference between honesty before men and honesty before God?
3. How do you evaluate your personal integrity?

Lifeline:

Integrity means "knit together," and integrates your walk and your talk.

1 CoRintHians

Only an hour's drive from the great city of Athens, Greece, lie the rediscovered ruins of ancient Corinth. Of all the places in the world I've ever visited, Corinth has been the most impressive. It was here that early Christians stood up to the culture's oppressive, sinful lifestyle. Corinth was a cultural crossroads with sin infiltrating from every side. Towering over the city like a huge, gold idol was a mountain where a thousand prostitutes practiced illicit sex as a heathen religious practice. Each day a Corinthian Christian awoke, he stood in the shadow of this looming reminder of sin.

Life in ancient Corinth was not unlike life in our society today. The TV set in my house, like the mountain above their city, is a daily reminder of how different my behavior is supposed to be from that of the nonbelievers around me. I respect the believers in Corinth who made the difficult choice to walk away from sin and to trust in God. We have much to learn from them as we go through 1 and 2 Corinthians.

Will Cunningham is a close friend, a director of one of the Kanakuk Kamps, and one of America's most gifted writers. He has written several books, including The Sunset Grill and The Sins of the Fathers. Will plays guitar like a concert performer and sings with the voice of a studio soloist. His big, warm smile could melt a springtime snow, and he is a wonderful model for how a man should love God, his wife (Cindy), and his children (Wesley and Peter).

Will joins me to write the following devotionals from 1 Corinthians. He has much experience as a professional counselor and an abiding love for God and His people.

DIVIDED WE FALL

"Now I exhort you, brethren, by the name of our Lord Jesus Christ, that you all agree and that there be no divisions among you, but that you be made complete in the same mind and in the same judgment. For I have been informed . . . that there are quarrels among you. Now I mean this, that each one of you is saying, 'I am of Paul,' and 'I of Apollos,' and 'I of Cephas,' and 'I of Christ.' Has Christ been divided? Paul was not crucified for you, was he? Or were you baptized in the name of Paul?"

1 Corinthians 1:10-13

Coaches get excited when their players are working together. Dads get even more excited when their kids work together. To the church at Corinth, Paul was both father and coach. Before his arrival, these unbelievers on the Aegean Sea had never had anyone explain the gospel to them, much less show them how to live by it. Paul's preaching had made him their spiritual father, and he was just as interested in coaching them to maturity. Unfortunately, the Corinthians were anything but unified. As other church leaders became popular, the church members began to argue like a football team squabbling in the huddle.

"I was discipled by Apollos," someone would say, "so I'm the quarterback!"

Another disagrees: "Paul was my mentor, so I get to call the plays!"

"Big deal! Peter's the main man, and that's who I follow, so both of you stand aside."

Not surprisingly, the church at Corinth was not having much success on the field, which made Coach Paul both angry and sad. His appeal to unity flows through his entire letter to them.

Teams go nowhere when they quarrel and fight. They succeed only if they work as a unit. This is what Paul wanted the Corinthian Christians to know more than anything else. And it is what God wants today's Christians to know, too.

Discussion Starters:

1. Football teams get penalized if they spend too much time quarreling in the huddle. What are some consequences the church faces when Christians don't work together?
2. What was the source of the Corinthians' squabbling? Do you ever see a similar problem in your own church?
3. What is one way you can become more unified with your fellow Christians?

Lifeline:

Just as an athletic team must unite, so we as Christians must lay aside our petty differences and be unified in the work Jesus has called us to do. Do you and your family members have any major differences that need to be laid aside to create unity?

FOOLS AND FIGHTERS

"For the word of the cross is foolishness to those who are perishing, but to us who are being saved it is the power of God."

↬ 1 Corinthians 1:18

As a boxer, Muhammad Ali was an unsurpassed warrior. Of all his fights, most memorable are his bouts with Smokin' Joe Frazier. Joe was a half foot shorter than Ali, but built like a block of granite and noted for his hard, straightforward punches. Frazier was known to pursue his opponents relentlessly, moving in tight, taking blow after blow, until he finally wore them down enough to move in for the knockdown. Ali was the champ, but many sports analysts were picking Frazier to win.

Those closest to Ali say that for weeks prior to the match, he did nothing but abdominal work—sit-ups and more sit-ups—even to the neglect of his other skills. It was baffling to the media, and Ali's explanation wasn't much clearer: "If you're coming to see me float like a butterfly and sting like a bee, you're in for a surprise! I'm going to use the rope-a-dope on Mr. Frazier, and he'll never know what hit him."

The rope-a-dope? No one had ever heard of it. But it seemed foolish for Ali to alter from his proven, flashy fighting style. When the fight began, Ali backed into the ropes. Frazier followed and pummeled Ali's mid-section for round after round, with little retaliation from Ali. Eventually it became evident that Frazier was the "dope" Ali had been talking about. Worn out by his unsuccessful attack on Ali's muscled torso, Frazier found little strength left in his arms. Soon the victory was Ali's. For weeks afterward, the media praised Ali's rope-a-dope tactics. What had once been considered foolish had become the epitome of boxing wisdom.

Paul knew that human wisdom could be a treacherous opponent to the gospel. At its core is the proud belief that we are good enough or clever enough to earn God's favor on our own. The thought of Christ dying on the cross to make it possible for people to live in heaven is foolishness. But in the end, when nonbelievers think God's people are on the ropes, it will be the power of the cross that delivers the final knockout blow to Satan.

Discussion Starters:

1. When was a time your human wisdom (or pride) hindered you from following Christ?
2. When was a time you felt foolish for following Christ but followed Him anyway?
3. Why does Paul call the cross "the power of God"?

Lifeline:

Spiritual fitness is the Christian's "rope-a-dope" strategy that will eventually defeat Satan.

SIMPLE TALK

"My message and my preaching were not in persuasive words of wisdom, but in demonstration of the Spirit and of power, so that your faith would not rest on the wisdom of men, but on the power of God."

⇝ I Corinthians 2:4-5

During the past year, I had dinner in the homes of two different ex-NFL linebackers. Both were godly men with good wives who treated me with such hospitality that you would have thought I was an ambassador. Their children were conversational. Their homes were in order. Even their pets were polite. From what I could tell as a guest, they seemed to live a perfect life.

Of course, I know things are not perfect for them all the time. But they had learned to experience a lasting peace—not from knowing they had earned Super Bowl rings, but because of their relationships with an awesome God. In both homes I noticed that their trophies were nowhere in sight. When I pressed them, one led me to the basement and the other to an obscure closet. The evidence of their careers was collecting dust.

In one home, a Super Bowl game jersey, long forgotten by the public, was tucked in a corner. Underneath a stack of boxes was the pair of shoes the owner had worn to run the 40-yard dash in 4.3 seconds. One day even Darryl Green, the fastest man in the NFL, will fade from people's memory. Somehow, my two linebacker friends had kept all the fame of their lives in proper perspective. Instead of talking about their accomplishments both nights, we spent our time together talking about the Lord.

These were two noted football players, yet they were not in the least flashy or ostentatious. Similarly, Paul was perhaps the best-known preacher of his time, yet he took great care to avoid sounding stuffy or talking over people's heads. He knew if he could just stand back and let God act, everyone would be a lot better off. My two NFL friends seem to have learned that lesson. I hope it sinks in for me and for you as well.

Discussion Starters:

1. If you won a Super Bowl or some equivalent honor, where would you display your trophies?
2. When have you relied on someone who let you down? Is it possible you were not relying enough on God?
3. When was a time you experienced the power of God?

Lifeline:

Take inventory of the things you rely upon. If they are anything less than God's Spirit, reconsider.

Mind Reader

"For who has known the mind of the Lord, that he will instruct Him? But we have the mind of Christ."

⟿ 1 Corinthians 2:16

I once read that every successful father knows one good magic trick. So I learned my trick and repeated it hundreds of times to the delight of squealing kids. Then came Henry. After I did the trick for him, he ran and told his mother I was a mind reader. Henry's mom came to see if her son's head was being filled with mumbo-jumbo.

I explained that my trick was only about 1 percent "magic" and mostly required distracting the kids while I prepared the deck. She still looked skeptical, and Henry didn't help things. "That's not true, Mom. He closed his eyes and told me to pick a card. Then he put his hand on my forehead, rubbed a little bit, and told me the exact card I picked. He's a mind reader!"

By now Mom was really frowning, so I held out the deck and said, "Henry, pick a card." I knew that without stacking the deck, there was no chance I would guess which card Henry chose. He would see there was nothing magic about my trick at all.

Henry picked a card. And I'll be the Queen of Artichokes if my wild guess wasn't the right one. Then he picked again. Once again, I guessed correctly! A *third* time Henry chose, and *again* I guessed which card he had.

At that point the mother hastened Henry away from what she must have considered my dangerous, magnetic gaze. As I watched them drive away, I promised to never again amuse a child with "magic"—a promise I have kept.

Yet when I read 1 Corinthians 2:16, I discover I *can* be a mind reader. It's as if Paul is saying, "I know it seems a little hard to believe, but we can know Christ's thoughts because *we have the mind of Christ.*"

If you're a Christian, you too have the mind of Christ. His thoughts are available to you in Scripture, and the Holy Spirit helps you remember and understand what you read. So why not open your Bible today and start practicing a little mind reading?

Discussion Starters:

1. When have you had the mind of Christ—a time when His thoughts helped you make a decision, withstand a temptation, etc.?
2. Have you ever sensed that Jesus was attempting to give you good directions, yet you followed your own mind? Explain.
3. What do you think about a personal God who is willing to share His thoughts with you?

Lifeline:

Every bit as important as asking "What would Jesus do?" is knowing what Jesus would think.

FOUNDATIONS FOR LIVING

"According to the grace of God which was given to me, like a wise master builder I laid a foundation, and another is building on it. But each man must be careful how he builds on it. For no man can lay a foundation other than the one which is laid, which is Jesus Christ."

⤷ 1 Corinthians 3:10-11

In my neighborhood we have what I would guess to be, oh, about 5,000 little boys, each with a bike and a dog. If eight of them come to your house for cookies, you can be sure there will be eight bicycles in your driveway and eight lazy dogs lying in your front yard.

The other day I was walking through our woods and noticed some of their handiwork. Every other tree had the beginnings of a tree house in it. Over here was a chunk of two-by-four nailed to the trunk of an oak. Farther off, an irregular piece of plywood formed a seat in the crook of an ash tree. But in the center of the woods was the grandfather of all tree houses—a finished product nestled high in the arms of an alder tree.

I use the word *finished* loosely, but to a 10-year-old boy it must have seemed so. More accurately, it was a ton of lumber teetering on a toothpick. It was a deathtrap! How could any child play there without plunging to his demise? I had the urge to call the Department of Urban Renewal, but then I remembered my own childhood, smiled to myself, and went on my way.

Unfortunately, a lot of people's lives are on foundations just as shaky as that tree house. Everything seems okay at first glance, but a closer look reveals that things aren't quite right.

Paul wanted the Christians at Corinth to know that only one foundation is stable enough to build a life upon. If we try to build our lives on things like money, accomplishments, physique, or possessions, those foundations will eventually crumble, and the fall will be tragic.

At all costs, I urge you to build on the foundation of Jesus—and nothing else.

Discussion Starters:

1. Are you building on some "foundations" other than Christ? If so, what are they?
2. When people have built on other foundations, is it better for them to "do the remodeling" themselves or wait until those foundations crumble? Explain.
3. What is the best symbol for your current relationship with Jesus: A shaky tree house? A log cabin? A brick home? A stone fortress? Other? Explain your answer.

Lifeline:

Discuss ways you can build your life on the foundation of Jesus Christ.

THE REAL THING

"Now if any man builds on the foundation with gold, silver, precious stones, wood, hay, straw, each man's work will become evident; for the day will show it because it is to be revealed with fire, and the fire itself will test the quality of each man's work. If any man's work which he has built on it remains, he will receive a reward."

⤷ 1 Corinthians 3:12-14

My friend Andy went to marvelous measures to ask his girlfriend to marry him. Being an actor, he invited her to a play in which the character he played (a very stuffy aristocrat) was in a marriage proposal scene but could not bring himself to pop the question. After the play, the curtain came down and the lights went on. But before people could exit, Andy stepped to center stage and, in front of his college peers, delivered two dozen roses to his girlfriend in the audience.

He announced: "My character in the play was unable to receive and give love. But I'm not him and he's not me, and I can think of nothing more wonderful than to share our love together for the rest of our lives. Will you marry me?" Then he pulled a box from his pocket and opened it to reveal a shining diamond ring.

The girl said yes. I think I was happier than most of the others in attendance, because she happened to be my daughter. Andy, who is now my son-in-law, won my admiration for a lifetime.

Now imagine if, after all the creative energy Andy poured into his proposal, he had offered Jamie Jo a cheap little plastic wedding band he'd gotten out of a gum machine. Trust me, the evening would have turned ugly.

Paul told the Christians at Corinth that it was their choice to build upon the foundation of Christ with either precious jewels or materials that were worthless. We have the same choice today. Of course, it is by God's grace that any of us will get to heaven in the first place. But our works determine the quality of the gift we present to Jesus when we get there. I'd much rather hand Him a diamond than a piece of plastic. How about you?

Discussion Starters:

1. What are some "works" that are jewels?
2. What are some "works" that are worthless?
3. Do you need to improve the quality of your "works"? If so, how and when will you do this?

Lifeline:

Jewels and precious metals survive the test of fire. Will the value of your work for Jesus endure, or will you stand before Him empty-handed?

DEAD MAN WRITING

"For, I think, God has exhibited us apostles last of all, as men condemned to death; because we have become a spectacle to the world, both to angels and to men."

⟿ 1 Corinthians 4:9

Twice I have written to a dead man. On both occasions, his response showed me I was less alive than he was.

When I sent my first letter to Darrell in the fall of 1998, I half expected to get back the ramblings of a stir-crazy inmate. After all, he had been on death row for over 10 years. How fluent can a man be in his situation? Yet his reply was immediate and filled with wit, country humor, and spiritual wisdom. It turns out that Darrell's only conversation partner is God—24 hours a day—so his letters are filled with scriptural references.

After entering Potosi Correctional Center, he gave his life to Christ. At that moment, his old self died—the old, awful self who had shot his former drug dealer and two other human beings with a 12-gauge shotgun. Since then, Darrell has become the self-appointed chaplain of death row.

Not long ago, I saw that Pope John Paul II had taken up Darrell's case and had asked the governor of Missouri to pardon him after 10 long years. Darrell's letters reveal that he believes he will one day be released.

In today's verse, Paul compares Christianity to a death sentence. Without crucifying our old, evil natures, we could never enter the perfection of heaven. But Christianity is also a *life* sentence—a full pardon that flings our cell doors open wide and frees us to walk with God.

Have you died to sin? Like Paul and Darrell, are you a dead-to-self person who now lives in the abundant life of Christ? If not, consider the cold, hard walls of your existence and the bleakness of your future. Then come to Jesus, the doorway to life, and leave your cell behind forever.

Discussion Starters:

1. Do you have the hope of eternal life with Jesus Christ? If so, who are some "imprisoned" people you know whom you could free with the good news of the gospel?
2. As believers in Jesus Christ, we are spectacles to the world (1 Corinthians 4:9). What does the world see in you: a dead person or a live one? A death sentence or a wonderful sense of freedom?
3. What old behaviors do you need to "crucify" to strengthen your relationship with Jesus Christ?

Lifeline:

The more dead you are to self, the more alive you will become in Christ.

CLIMBING TOWARD SERVANTHOOD

"To this present hour we are both hungry and thirsty, and are poorly clothed, and are roughly treated, and are homeless; and we toil, working with our own hands; when we are reviled, we bless; when we are persecuted, we endure; when we are slandered, we try to conciliate; we have become as the scum of the world, the dregs of all things, even until now."

⟿ 1 Corinthians 4:11-13

In the world of technical climbing, one person leads the group and another follows behind. The leader has the job of getting the team of climbers safely up the cliff by "setting protection" along the way. Into one crevice he places a cam; into another, a chalk or a wedge. And into each of these devices he fastens the climbing rope. The safety of his comrades depends on how well he does his job. If the climb is successful, the lead climber gets the glory.

On the other hand, the climber who follows—known as "the cleaner"— has the unheralded job of unfastening ("cleaning") the protective devices set by the lead climber as the team advances up the cliff. There is nothing flashy about the role he plays. Consequently, he rarely gets acknowledged.

The role of the Christian servant is like that of "the cleaner" on a treacherous mountain climb. If he does his job well, the whole team advances. But his negligence can result in disaster. I knew a man who broke his leg on an ice climb—snapped the bone in two—because the cleaner had not paid attention to his job.

Paul wanted the Corinthians to take servanthood seriously. He didn't try to hide the challenges and "down" sides of service because he knew the rewards were even greater. And he made it clear that he was right there with them, even admonishing his readers to imitate his example (1 Corinthians 4:16).

Whether God calls you to be a "lead climber" or a "cleaner," there is no place for arrogance in the Body of Christ. We are all servants, just as our Lord Jesus was a servant. When we get this point straight, our journey upward will be a thrilling one. And the view from the top, when we finally get there, will be glorious.

Discussion Starters:

1. Do you see yourself more as a "lead climber" or a "cleaner"?
2. Are you aware of any disasters that have happened because Christian leaders were either arrogant or negligent?
3. Think of one servant-leader you know. What characteristics distinguish his or her servanthood?

Lifeline:

Discuss the ways you and your family can be servants:
- to each other
- to the church
- to your neighborhood

WEEDS AND WORSE PROBLEMS

"It is actually reported that there is immorality among you, and immorality of such a kind as does not exist even among the Gentiles, that someone has his father's wife. You have become arrogant and have not mourned instead, so that the one who had done this deed would be removed from your midst."

⤿ 1 Corinthians 5:1-2

A tick imbedded in your skin.
A high cholesterol count.
A rumor.
A child near a socket with a paper clip.
A fever.
A disagreement with the wife or kids.
A disagreement with *anyone*.
A bag of weed in Johnny's bedroom.
A spot on an X-ray.
The letter "E" on the gas gauge.

Some problems in life are trivial and can be ignored. Others, such as the ones listed here, demand immediate attention. If we don't take action, they will only get worse.

The church in Corinth had a serious problem that needed to be addressed immediately. One of the church members had an ongoing sexual relationship with his mother (or stepmother) but kept coming to Sunday services as if nothing were wrong. Amazingly, no one in the church was doing anything about it. In fact, it had become a point of arrogance for them. They thought it made them seem cool and free-thinking—sort of like a guy who brags about how many beers he drank at last night's party. But such an attitude always brings you down eventually.

Paul's advice was twofold: (1) they should change their attitude about the sin before it infected the entire body; and (2) they should remove the man from their midst until he repented.

Are any problem areas being left unattended in your own life that could do you harm? If so, take action. Don't let the weeds of today become the woes of tomorrow.

Discussion Starters:

1. Do you think it's okay for churches to kick out people who don't conform to biblical teachings? Why or why not?
2. Think of something you need to repent of right now and, if you are willing, share it with someone else.
3. What do you think might happen if you don't repent?

Lifeline:

Unconfessed sin always creates an incomplete relationship with the Lord.

CRATE EXPECTATIONS

"I wrote to you not to associate with any so-called brother if he is an immoral person, or covetous, or an idolater, or a reviler, or a drunkard, or a swindler—not even to eat with such a one."

⌐ 1 Corinthians 5:11

I have helped train several Labrador retrievers, so I can chuckle as I watch my son-in-law go through the same painful process. Andy doesn't have a single mean bone in his body. His pupil, Ty, on the other hand, is a tail-wagging terror. It is high comedy watching the gentle master with his not-so-eager pupil.

Yet I get more than grins from observing Andy and Ty. Their back-and-forth struggle reminds me that love is not always comfortable. At times one must direct a dog with painful consequences in order for him to become more teachable, more useful, and, in the long run, happier. The same is true of people. In spite of what we hear in this age of leniency and political correctness, our failure to apply discipline in our deepest relationships has led to the breakdown of families, businesses, governments, and even churches.

One of the hardest things for a dog trainer to do is put his animal in a crate. It separates the dog from the company of all living creatures by confining him to a box barely bigger than a suitcase. But the procedure is necessary when the trainee habitually rebels against the trainer's voice. After the confinement, when the doors to the crate are flung wide again, it is often a much more submissive dog that emerges.

Paul was confronted with a problem in the Corinthian church that went beyond the usual issues—a man was sleeping with his own mother (or stepmother). The church leaders had apparently given their stamp of approval, so Paul felt obliged to step in.

"Crate the man!" he says in essence. "Remove him from the presence of the congregation until he can hear and obey his Master's voice again." So the man was sent away.

Tough love? Certainly. But that's sometimes what it takes when people don't respond to "soft" love. A church unwilling to practice complete obedience to God is destined to go to the dogs.

Discussion Starters:

1. What is a situation where you have seen "tough love" applied? What were the results?
2. What might have happened if a softer approach had been taken?
3. How can people avoid finding themselves in a spiritual "crate" to be disciplined?

Lifeline:

Loving parents will express tough love to their children when necessary. Really loving parents will also accept tough love from their children.

COURT ADJOURNED!

"I say this to your shame. Is it so, that there is not among you one wise man who will be able to decide between his brethren, but brother goes to law with brother, and that before unbelievers? Actually, then, it is already a defeat for you, that you have lawsuits with one another. Why not rather be wronged? Why not rather be defrauded?"

↜ 1 Corinthians 6:5-7

Several years ago, a woman sued a major fast-food chain after receiving a serious burn from spilling a cup of coffee in her lap. Never mind that in her haste to pull away from the drive-through, she had placed the cup between her legs instead of in a cup holder. Rather than assuming responsibility for her haste and acknowledging that "accidents happen," she hired a lawyer and charged the restaurant with serving coffee that was too hot. The amazing thing is, she won.

In an age when people would rather sue than accept the consequences of their actions, Paul's words in 1 Corinthians 6:1-11 are a breath of fresh air. The passage exposes what is at the heart of so many of our lawsuits: greed, a desire for vengeance, and a disregard for the forgiveness we have received.

Paul explained that the whole church suffers whenever Christians "air their dirty laundry" in public. Lawsuits in a secular court of law may be unavoidable at times. But more often than not, we Christians should be able to settle our differences without the aid of attorneys—even if we agree to receive less than what we had hoped for. Paul points out that one day we are to "judge angels" (v. 3), so we should be eager to concern ourselves more with God's style of justice (which is heavy with mercy and forgiveness) rather than demand a precise eye-for-an-eye compensation.

Do you have a grievance with a friend? A teacher? An employer? A spouse? Rest assured that for each of your gripes there is a lawyer who would like to turn it into money for you (and him). With Paul, I urge you to resist the temptation to pursue quick financial gain, striving always to settle your disagreements in a godly manner.

Discussion Starters:

1. What is the silliest lawsuit you've heard about lately?
2. How do you think so many people's haste to sue one another has affected our country? How might it affect the church?
3. When was the last time you willingly let someone else take advantage of a situation in order to put a quicker end to a conflict? How did you feel? (You can be honest!)

Lifeline:

Whenever you think of someone you would like to sue, ask Jesus to help you to settle out of court.

HOW'S YOUR APPETITE?

"Or do you not know that your body is a temple of the Holy Spirit who is in you, whom you have from God, and that you are not your own? For you have been bought with a price: therefore glorify God in your body."

⮑ 1 Corinthians 6:19-20

If you hang around kids for a weekend, you'll hear them say some pretty funny things. One of my camp directors coaches a second-grade boys' basketball team in his spare time, and one of his players told him, "My sister can't eat much 'cause she has a little stomach. But I can eat 17 pieces of pizza. Deep dish."

That guy sounds like a classic overachiever. Don't you get a sick feeling picturing 17 wedges of meat sauce, cheese, and bread dough all mashed together inside a single second-grader? Such a binge may be legal, but it can't be natural.

The people of ancient Corinth had some heavy appetites as well—but not for food. Their city was known for temples housing fertility cults. It was not only lawful, it was fashionable to have sex with prostitutes who lived on the premises. It was even their religion and was done on a regular basis! Supposedly, the sexual acts were to gain favor from the gods so they would bring blessings on the person's crops. (Sounds like a pretty lame excuse to me.)

Paul wanted the Corinthians to acquire a righteous repulsion to their city's involvement with such cults. He used the examples of both food and sex to make the point that our bodies are not our own. We belong to the One who bought us with everything He had—five pints of blood and all the glory in the universe. How dare we allow ourselves to become mastered by our inner appetites, whether culinary or sexual!

Whether it's a little boy packing 17 slices of pizza into his belly, or a teenager allowing his or her hormones to run rampant and becoming a slave to sex, we ought to be grieved by any out-of-control appetites. Paul concludes with the best reason in the world for submitting our passions to the Lord: "You have been bought with a price: therefore glorify God in your body."

Discussion Starters:

1. Not including food, what are three human appetites that affect a lot of people?
2. Why are human appetites so difficult to master?
3. What appetites do you struggle with? What is the secret to mastering them?

Lifeline:

If an appetite is too strong, perhaps something else is missing from your life to cause the imbalance.

THE WEDDING SINGER

"The husband must fulfill his duty to his wife, and likewise also the wife to her husband. The wife does not have authority over her own body, but the husband does; and likewise also the husband does not have authority over his own body, but the wife does. . . . One who is unmarried is concerned about the things of the Lord, how he may please the Lord; but one who is married is concerned about the things of this world, how he may please his wife, and his interests are divided."

~ 1 Corinthians 7:3-4, 32-34

A friend of mine used to sing in a lot of weddings . . . until one particular ceremony cured him of the habit. He was early, his guitar was in tune, and he was sure he had the Gordon Lightfoot song down perfectly. Then the worst happened.

Smack in the middle of the song, all recollection of the English language fled from my friend's memory. He stood there gaping like a codfish for a split second and then immediately plunged into wedding singer suicide—he improvised. He made up words and even attempted to hideously wedge both the bride's and groom's names into the lyrics. The result was a cross between a singing telegram and a fortune cookie.

Now, whenever my friend is asked to sing in someone's wedding, he has a pat answer: "The marriage of two people is such a beautiful thing. Why would you want me to go and mess it up?"

Paul, too, believed that marriage is a beautiful thing. Yet he also knew about some potential problems that are unforeseen by many single people. As soon as you say "I do," two things change: (1) your body is no longer yours (v. 4); and (2) your interests will forever be divided (vv. 32-34).

During our single years, we have only ourselves to think of. Marriage quickly changes that, and Paul wants us to be prepared rather than surprised. Are you selfless enough to sacrifice your body for another? Your quiet times? Your needs, interests, hobbies, and more? If so, you are a candidate for marriage. Just remember—there's no need to rush it.

Discussion Starters:

1. What does Paul mean when he says that husbands and wives no longer have authority over their own bodies? Is this only in a sexual sense, or might it be interpreted more broadly?
2. Why did Paul feel compelled to warn prospects for marriage about their interests becoming divided?
3. What are the advantages of postponing marriage until after your teenage years, or even longer?

Lifeline:

Over the institution of marriage hangs a big sign that reads: Prepare to give yourself away, all ye who enter here!

FIERY LOVE

"It is better to marry than to burn with passion."

⟻ 1 Corinthians 7:9

Most of us are drawn to a fire in the dead of winter. When all is bleak and white outside, nothing beats sitting around a crackling campfire with close friends, sharing stories and a bag of marshmallows. But we grow somber when witnessing the terrible devastation of a fire out of control. Fires remind us that every good gift of God can go awry if not managed properly.

Sex is a gift from God, intended to be the fiery fulfillment of monogamous marriage. I am intrigued by the analogy of fire and human sexuality. Every good fire requires three elements: fuel, oxygen, and spark. Remove any of these elements and you decrease the possibility of combustion. Let's think of the "spark" as our hormones, the "oxygen" as our environment, and the "fuel" as our emotions. We can't do much about our hormones or environment, so let's focus on the fuel of sexual involvement: emotions.

We have a choice of fuels. One common one, though not a particularly good choice, is fear. Have you ever been so afraid to try something that you actually got a "rush" when you finally did it? That's why snowboarding, whitewater rafting, roller coasters, and similar things are so popular.

Lots of dating couples start having sex and experience the "fire" fueled by fear. Will they get caught by someone? Get pregnant? Catch an embarrassing disease? But using fear as a fuel for sex is like replacing your dinner candles with a big bowl of gasoline. By the time the couple marries (if they ever get around to it), little fuel remains. The flames of their passion burn less brightly, and many quickly decide they are "no longer in love."

The fuel of genuine love, on the other hand, will never ignite the sexual fire prematurely because love is patient. But on your wedding night, love will produce fireworks galore—and the fire will never go out. Indeed, genuine love just burns warmer the longer you stay together.

You're going to have a fire one way or the other. Just choose your fuel wisely.

Discussion Starters:

1. What are some ways people can get "burned" by experimenting with premarital sex?
2. Besides fear, what are some other emotions that may tend to ignite a sexual relationship between two people not yet married?
3. With hormones and environment creating a sexual drive within you, what steps can you take to remain faithful to God and your future spouse by saving sex for marriage?

Lifeline:

Sex outside of marriage is sin, but God forgives all kinds of sins. If your past already includes a sexual history, He will honor your decision to start fresh today.

WHAT DO YOU KNOW?

"Knowledge makes arrogant, but love edifies. If anyone supposes that he knows anything, he has not yet known as he ought to know; but if anyone loves God, he is known by Him."

↜ 1 Corinthians 8:1-3

Just when I think I know everything, someone asks me a question I can't answer. Here's one that humbled me recently: "What is uglier than the devil, more beautiful than God, possessed by the poor, and desired by the rich?"

If you said "nothing," you are smarter than I.

Sometimes on the ladder of knowledge, a person must be knocked down a step or two in order to realize how little he or she truly knows. The universe is a vast vault of secrets still undiscovered by even the world's greatest thinkers.

Know-it-alls are like party balloons, all puffed up and full of themselves. Yet it only takes one simple question they can't answer, one tiny pinprick of doubt or ignorance, for their pride to be popped. Then everyone can see them as they truly are—empty windbags.

Paul tells us that loving God is more important than accumulating an ever bigger database of facts and figures. Knowledge can make you look good to others, and you may feel good that others look up to you, but it's a false sense of security. As we begin to believe we know it all (or at least most of "it"), we develop an arrogant attitude. Frequently people with strong personalities and opinions have a hard time learning from others and listening to God.

We must come to realize that if we have developed that kind of sinful mind-set, we *don't* know it all. We still have a lot to learn about love. "Love edifies," says Paul, meaning that it builds other people up. Love is more important than worldly knowledge because it is the key to tapping into *God's* knowledge. A genuine love for God soon blossoms into an active love toward others by becoming compassionate and attentive to their needs. If you learn to do that, you won't need to know it all. You'll already have more friends than you know what to do with.

Discussion Starters:

1. Knowledge can be both a blessing and a curse. Give examples of each.
2. What is a particular area of knowledge that you know a lot about? Have you ever found yourself becoming a bit proud (even arrogant) because you were smarter than other people in that area?
3. How do you feel about know-it-alls? How can you avoid becoming one?

Lifeline:

All that you know, though it may be a vast amount, is like a grain of sand on the shore of all that you don't know.

IN A CORNER

"But take care that this liberty of yours does not somehow become a stumbling block to the weak."
— 1 Corinthians 8:9

Many times I have "painted myself into a corner" in a symbolic sense. But never have I seen this saying fulfilled quite as literally as when I worked with Tom Boggins.

It was a hot day in June. We were hard-pressed to paint six tennis courts before foul weather arrived, as the weatherman had predicted. "Slop it on good and fast," I ordered the crew as I eyed the sky.

Tom took his paint tray and long-handled roller and headed for the spot where we had stopped the day before. I left to go make my rounds and check on several other projects. When I got back, Tom Boggins stood on a tiny island. All around him was an ocean of wet blue paint—and nowhere to go.

I told him to stand still until the paint dried, and he did just that—all the way through lunch and supper. Then, when the paint was finally dry enough, Tom tiptoed back to freedom. To my knowledge, he has not picked up a paint roller since.

But when all the facts were in, it became clear that Tom hadn't painted *himself* into that predicament. His fellow workers had been so free with their brush strokes that they had isolated Tom and forced him to forfeit some of his own freedom. They just hadn't been thinking.

Do you ever behave so freely that you don't notice how you're causing other people to struggle? Paul warns us not to cause others to stumble. If our Christian liberties cause them annoyance or discomfort, it's not much of a personal testimony. Paul had no problem eating meat offered to idols because he knew idols were nothing more than sticks and stones. If others took offense, however, Paul didn't eat that particular food anymore. We might substitute drinking or wearing tattoos—things that are lawful for Christians but may cause others to stumble in their faith.

As you paint the canvas of your life, do you notice all the others around you? Or do you slop paint so freely that they will eventually find themselves isolated?

Discussion Starters:

1. How has some other Christian's behavior caused you to stumble?
2. In addition to drinking and getting tattoos, what are some practices Christians could feel free doing but might want to voluntarily avoid in order not to cause others to take offense and stumble?
3. Have you ever been a stumbling block for others? How? What have you done about it?

Lifeline:

If any of your freedoms cause others to stumble, choose today to become less "free" in that area.

RIGHT OF WAY

"If we sowed spiritual things in you, is it too much if we reap material things from you? If others share the right over you, do we not more? Nevertheless, we did not use this right, but we endure all things so that we will cause no hindrance to the gospel of Christ."

↪ 1 Corinthians 9:11-12

I once saw a man's car get smashed on his left while he was exercising his rights. "But I had the right of way," he told the officer who surveyed the scene. "The other guy didn't stop at the intersection." The officer replied, "Sometimes our rights don't keep us from getting wronged."

I am astounded by the rights entitled to any United States citizen. If I choose to do so, I can own a gun to protect my family against evil intruders. I can get legal representation in a court of law even if I can't afford it. I can disagree openly with our government. These rights and dozens like them are unheard of in many countries. In fact, we have so many rights that we have begun to expect everything we want. Some of us have even begun to identify wrong as "right" and the pursuit of wrong as a right endeavor.

A popular TV network tells its viewers that "kids rule." A recent hit song declared, "You've got to fight for the right to party." Call me old-fashioned, but I don't believe kids have the right (or the maturity) to rule, and I still think that life, liberty, and the pursuit of happiness are nobler goals than partying.

The next time you feel like demanding your "rights," stop and recall the words of today's passage. Paul knew he had rights. When the situation was appropriate, he applied them with great skill. (See Acts 16:35-39.) Yet if more people could have been won to Christ, Paul was willing to give up all entitlements, even the meager income he made from preaching. In short, Paul exercised his rights with wisdom. We should learn from his example that it is always more important to do right than to demand rights.

Discussion Starters:

1. People who don't always stand up for their rights are often seen as spineless or weak. But for what other reasons might they concede their rights?
2. What rights did Jesus Christ give up?
3. Have you ever yielded your rights, even though it was very hard to do? Why?

Lifeline:

Jesus Christ and the apostle Paul gave up their rights, and great numbers of people received the love and forgiveness of God as a result. What rights could you give up that might help more people come to know Christ as their Savior?

DECKS

"For though I am free from all men, I have made myself a slave to all, so that I may win more. To the Jews I became as a Jew, so that I might win Jews; to those who are under the Law, as under the Law though not being myself under the Law, so that I might win those who are under the Law; to those who are without law, as without law, though not being without the law of God but under the law of Christ, so that I might win those who are without law. To the weak I became weak, that I might win the weak; I have become all things to all men, so that I may by all means save some."

⌇ 1 Corinthians 9:19-22

It was brought to my attention this summer that some of my staff members had gotten creative in their quest to keep in shape. "They're doing decks," my source told me. Two (or more) guys, eager to pump up their pectorals, would take turns drawing a card and doing that number of push-ups until they had gone through the entire deck. Depending on the luck of the draw, one participant could end up doing a lot more push-ups than the other guy. You ought to see some of my counselors go at it. Talk about a passion for winning!

Paul expressed the same kind of tenacity when he used the phrase "I might win" five times in four verses. He was trying to win souls—any souls. Paul prioritized evangelism over every other aspect of his life.

Paul even had a "workout regimen" to help him achieve his spiritual goals (vv. 26-27). Because he could not bear the thought of anyone missing out on the salvation of God, he was always willing to go the extra mile, do the "extra push-up" for the sake of those who were lost. He worked hard . . . prayed hard . . . preached hard . . . traveled hard . . . loved hard . . . and trained hard.

And he wanted to know, 2,000 years before Nike asked the question, "What are *you* training for?"

Discussion Starters:

1. What word would you use to describe your "walk" with Christ: Stroll? Jog? Run? Sprint? Marathon? Other? Explain.
2. What are you training for, in a spiritual sense? Do you have a spiritual workout schedule? If so, describe it.
3. When you're passionate about something, you automatically work harder at it. How can you become more passionate and disciplined about sharing the gospel?

Lifeline:

If spiritual performance were an Olympic event, what score do you think you would receive from the judges? Why?

RATTLER

"Let him who thinks he stands take heed that he does not fall."

⌐ 1 Corinthians 10:12

Bill was a rancher, which meant he spent a lot of time alone. He quickly developed a habit of taking action at the first sign of trouble. One night he went to bed and felt something move against his leg beneath the sheets, so up he sprang, grabbing a broom to defend himself. *Whack! Whack! Whack!* With no electricity in the bunkhouse where he slept, Bill beat the bed blindly until he broke a sweat. He stopped to catch his breath and listen. Silence. Bill turned back the covers and swept vigorously until he was sure the mysterious bedfellow was gone. Then he lay back down and went to sleep.

Just before dawn, Bill was awakened by a noise—a sound every rancher has learned not to ignore: a *rattle*. As the sound grew louder, an object fell onto the bed from the bookshelf above. Up Bill sprang again with his trusty broom. *Whack! Whack! Whack!* He pounded until the broomstick snapped and flew across the room. This time he dared not go back to bed but decided to take his chances under the stars.

The next morning, when Bill returned to the bunkhouse, he found a six-and-a-half-foot rattlesnake, dead, stretched out in a patch of sunlight. From that point on, whenever Bill hears the sound of a rattlesnake's rattle, he associates it with the goodness of God's protection.

First Corinthians 10:1-12 is a passage filled with warnings telling us to walk carefully, keep a sharp eye out, and avoid the mistakes of the Israelites (idolatry, immorality, discontent, grumbling, etc.). Just when we think we're immune to these things, they strike. So as today's verse says, we need to "take heed." If we keep our ears open to God's voice, we'll always hear the "rattle" before such dangers can get close enough to hurt us.

Discussion Starters:

1. What are the warning signs that someone's life is being threatened by idolatry? Immorality? Grumbling?
2. In each of these areas, how can the person heed the warning signs?
3. What are the things that regularly threaten to trip you up and make you fall?

Lifeline:

Identify any "idols" in your life. What steps must you take to diminish each idol's power?

ESCAPE ROUTE

"No temptation has overtaken you but such as is common to man; and God is faithful, who will not allow you to be tempted beyond what you are able, but with the temptation will provide the way of escape also, so that you will be able to endure it."

&#x21 dc; 1 Corinthians 10:13

I heard about some snowmobilers in Lake City, Colorado, who ignored a winter storm alert they heard during a lunch break. An hour later they were high atop Bristol Head, groping along in a whiteout, when suddenly the ground dropped from under them. Days later a rescue team found their shattered bodies at the base of an enormous cliff. Because they ignored a storm warning, they found themselves in a whiteout. Because of the blinding snow, they missed the sign that warned of the dangerous cliff. And because they missed the sign, their lives were tragically cut short. It is now impossible for me to pass that landmark without thinking of the terror that must have been theirs during that unexpected plummet.

When I read 1 Corinthians 10:13, I find both comfort and caution. It's a relief to know that I'm not the only person experiencing the strong temptations I face. But in spite of this comfort, I realize that even a "common" temptation can lead to a disastrous fall if I yield to it. So I must look for God's "way of escape" before I end up endangering myself.

Many are the imprisoned guys and pregnant girls who say, "When I was tempted, God didn't provide *me* with a way of escape. Now look at the mess I'm in!" Yet if you press them, they know that what they did was wrong and that God had provided a clear sign that read: "DO NOT PROCEED BEYOND THIS POINT."

Oh, how I wish teenagers would look ahead far enough to see the tragedies that might result from giving in to common temptations! The longer we ignore God's initial "way of escape," the more impaired our vision becomes and the more difficult it is to find our way back to safety.

Watch for God's signs today. And when you see one, don't just read it and roar past it. *Heed* it and soar successfully through life.

Discussion Starters:

1. What are some "common" temptations you regularly face?
2. Is it comforting to know that lots of other people face those same temptations? Why?
3. Have you ever suffered after recognizing, yet refusing to heed, God's "way of escape"? What were the results? What potential problems have you avoided by heeding God's signs for righteous living?

Lifeline:

God's ways of escape will always be on His paths, not ours.

ORDER AND TEAMWORK

"But I want you to understand that Christ is the head of every man, and the man is the head of a woman, and God is the head of Christ."

⮝ 1 Corinthians 11:3

"Who wants to play quarterback?" the coach asked at the first football practice of eight-year-old gridiron warriors. He then had to explain why 15 quarterbacks might be a few too many. So most were doomed to become linemen. A few were chosen as running backs or for other positions of honor. And finally Zach became the object of envy when he was named quarterback. As the coach told him, "You da man."

Zach beamed. He had never felt so elated in his life. He was "da man." And he lived in that blessed state until Saturday, a minute and 20 seconds into the first quarter of game one. As he looked up from the indentation he had just made in the ground after being sacked by the other team's linemen, he suggested: "Maybe someone else would like a chance to play quarterback."

Those eight-year-olds learned a lesson that day: without organization, every team fails. Players must accept their positions and play heartily for the good of the team. The people scoring touchdowns and kicking field goals usually get more recognition than others, because points win games. But without those mud-encrusted linemen doing their jobs equally well, no one's going to score many points.

In a society that values political correctness, a lot of people like to skip 1 Corinthians 11. But the Bible indicates there is order in marriage relationships, just as in peewee football and in heaven between Jesus and His Father. What Paul is saying is that, yes, a husband is the "head" of a woman in the same way that God is the head of Christ. Can you imagine Jesus and God getting into a screaming contest over who's number one? No way! They have an order in their relationship that has nothing to do with personal value and everything to do with function.

When men and women get this straight, their mutual *inter*dependence brings glory to God. Failure to accept it brings chaos—and lots of fumbles.

Discussion Starters:

1. Why are many people offended when they first hear that "the man is the head of a woman"?
2. Paul also says, "Christ is the head of every man." How would you describe His "headship"?
3. Is it possible for people to practice the same kind of headship as Christ? If so, how?

Lifeline:

Identify what you think your "position" is on Jesus' team at this point in your life.

THE HEART OF THE MATTER

"Therefore whoever eats the bread or drinks the cup of the Lord in an unworthy manner, shall be guilty of the body and the blood of the Lord."

1 Corinthians 11:27

Some of our camp catalogs feature pictures of our staff, many of whom are awesome athletes in their off-seasons. As you might imagine, they have bigger-than-average appetites. (You should see our flapjack budget!)

I'll never forget one lineman from Texas Tech—I'll call him Alex—who had the biggest biceps I've ever seen and could eat more food than any two other men. Because he was a gentle giant, Alex was assigned to counsel our smallest campers. One day I noticed Alex engaged in a classic contest with a boy the size of his thigh. They were spinning a spoon to determine who got the last pancake on the plate.

Alex won. Just as he was about to take his first bite, he saw the boy was crying. With little ado, Alex simply slid the pancake over to the boy's plate. Later I discovered Alex had been tending to one of his sick campers in the infirmary that day and was late to breakfast. That last pancake was going to be his *only* one to prepare him for a long day of hard work.

After Alex left camp, I never heard of him again. But that day in the Kanakuk dining hall, he became an all-American in my book.

The mark of an all-star Christian is love. Paul's big beef with the Corinthians was that they were treating the Lord's Supper as if it were a buffet table rather than a holy sacrament. They were beginning to fight over it as if it were the last pancake.

The early church combined its communal "agape" meal (sort of like our potlucks) with the Lord's Supper (which highlights the symbolic significance of the bread and wine). This meal was meant to commemorate the most selfless act of all times, the Crucifixion, yet it had sadly become a me-first grabfest. Some church members were eating their fill while others went hungry. And Paul was angry about it.

Do you get more satisfaction from beating everyone else to the last pancake, or from passing it up so someone else can benefit? Your answer will tell me a little about your stomach. But it will tell me much more about your heart.

Discussion Starters:

1. Besides food, what other appetites reveal a person's heart?
2. What are some of your appetites? How do you handle them?
3. What are some ways that people can still abuse the Lord's Supper?

Lifeline:

Jesus is the bread of life (John 6:48). Are you sharing that "bread" with others?

THE FIVE-LEGGED STEER

"To each one is given the manifestation of the Spirit for the common good."

⌐ 1 Corinthians 12:7

In the grammar school I attended, the boys couldn't wait until sixth grade and Mr. Cottle's field trip to see the five-legged steer. We endured the first five years of school primarily for the opportunity to board the bus for the field trip we knew would be the zenith of our lives. (The girls were less enthusiastic.) After a 65-mile trip discussing where the fifth leg would be on this steer and how much faster it should be able to run, we finally arrived at "Lester's Little Sahara—Home of Exotic Delights."

Before seeing the star attraction, we looked at newborn baby pigs, a bunch of tarantulas, some ostrich eggs, live rattlesnakes, and a three-ton prairie dog made of crumbling plaster. But our eyes didn't light up until we reached a door on which was scrawled, "Behold the Five-Legged Steer."

It is with the deepest regret that I must tell you it was one of the biggest disappointments in my life, over in a matter of seconds. We were hurried past a dismal-looking bovine with what looked like a woman's stocking filled with sawdust strapped to its back. Then we went through another door and found ourselves back in the parking lot, blinking at one another in the bright sunlight. Sadly, the highlight of our trip was the stop at Dairy Delite on the way home. But you can bet that when we got back we bragged about the five-legged steer as if we had seen the Taj Mahal.

If the apostle Paul had been in Mr. Cottle's class, he might have subtitled 1 Corinthians 12: "Beware the five-legged steer!" Church members were envying one another's God-given gifts and were trying to be things they weren't. Subsequently, the "body of Christ" was taking on the grotesque demeanor of a five-legged steer. (Paul used equally ludicrous examples of feet trying to be hands and "bodies" consisting of a single large eye or ear [vv. 15-17].)

God knows what He's doing, so don't let envy of other Christians turn you into a useless appendage. If each of us does as God directs, we'll really be some body!

Discussion Starters:

1. What are a few things that *all* Christians should be involved with in the church?
2. Who are some people you know who have unique and specific spiritual gifts?
3. When have you tried to be just like someone else, only to experience problems?

Lifeline:

If you don't want to feel like a useless fifth leg, you need to identify what special gifts God has entrusted to you. How can you begin to discover your individual gift(s)?

MARCHING ORDERS

"Now you are Christ's body, and individually members of it."

⤳ 1 Corinthians 12:27

When my friend Bill was in the military, he was assigned to a platoon of illiterate men, so he went to his superiors to request a transfer.

"Request denied," they told him.

"But I have an education," said Bill. "I can read."

"Sorry, there's too much red tape involved. Besides, we need a leader in this group of ragtags. I guess you're it."

At first Bill was angry, but soon he began to feel honored. After all, he had two years of college and was planning to go to medical school. He could lead these men. He could teach them to read. Why, he might even get a medal for it!

Because of Bill's height, he was given the lead position in the marching formation, which meant he was in front of everyone. The first day of drills, a sergeant was barking out commands, but not very clearly. Bill guessed right on the first two turns, but the third time he went right when everyone else went left. He didn't notice for several paces. After the other men had a good laugh, the sergeant gave Bill a brick to carry in his right hand for the rest of boot camp (to help him learn right from left). In the end, Bill made a fine soldier, spending months in the Philippine Islands as a radio operator. On breezy days, he kept his door propped open with a brick—the same brick that would keep him humble until he died at the age of 69.

It's easy for Christians to get a "big head." We love to be perceived as spiritual giants, but we need to be reminded daily that there is only one head of this platoon of Christian soldiers—Christ Himself.

Paul makes it clear that love must prevail in the church so we as individuals can achieve unity. We're all marching in the same direction. The better we keep in step, the more pleasant and efficient will be the journey to our final destination.

Discussion Starters:

1. How is it possible for people in positions of Christian service to become arrogant?
2. What does it mean to submit to Christ? Give some examples.
3. When have you been humbled in front of a crowd? What is a "brick" you could carry with you or post in a prominent place to remind you to be humble?

Lifeline:

It's a lot less embarrassing to humble ourselves than to have others do it for us.

"X" DOESN'T MARK TRUE LOVE

"Love never fails. . . . But now faith, hope, love, abide these three; but the greatest of these is love."

⇜ 1 Corinthians 13:8, 13

I opened a valentine the other day and saw a string of X's at the bottom of the card, accompanied by the words "I love you, Dad." After being touched by the sentiment, I began to ask myself one of the age-old questions: What is love? Psychologists tell us that without love we shrivel up and die, yet hardly one in a hundred people could come close to defining it.

Many people who sign an X to a card or letter simply intend it to represent a kiss. Actually, however, the sign goes back to the days of the early Christians. "X" was the first letter in the Greek word for Christ as well as a symbol for the cross. As a symbol it conveyed the power of an oath, and because it was associated with goodness and honor, it became an acceptable substitute whenever a signature was needed from an illiterate person. So, in an age when few people could write, the "X" began to appear on many documents. To prove the sincerity of a transaction, a person would kiss the "X." It was this practice that led to its becoming a symbol of a kiss.

So much for our fascinating history lesson, but we still haven't defined love. It seems easier to nail Jell-O to a tree than to arrive at a good definition. It's more than an emotion, more than a decision. The best definition I can offer is found in 1 John 4:8: "God is love." Love must ultimately be defined as a person, and must include all the traits that person possesses.

God's loving characteristics are found in 1 Corinthians 13. Read the entire chapter and substitute the word *God* wherever the word *love* appears. Your daily need for more of God in your life will quickly come into focus.

Love is not a string of X's. It is not merely an emotion, a decision, or even an action. True love is a Person—God Himself. Be filled with God, and you can't help but be filled with love.

Discussion Starters:

1. Read through 1 Corinthians 13 and write down all the qualities of love.
2. How many of these descriptions can you say are true of you? Which ones are most lacking?
3. How can you "fill in the gaps" so your demonstration of love toward others can be more complete?

Lifeline:

You can't have love without sharing it with other people. Otherwise, it's not genuine love.

DROOPY DRAWERS

"When I was a child, I used to speak like a child, think like a child, reason like a child; when I became a man, I did away with childish things."

~ 1 Corinthians 13:11

I have a friend—I'll call him Reggie to spare him some embarrassment—who has a great underwear story. Every teenage boy knows that when you wear a pair of boxers for too long, the elastic waistband gives out. What starts as size 32 quickly becomes, roughly, size 58. Reggie had one such pair that he had failed to retire to the rag box. In a hurry to get to a game, he put on the only pair in his chest of drawers and rushed out the door.

He had no problems during the pregame warm-up. But when the game began and the sweat started to roll, his undies started a migration south. At first only a hint of white cotton appeared below the hem of Reggie's blue basketball shorts. But after a few more trips down the court, they became a white flag, flapping at his knees.

Every time there was a break in the action, Reggie would try to tuck everything back into place, but nothing worked for long. He says, "My face was red, my boxers were white, and my uniform was blue—I must have looked like Old Glory with high-tops on."

Reggie went on to play for the Arkansas Razorbacks, and then for the Spirit Express, a Christian team that travels around playing exhibition games and sharing the gospel. But he never again left for the gym without checking the waistband of his underwear.

Sometimes it's harder to change a childish habit than to hide a pair of droopy drawers. Paul's comments in today's passage most likely refer to the unloving, childish ways Corinthian church members were using their spiritual gifts. He was telling them, in a nice way, "Oh, grow up!"

You probably know gifted people (ones who *know* they are gifted) who flaunt their gifts and become rather difficult to tolerate. But God has gifted *all* Christians. When we properly apply our gifts, the church grows stronger. But if we use them to elevate ourselves rather than God, then we are no less an embarrassment to the Body of Christ than a pair of droopy drawers.

Discussion Starters:

1. Have you ever seen people abuse or misapply their spiritual gifts (teaching, preaching, evangelizing, etc.)? In what ways?
2. What would be a mature way to apply each of the gifts you have observed?
3. How can *you* prevent becoming a source of embarrassment to the Body of Christ?

Lifeline:

The gifts God gives us are of little benefit unless we "open" them and put them to use.

PAUL'S TOP FIVE

"In the church I desire to speak five words with my mind so that I may instruct others also, rather than ten thousand words in a tongue."

⮜ 1 Corinthians 14:19

Just over a year ago, Julia went in for routine thyroid surgery. But while she was on the operating table, the surgeon severed one of her vocal cords with the scalpel. Immediately, her voice was reduced to a painful whisper. Attempts at rehabilitation weren't working well. But exactly a year after the surgery that rendered her mute, Julia again found herself on an operating table—with a different doctor. This time the surgery was successful and Julia had her voice back.

Her new doctor advised her to take it easy for 10 days until he was sure her voice would still work. But Julia decided that if there was any possibility her voice might disappear again, she was going to make the most of the time she had. She used her newfound voice like there was no tomorrow.

She told her husband, "I love you," 50 times a day. She told her kids how proud she was of them. She told knock-knock jokes, read bedtime stories, sang in the shower, and laughed at every opportunity. And she made sure every night to say "thank You" to God for returning her voice—even if it was just temporary. I'm glad to report that after two months, her voice is still going strong.

As I read today's passage, I think of Julia and wonder why Paul chose "five words" instead of two, or 12, or 25. Something tells me Paul was a lot like Julia in that both had learned the value of speech and were eager to use their voices as a blessing for others.

I don't think Paul had five specific words in mind, but if he did, I suspect they might have been "Jesus Christ, God's Son crucified." That phrase was the basis of everything Paul stood for, a common theme in his writings, and a bond that united a thriving church. Uninterpreted tongues could never have the same effect as those five words.

Spend some time thinking about your own words. Do you use your tongue to edify others? Or would the world be a better place if you were mute?

Discussion Starters:

1. What does your speech tell others about your heart?
2. Who has the most edifying speech that you know? What makes that person stand out?
3. What can you do to build up others with your words?

Lifeline:

What five words best describe your feelings about God? How can you influence others with those words?

TONGUES OF FIRE

"So then tongues are for a sign, not to those who believe but to unbelievers. . . . Therefore if the whole church assembles together and all speak in tongues, and ungifted men or unbelievers enter, will they not say that you are mad?"

⟿ 1 Corinthians 14:22-23

A friend of mine shared a story I would like to pass along as he told it to me:

"A boy named Larry lived on my street, and he was a bona fide pyromaniac. One Christmas his parents gave him a magnifying glass. When he got tired of using it to melt tar and herd bugs, he gave me a call. I think he was looking for an accomplice.

"I met Larry beside a Dumpster at the Piggly Wiggly supermarket. Next to the Dumpster was an old mattress, its cottony guts protruding from a gash down the middle. Larry had found (or maybe stolen) a gross of bottle rockets and had dumped their gunpowder into a substantial pile in the center of the mattress.

"'This is going to be cool,' he bragged. 'Since we're not using any matches, there'll be no evidence to prove who did it.'

"Larry carefully focused the sun's rays through the glass until a tiny, orange tongue of fire sprang up. Larry leaned closer to study his project just as a gust of Oklahoma wind reached the flame, igniting the gunpowder. A flash blew Larry's eyebrows from his forehead, and he stumbled back into the Dumpster. In a matter of seconds, the flames had reached the Piggly Wiggly.

"We ran away as fast as we could and then watched the arrival of the fire department from a nearby tree house while eating Oreos. The blaze was out in less than 10 minutes, but the lesson has lasted a lifetime—at least for me. It wouldn't surprise me if Larry is still somewhere playing with matches in a prison cell."

Christians disagree on the significance of tongues in today's church. But Paul makes it clear: Misusing the gift of tongues can be as dangerous as a fire out of control. Used inappropriately, speaking in tongues can create confusion, disunity, and even ill feelings toward the church. A fire under control can be a blessing, but fire in the hands of folks like my friend's friend Larry is always destructive.

Discussion Starters:

1. What's your opinion about the gift of tongues?
2. How might this gift be threatening to others?
3. How can it can be a blessing when used appropriately?

Lifeline:

When kids abuse new toys, they break. Similarly, the misuse of *spiritual* gifts is always disappointing and unrewarding.

THE SPOTLIGHT OF TRUTH

"For I delivered to you as of first importance what I also received, that Christ died for our sins according to the Scriptures, and that He was buried, and that He was raised on the third day according to the Scriptures, and that He appeared to Cephas, then to the twelve."

⮑ 1 Corinthians 15:3-5

We've all seen a police helicopter whirring across a city sky, its spotlight probing the ground for some fleeing villain. But one of my friends actually witnessed one that had the hunted person pinned down in a circle of light.

"I was coming home from church with my family one night," he told me. "We had just entered an overpass, and below us the highway was dotted with traffic. Suddenly, my son shouted, 'Hey, Dad, look at that car down there. It looks like it's on stage.' Sure enough, ahead of the other cars sped an old, black van—smack-dab in the middle of a fluorescent halo. Above it, flying as low as possible, a police helicopter kept its search beam trained on the suspect. The light was so bright that every detail of the van stood out—license number, missing taillight, rust on the back. Nothing was hidden from view. No doubt, the police had their man."

In 1 Corinthians 15, Paul has his spotlight trained on the resurrection of Jesus. His light shines so brightly that nobody can be mistaken about the identity of the man "on stage." The man had a name: Christ Jesus. The man had a purpose: to die for our sins. The man was buried and stayed in the grave for three days. The man was raised from the dead. Finally, the man appeared to many people after His resurrection, and in a specific order: first to Peter (Cephas), then to His disciples, then to a group of 500, then to James, then to the apostles, and finally to Paul (vv. 5-8).

In short, the Resurrection is illuminated by facts and eyewitnesses. When we study it in light of Paul's evidence, we can arrive at only one conclusion: Jesus Christ most certainly rose from the dead. Case dismissed.

Discussion Starters:

1. Without looking at today's text, what are four pieces of evidence that verify Christ's resurrection?
2. In 25 words or less, how does the Resurrection give you hope?
3. If it were your job to try to disprove the Resurrection, what questions would you ask? Do you have a satisfactory answer for each of those questions?

Lifeline:

When Christians take the spotlight of their faith off the resurrection of Jesus, they are usually left in the dark.

THE LAST TRUMPET

"Behold, I tell you a mystery; we will not all sleep, but we will all be changed, in a moment, in the twinkling of an eye, at the last trumpet; for the trumpet will sound, and the dead will be raised imperishable, and we will be changed."

↞ I Corinthians 15:51-52

For years at Kanakuk, we began each morning with reveille. How would you like to be responsible for waking up 220 sleepy, grumpy boys and men every morning? No, you didn't get to quietly sing them awake or entice their eyes open with a terrific-smelling breakfast.

Here's how reveille works. A young boy is enlisted for his musical talents (primarily being that he owns a trumpet). It becomes his job to rise early, pull a T-shirt over his nappy head, grab his instrument, and shuffle to the bluff that overlooks beautiful Taneycomo Lake. There he starts blaring on his trumpet as loudly as he can—occasionally hitting the correct notes. To his sleeping peers he is, in every sense of the word, "unpopular."

Once an anonymous hero arose in our midst. In the quiet hours of the night he sneaked into the reviled bugler's cabin and plugged his horn with a big, wet wad of toilet paper. When the boy tried to bugle, nothing came out. We had 15 minutes of extra sleep that day, and the anonymous vandal gained the admiration of the masses.

The apostle Paul tells of another "bugle"—a trumpet that will one day sound so loudly that no plug can mute it. No one will sleep through it because even the dead will be awakened. In fact, it will be those of us who are awake and ready who will respond positively to this heavenly trumpet call. In an instant we will be changed, given immortal bodies that are fit for heaven in every way.

How can someone prepare for this day? He or she must be a Christian, rescued from the clutches of death by Christ Himself. Those who are not ready will never hear the bugle again. For them, there will be no more mornings to wake up to. Are *you* ready?

Discussion Starters:

1. Christ's return to earth seems too fantastic for some people to believe. Why do you think this is so?
2. Would you like to be living when Christ returns? What do you think it would be like to go straight from algebra class to heaven?
3. How does someone know if he or she is ready to meet Christ?

Lifeline:

Spend an hour or so determining how to be ready to hear that final trumpet.

THE STICKIES

"On the first day of every week each one of you is to put aside and save, as he may prosper, so that no collections be made when I come. When I arrive, whomever you may approve, I will send them with letters to carry your gift to Jerusalem; and if it is fitting for me to go also, they will go with me."

↝ 1 Corinthians 16:2-4

At least twice a year, "the stickies" would arrive. You could always recognize them by the fingerprints on the packaging and the card that read: "I lov yew, Dady." They came at Christmas, on my birthday, and sometimes for no special occasion at all. The stickies were always the same—a scrap of cloth, a tattered item from the garbage can, or perhaps a little wad of yarn with feathers glued randomly to it.

One time I ran my fingers across the colorful plumage and remarked, "Gee, Cooper, this is the most beautiful bird I've ever received."

Silence intruded—followed by correction.

"It's a hand gwenade."

His hand grenade is only one of the many tokens of love I've received from my kids over the years. They were always so touching, so personal . . . so sticky. But it didn't matter that they were coated in the goo that covers every child's hands. They were *sincere*, and I would never dream of throwing them away. I keep them in a special drawer, where my now-grown children can one day bring their children to rummage through the stickies.

Paul's closing instructions to the Corinthians begin with an appeal to practice *sincere* giving. Perhaps no mark of Christianity is more significant than one's willingness to give to others. And Paul didn't just instruct the Corinthians to give; he told them to give *habitually*—once a week, as soon as the paycheck comes in.

The Corinthians' gift was headed to the church in Jerusalem from where Christianity had spread. When we remember people or ministries that have been instrumental in our spiritual lives, we should ask God to bless them. Then *we* should bless them with a gift they'll never forget.

Discussion Starters:

1. Who would be the top three people or ministries you might want to give to?
2. Other than shelling out money, in what ways do you give?
3. In what ways would you like to become more giving?

Lifeline:

We don't actually give to God. The best we can do is return some of the abundant gifts with which He has blessed us.

TINY DOORS, WIDE OPPORTUNITIES

"I will remain in Ephesus until Pentecost; for a wide door for effective service has opened to me, and there are many adversaries."

↩ 1 Corinthians 16:8-9

I have been blessed to oversee several pieces of God's great earth. One of them, a cave in northern Arkansas, has become a favorite of mine. I enjoy taking people to explore it.

The sport of cave exploration is technically called *spelunking*, but most people just call it "crazy." Admittedly, it is a little nuts for a person to enjoy crawling into a hole, through mud, beneath tons of limestone, into the blackest darkness you can imagine. But the payoffs are out of this world— or should I say, *under* this world?

My cave has an entrance no bigger than a microwave oven. Most adults can squeeze through, but recently a large lawyer friend got stuck. He was helpless, with his front half in the hole and his hindquarters outside with us—in just the position many people dream of seeing lawyers. We greased his belly with good Ozark mud as if we were buttering a piece of corn, gave three hefty shoves, and his legs disappeared through the hole. Twenty minutes later, we all stood at the back of the cave, admiring the crystal stalactites and stalagmites.

Sometimes the greatest opportunities of life lie just beyond tiny doors. Ephesus was but a single town on the eastern shore of the Aegean Sea. Many Roman emperors saw Ephesus as a gateway to the Eastern world, which they hoped to incorporate into their empire for its wealth. Yet Paul saw Ephesus as a "wide door for effective service" through which he hoped to minister. The only wealth he was interested in were the unsaved souls which could be redeemed for God.

The Bible speaks of another door—one that leads to your heart. Jesus stands and knocks, but He won't enter until you choose to open the door (Revelation 3:20). Have you swung wide that door to let Him in? Or is He still standing outside, knocking, just waiting for you to discover the wonderful opportunities that await as soon as you invite Him in?

Discussion Starters:

1. Can you identify any potential "doors of opportunity" to which God is leading you?
2. Paul mentioned his adversaries (1 Corinthians 16:9). Do you face any adversaries as you pursue a Christian lifestyle?
3. Who are some trustworthy colleagues you can call on to give you good advice for which doors to pursue, and to help you stand against your adversaries?

Lifeline:

Identify any dark and/or tiny doors you are faced with today. How will you get through?

2 Corinthians

Second Corinthians is Paul's second biblical letter to the church at Corinth. This fantastic letter is one of my personal favorites because it is packed full of godly wisdom. It relates to teenagers with amazing clarity and gives us a chance to see a spiritual X-ray view of the apostle Paul's heart. You see his highest highs and lowest lows. His openness and his honesty will help you see God and yourself in a way that will probably influence you for a lifetime. I pray that through our time together in this tremendous book, it will touch your heart and your character the way it has mine.

BRAVERY

"Blessed be the God and Father of our Lord Jesus Christ, the Father of mercies and God of all comfort, who comforts us in all our affliction so that we will be able to comfort those who are in any affliction with the comfort with which we ourselves are comforted by God."

⌐ 2 Corinthians 1:3-4

War Memorial Stadium in Little Rock, Arkansas, is not the place to be when the Razorbacks boast the number-two team in the nation and you're dressed in the red, white, and blue uniform of Southern Methodist University. My 20-year-old rookie legs shook as I staggered onto the field for the opening kick-off. My dismay intensified as the Razorbacks scored 35 unanswered points.

With 10 minutes, 53 seconds left in the game, we were still behind 35 to zero. That's when a fiery-eyed linebacker named Bruce Potillo pulled our battle-weary defense together and screamed to us above the Arkansas roar, "Men, these guys aren't that good. We're better than they are. They're not going to make one more first down for the rest of this game. Let's go out there and play like we are capable of playing."

Our offense scored on the next series. Our defense stopped them like a concrete wall. Three more times our offense scored. Three more times our defense held. As the clock ticked down to 28 seconds remaining, the stadium had become deathly quiet. We had held the powerful Razorback offense yet again.

Our offense had one more shot at the ball—or so we thought. Somehow the refs let the clock tick down to zero. Game over. We were certain that if we had touched the ball just once more, the upset of the year would have taken place. Although our 28-point scoring spree left us one touchdown short of catching up, I would never again experience a "victory" so sweet, because a word spoken by a friend gave our entire team the "bravery" (which is exactly what the biblical word *comfort* means) to pick ourselves up, return to the battlefield, and play like we had never played before. Whether you need comfort or courage, you'll find both in Paul's words as we begin this series in 2 Corinthians.

Discussion Starters:

1. How does the Holy Spirit give you "bravery" (comfort) when you need it most?
2. How do you transfer the comfort you receive from God to others who need it?
3. What trials have you faced (and endured) that allowed you to later minister to someone going through the same thing?

Lifeline:

Comfort is never found in attempting to sidestep difficult circumstances, but in bravely facing them with the strength God provides.

THE PLEDGE

"Now He who establishes us with you in Christ and anointed us is God, who also sealed us and gave us the Spirit in our hearts as a pledge."

∽ 2 Corinthians 1:21-22

The air seeped out of the front right tire of our van with a steady swoosh. It was just after midnight and definitely no time for a flat tire, especially for a group of weary travelers with no spare who were planning a nine-hour, all-night drive to Kansas City. To my amazement, we found an open tire store with one tire on the shelf exactly the right size. As I reached for my billfold, I realized I had left it—with all my travel money—at a McDonalds across town. With frantic determination, I pleaded with the mechanic to trust me and put the tire on our van while I hitched a ride to retrieve my billfold.

"How do I know you'll return to pay me?" he asked with a shout.

"I'll leave Brad Friess with you. He's my close friend," I said clumsily.

It was enough to seal the deal. Brad was my friend, and no fool would abandon a friend for the price of one measly tire! Besides, he was a handsome, intelligent, talented, 6'5" basketball standout for the University of Arkansas cagers.

When I returned with billfold in hand, I received Brad back along with the new tire. During our starlit trip to Kansas City, my friends laughed at me all night long for exchanging Brad for, of all things, a steel-belted radial worth no more than $99. But I didn't trade Brad. He was my *pledge* to the mechanic. It's how he knew I would return.

When Jesus had to go away, He knew some of His followers might be afraid He would never return. So, as Paul tells us, He left the Holy Spirit as His pledge. When Jesus returns, we'll all be together again. Until then I can take Him at His word because I am holding His pledge—one I trust even more than my friend Brad.

Discussion Starters:

1. When a person receives Christ as personal Savior, what is the significance of the Holy Spirit entering his or her heart to stay?
2. Sometimes Christians talk about "the security of the believer." In light of today's passage, what does the phrase mean to you?
3. What does it mean that God "sealed us"?

Lifeline:

The most hope-inspiring words in Scripture may be "I will never leave you or forsake you" (Deuteronomy 31:6; Hebrews 13:5).

FORGIVEN

"But one whom you forgive anything, I forgive also; for indeed what I have forgiven, if I have forgiven anything, I did it for your sakes in the presence of Christ, so that no advantage would be taken of us by Satan, for we are not ignorant of his schemes."

⤳ 2 Corinthians 2:10-11

The chair lift in Park City is the longest one in Utah. I was riding with my 22-year-old friend Emily, an energetic snowboarder who can run circles around this "gray-haired knuckle dragger" (as the young snowboarder crowd terms old guys like me). It took the entire trip for Emily to tell me her emotional life story. At age 15 she thought she had a model family until her mother announced she was in love with the school music director and would be leaving home with all the furniture and as much of the family's savings as she could get her hands on. Emily's world immediately shattered into small fragments.

In contrast to her gentle-spirited, forgiving father, Emily's rage toward her mom boiled inside. Her anger seemed unquenchable. The inner fire of hatred blazed hotter with each passing year as her mom demanded more and more from the family and updated them on her continuing extra-marital affair.

Five years later, Emily showed up at our sports camp to counsel teenagers. From all appearances, she was a talented athlete with a smile as beautiful as a Rocky Mountain sunrise. Yet in addition to all her talents and Christ-filled beauty, Emily also brought a loaded suitcase of bitterness that was crippling her like a case of spiritual arthritis.

During staff training week, I spoke frequently of God's amazing love for us and of my boundless love for my wife and kids. During the week, the Holy Spirit purposely and mysteriously melted Emily's hard heart toward her mom, allowing her to completely forgive her mother for five long years of hurt. Like a mighty wall of water caged behind a huge concrete dam, the healing power of forgiveness was released to flow into Emily's life and enable her to be truly well, truly whole, and truly free.

Discussion Starters:

1. Why does God expect us to forgive others as He forgives us?
2. What specks of bitterness might be hidden in your heart that you need to get rid of today?
3. Review today's passage. How does Satan take advantage of us when we refuse to forgive one another?

Lifeline:

The healing power of forgiveness is God's greatest medicine for you and your family.

BOY, DO WE SMELL!

"But thanks be to God, who always leads us in triumph in Christ, and manifests through us the sweet aroma of the knowledge of Him in every place. For we are a fragrance of Christ to God among those who are being saved and among those who are perishing; to the one an aroma from death to death, to the other an aroma from life to life."

↪ 2 Corinthians 2:14-16

My walk along the 2,000-year-old original stone Appian Way into the ancient walled city of Rome is without a doubt the most memorable of my life. Peter and Paul walked on those very stones as they went about their historic, gospel-spreading ministry. On those stones, too, marched Roman soldiers attempting to silence the testimony of early Christians, bringing capital punishment as a final judgment to many who faithfully gave testimony of their risen Savior.

The Appian Way into Rome was also "Main Street" on which the Roman armies would return in their famous "parade of triumph." Proud generals would display their troops, as well as throngs of captured slaves and condemned prisoners, while wildly cheering crowds lined the thoroughfare into the heart of the city.

According to tradition, burning aromatic incense would accompany the chariots and officers in the parade. To the Roman conquerors, it was an aroma of life. To the prisoners, it was an aroma of death because this would very likely be their final walk. A cruel death awaited, perhaps the same fate that was given to Jesus, or something almost as cruel.

Paul passes along the good news that those who are led by God *always* march in triumph. For us, the stench of death is left behind and replaced by salvation and victory in Christ. As Christians, we are a "fragrance of Christ to God." As far as God is concerned, we really smell! And we can be happy we do.

Discussion Starters:

1. As you speak up for Jesus, Christians may support you while others give you a hard time. Why is your witness an "aroma of life" to one group and an "aroma of death" to the other?
2. What's the worst you've ever suffered because you were a Christian? How does that compare to the treatment received by Peter, Paul, and other early Christians at the hands of the Romans?
3. How noticeable is your "aroma of triumph"? How can you make it stronger?

Lifeline:

Commit each day to be an "aroma of life" to your family.

A STRANGE-LOOKING LETTER

"You are our letter, written in our hearts, known and read by all men; being manifested that you are a letter of Christ, cared for by us, written not with ink but with the Spirit of the living God, not on tablets of stone but on tablets of human hearts."

⟿ 2 Corinthians 3:2-3

The highways that lead into our highly traveled tourist town of Branson, Missouri, are lined with huge, illuminated billboards that literally number in the thousands. Numerous country music stars have elegant theaters here, each seating from 2,000 to 4,000 people. Music fans travel here by the millions. The billboards are part of a strategy that marketing experts call "intercept marketing," and are intended to influence the plans of tourists who don't have their vacation schedules finalized.

I'm not sure how the tourists feel about the billboards. But to many of us who live here, the signs are flashy . . . glitzy . . . gaudy . . . and nauseating.

Believe it or not, you and I have billboards around our necks, on our cars, in our homes, in our classrooms, and where we work. As true believers, our billboards all display the same message: "JESUS LIVES HERE!" It's a simple but profound statement. *Jesus* lives here. Jesus *lives* here. Jesus lives *here*.

Surprised? It is true. We are part of God's intercept marketing. Many people sense they are headed for death and hell, but they haven't finalized their decisions yet. Any one of the Christian "billboards" God puts in front of them might sway their decision so that their destination becomes eternal life in heaven.

Sometimes I realize my billboard needs a bit of repair. Perhaps the light is beginning to burn dimly or I need a fresh coat of paint to make the message easier for others to see. How about you? You will reach dozens (or hundreds, or thousands) of people I'll never see. The way you talk, act, and treat others will make your billboard either a repulsive sign that causes them to reject the message or perhaps the most attractive piece of artwork they will ever see. Shine on!

Discussion Starters:

1. A popular chorus says, "They'll know we are Christians by our love." What kind of love will attract your friends to Jesus?
2. Who is someone who consistently displays a "Jesus Lives Here" billboard that gets your attention? Why does that person stand out for you?
3. What can you do this week to make your message more clear to others?

Lifeline:

Someone may be looking for a "sign" from God, and you just might be it!

LET FREEDOM RING

"Now the Lord is the Spirit, and where the Spirit of the Lord is, there is liberty."

⌐ 2 Corinthians 3:17

The liberated woman . . . "peminism."

The liberated man . . . "machoism."

The liberated politician . . . "abortion advocate."

The liberated newscaster . . . "left-wing humanist."

The liberated teen . . . "drugs, sex, and alcohol."

The liberated Christian . . . free from guilt, free from the power of sin, free to forgive, free to live with purity, free to know God, free to receive God's grace and go to heaven.

Somehow it seems that in the secular world, "liberated" quickly translates into "liberal." But when it comes to active Christians, the press calls us fundamentalists . . . narrow-minded . . . shallow . . . judgmental zealots.

Amy and Marcus had been dating for over a year. Marcus convinced Amy that if she would be more open to sex, she could be *free* from her parents' grip on her life and could experience "free love" in their relationship. Three months later Amy stares into the impersonal eyes of an abortion doctor, trapped in a web of guilt that only Christ can unlock. Marcus is nowhere to be found.

Steve, Jason, and Jared hounded their friend Sam for four solid months to party with them. "C'mon, Sam, you're *so* enslaved to that cross you wear around your neck. Have some fun, man. Loosen up a bit." Sam started going to their parties and has become a serious teenage alcoholic. Jason is in drug rehab.

Melissa used to party. She thought she had to be high to get friends to like her, but she didn't even like herself for what she had become. At a Young Life Club she met a man named Jesus. Her new life with Christ has released her from her guilt and given her freedoms she had never known—including the freedom to enjoy staying at home sometimes on Saturday night, or going to church with her family on Sundays.

Paul says, "Where the Spirit of the Lord is, there is liberty." And he should know, because he learned it from a master—*the* Master—who promises, "If the Son makes you free, you will be free indeed" (John 8:36).

Discussion Starters:

1. How is the word *freedom* abused in today's society?
2. How does Satan twist the meaning of so many biblical words, such as "freedom," "love," and "fun"? Why does he do it?
3. What does being "free indeed" mean to you?

Lifeline:

Every day we choose to be either more free or less free.

PEANUT BUTTER JARS

"But we have this treasure in earthen vessels, so that the surpassing greatness of the power will be of God and not from ourselves; we are afflicted in every way, but not crushed; perplexed, but not despairing; persecuted, but not forsaken; struck down, but not destroyed; always carrying about in the body the dying of Jesus, so that the life of Jesus also may be manifested in our body."

↩ 2 Corinthians 4:7-10

When I was a kid, my dad worked hard to provide for us. We didn't go hungry, but we ate a lot of beans, burgers, and peanut butter and jelly. And our dog, Pixie, never got fat on leftovers because we hardly ever had any.

My mom was a champion at stretching a dollar, and she would save everything that had any potential value. Nothing went into the trash. Her mom had taught her to save buttons, rare coins, toy marbles, trading stamps, and other things that could be put to use at some time in the future. She accumulated these things in the numerous peanut butter jars we accumulated. I remember one Friday night we even put a bunch of fireflies in a peanut butter jar to create a natural flashlight for a game we played in the darkness of our room.

Treasures in peanut butter jars! It sounds contradictory, but it's a biblical image that's important to understand. The basic concept is that God is great and powerful, and we're pretty insignificant in comparison. Yet God Himself chooses to live within us when we turn to Him for salvation. Paul refers to this as "treasure in earthen vessels" (or some versions say "jars of clay"). In other words, the jar is only valuable because of what it contains.

I thought my family kept some pretty good treasures in our peanut butter jars. But when I think of God putting His greatest treasure into someone like me with all my failures and weaknesses, I am humbled and ecstatic at the same time. It's the least I can do to try to share my "hidden treasure" with folks who come my way.

Discussion Starters:

1. How valuable is an empty peanut butter jar? How valuable are you without Jesus?
2. According to today's passage, what are some benefits of having the treasure of God within us?
3. How might this passage motivate you to be more humble?

Lifeline:

When empty, the jar that I am will easily break. When filled with the treasure of God Himself, it is the strongest treasure chest on earth.

SKIN DEEP

"Therefore we do not lose heart, but though our outer man is decaying, yet our inner man is being renewed day by day. For momentary, light affliction is producing for us an eternal weight of glory far beyond all comparison, while we look not at the things which are seen, but at the things which are not seen; for the things which are seen are temporal, but the things which are not seen are eternal."

↜ 2 Corinthians 4:16-18

"Man, she's hot!"

"If I could only lose 10 pounds."

"My Daddy always reminds me how fat I am."

"Honey, you could stand to shape up a little."

"If we only had a newer car. This one is last year's model!"

Lusty TV shows, size two dresses, *Playboy* centerfolds, low-cut blouses, 17-inch biceps, flat stomachs, fat-free thighs . . . we are driving ourselves crazy with an obsession to be "perfect" (whatever that is). As the morals of our country continue to slide, we continue to concern ourselves with shallow, surface issues.

We need a reminder about stark reality from the commonsense writing of David: "As for man, his days are like grass; as a flower of the field, so he flourishes. When the wind has passed over it, it is no more, and its place acknowledges it no longer" (Psalm 103:15-16).

Imagine the freedom we would find if, instead of a size two dress, we concentrated on having a Jesus-sized heart!

Think how enormous our love for God could become if we encouraged spiritual growth in each other as much as we stress muscle growth.

If we started "working out" to purify our hearts and build up *others* instead of building our bodies, think how pleasant our homes, schools, and workplaces could be.

No doubt, beauty *is* only skin deep. But that soft, supple skin is destined to decay one of these days. The sooner we abandon our fixation with the outer shell and concentrate on what's beneath the skin (our hearts), the happier and spiritually healthier we will be.

Discussion Starters:

1. What are some influences that attempt to get us to focus primarily on external beauty?
2. What happens if we are deceived into a fixation on external things rather than eternal ones?
3. How can you, in your home, minimize the impact of potentially destructive influences?

Lifeline:

Look at the heart and see the face of God.

EARTH SUITS

"For we know that if the earthly tent which is our house is torn down, we have a building from God, a house not made with hands, eternal in the heavens. For indeed in this house we groan, longing to be clothed with our dwelling from heaven, inasmuch as we, having put it on, will not be found naked."

⟿ 2 Corinthians 5:1-3

Randy Odom is a counselor at Kids Across America, our summer sports camp reserved for some of America's most deserving kids who come from the financially challenged concrete world of urban inner cities. Not only does Randy love God, but he also loves urban kids with a passion.

One stormy spring day, Randy pulled up in front of his trailer home at the exact moment a tornado hit. In haste he jumped out of his car (as the door was ripped from its hinges), dove into his "home on wheels," and was met by another door flying down the hallway. The door pinned him to the floor as his whole house was literally demolished above him. Although his home and possessions were scattered for city blocks, Randy was protected by the door and escaped without injury.

The bodies we inhabit are about as reliable as Randy's mobile home in a tornado. They are like "earth suits" we wear while we're here. But like NASA's "moon suits," they will eventually wear out and need to be replaced. We can exercise them, feed them, and doctor them all we want, but the tornado of time will eventually reduce them to dust.

We can thank God that when Christians die, our bodies (which are no longer needed) are like trade-ins for permanent, eternal bodies (1 Corinthians 15:40-44). In addition, our spirits are eternal, protected from destruction by the Spirit of Christ. Your spirit, sealed by grace for eternity, is destined to live with God forever—unscathed, unharmed, free to live, and fit for a King.

Discussion Starters:

1. What do you like best about your body? How would you feel if those features were lost or diminished?
2. What blinds us to the important things in life and causes us to focus so much time and attention on an "earth suit" that will deteriorate?
3. How can you rearrange your priorities to stay focused on the part of you that will live forever?

Lifeline:

When you start thinking about living forever, you'll be more likely to dwell on things that are eternal.

METAMORPHOSIS

"Therefore if anyone is in Christ, he is a new creature; the old things passed away; behold, new things have come."

↬ 2 Corinthians 5:17

After grammar school we take metamorphosis for granted, but think about it for a moment. The entire biological makeup of a creeping caterpillar somehow transfers into a majestic butterfly. And that butterfly can travel from deep in the heart of Mexico to the exact tree in the northernmost part of the United States where its ancestors lived! God is supernatural. He is unexplainable. He is unprovable.

To God, the caterpillar-to-butterfly and tadpole-to-frog transformations are a breeze. Even more amazing is the metamorphosis of a vicious murderer into a tenderhearted minister . . . a "hopeless" alcoholic into a trustworthy husband and father . . . lost and depressed teenagers into dynamic teachers, sports figures, counselors, musicians, and all sorts of other successful adults.

Recently a 17-year-old boy told me at a youth rally, "Last year when you spoke here, I was a heroin addict. But I became a Christian a month later, my drug habit has ended, and now I've been called to be a pastor someday."

I have failed in this life way too many times to count. So I can tell you from experience that when you feel like a caterpillar, the best thing to do is crawl into the "cocoon" of God's grace. Before long, like a butterfly, you'll be lighter than air and flying high.

Discussion Starters:

1. What does it mean to be a "new creature"?
2. Have you been through a spiritual metamorphosis? Is the transformation complete, or is it an ongoing process? Explain.
3. What other "new things" (2 Corinthians 5:17) do you have to look forward to?

Lifeline:

Try to always forgive the "caterpillar" state of others, and look for the "butterfly" in everyone around you.

BOUND TOGETHER

"Do not be bound together with unbelievers; for what partnership have righteousness and lawlessness, or what fellowship has light with darkness?"

↶ 2 Corinthians 6:14

Imagine that you are an ox named Bill, and your job is to pull the king of Turkey in a cart. You love the king and serve him willingly. After all, this is a pretty good gig for an ox. But one day someone places you in a yoke with Sam. Although Sam is a big, strong ox, he also turns out to be lazy, rebellious, and stubborn. Although you work hard, you can't compensate for Sam's hoof dragging. The king becomes frustrated with both of you and sells you to a much less compassionate owner. Your heart is broken because you really liked the king.

Yes, I know oxen don't have hearts that can be broken or a strong love for their owners! But the story presents an image similar to what Paul is warning about in today's passage. Many teen letters I've received tell the same story. Here are a few examples:

"My friends told me that getting high would make my problems go away. That wasn't true at all. First we tried speed, then pot, angel dust, and LSD. Although I only tried LSD once, it was an experience I'll never forget."

"He told me he loved me and that we'd get married someday. He talked me into sex and then we broke up. I was crushed."

"I began to hang out with the wrong friends. They were always partying and drinking. Before long, they took me down with them."

And here's one from an adult Christian businessman:

"The worst mistake I ever made was building a business partnership with [an unbeliever]. I'll be paying for it (literally) for years to come."

Christians are not to ignore unbelievers—by no means. We need to share the gospel with them and show them the love of God. But we must beware of becoming "bound together" with people who don't have our same moral base or faith in God. The pairing might be in a business partnership, marriage, dating relationship, etc. It may start out well, but it would be only a matter of time until the "yoke" became too much to contend with. When the separation eventually comes, your heart will be broken.

Discussion Starters:

1. Can you relate to being "bound together" with a nonbeliever? In what ways?
2. If you find yourself "unequally yoked" with someone, what do you need to do?
3. If you feel an attraction to a nonbeliever, what can you do *before* serious problems arise?

Lifeline:

Pull your own weight in helping your family to continue growing strong.

AN INSIDE WEDDING

"For we are the temple of the living God. . . . 'I will be a father to you, and you shall be sons and daughters to Me,' says the Lord Almighty."

$\backsim$ 2 Corinthians 6:16, 18

Candy Irwin was stunning on her wedding day as she walked slowly and deliberately down the colorfully laced pathway into the picturesque outdoor chapel. It was without a doubt the most beautiful wedding my eyes have ever beheld. Her wedding budget was a mere $100. Candy was a country girl and money was scarce. She had spent all summer hand-sewing beads and sequins to a simple white dress until she had produced a wedding gown far superior to anything Saks Fifth Avenue ever dreamed of. Candy had no money for flowers, but God took care of that with majestic splendor. The silver leaf maple trees surrounding the outdoor chapel had turned a myriad of fall colors. The gentle Ozark breeze blew brilliant leaves across the ground where they decorated her footsteps.

By the time Candy arrived at the wedding altar, I was speechless and her groom was in tears. The anticipation of this moment was overwhelming for him. He had patiently waited for three years while Candy attended to an ailing grandmother every day until her hero went to her heavenly rest. The thought of Candy's pure and loving heart intensified her beauty as she stood at the altar.

Yet as breathtaking as Candy's wedding scene was, it pales in comparison to a ceremony that takes place within each Christian. For at the "temple" of your heart, your soul becomes "wedded" to the Holy Spirit of God. No artist or architect could design a more beautiful interior wedding chapel than your heart, handcrafted by God to become His Spirit's dwelling place.

Paul says that each Christian is "the temple of the living God." That's why Scripture calls us to a high standard of holy living. That's why we're selective with our music, movies, television viewing, and conversation. That's why we don't ingest alcohol, drugs, or tobacco into our bodies. That's why we don't run rampant having indiscriminate sex.

But if we're happy in our "marriage," we won't mind a bit.

Discussion Starters:

1. How do you feel about your body being God's "temple"?
2. How do your eyes and ears allow things into the temple that ought not be there?
3. If your temple needs a good "housecleaning," how can you go about it?

Lifeline:

The joy of a wedding ceremony with Jesus Himself should quickly flow into your home.

PERFECTING HOLINESS

"Therefore, having these promises, beloved, let us cleanse ourselves from all defilement of flesh and spirit, perfecting holiness in the fear of God."

↜ 2 Corinthians 7:1

Erin can laugh now at her earliest athletic setback—getting kicked off the gymnastics team at age eight for being "too fat." She also laughs off the fact that her high school peers recently voted to bestow upon her the title of "Best Body." The honor was far from being a joke, yet Erin doesn't let other people's comments, positive or negative, affect how she feels about herself. She's a committed Christian who has dedicated her mind and body to Christ. As good as she looks on the outside, her heart is definitely her most beautiful attribute. To put it simply, Erin is "pure" and has dedicated herself to staying that way.

My son Cooper is one of Erin's close friends, and they frequently go out on weekends. She recently asked him to the prom and wrote him a "love letter," which he shared with me. It had a hand-drawn picture of a flower and looked something like this:

God's
Riches
At
Christ's
Expense

Dear Cooper,

Did you know the Bible mentions grace 131 times? Isn't that cool! See you Saturday. Erin

Seventeen magazine says that prom is like a miniature honeymoon for many couples. Supposedly more virginity is lost on prom night than any other night of the year. Not so for Erin. The grace she knows as a true believer has given her the determination to save her "best body" (every inch of it!) for her husband.

My oldest son, Brady, recently asked Erin what she liked best about Cooper. She was quick to respond, "His Christian character." When the question was reversed, Cooper replied with eloquent, football-player candor: "Same for her."

Most of us are willing to "dabble" in holiness, but Paul reminds us that our ultimate quest should be "perfecting" holiness. May we all come a little closer to perfection week by week.

Discussion Starters:

1. What does the term "purity" mean to you?
2. Why is purity such an attractive quality?
3. How do you interpret "perfecting holiness" when it comes to the way you live your life?

Lifeline:

A pure heart permeates all the senses: what you see, what you say, what you hear, what you touch, and what you feel.

WITHOUT REGRET

"For the sorrow that is according to the will of God produces a repentance without regret, leading to salvation, but the sorrow of the world produces death."

M. Scott Peck's insightful best-selling book *The Road Less Traveled* begins with a profound insight: "Life is difficult."

The French say *la vi est dure* ("the road is difficult"). But this popular phrase is immediately followed by *mon dieu est bon* ("my God is good").

In case you haven't noticed, this planet we live on is not heaven. Satan wreaks havoc on us in the form of crime, disease, heartaches, and heart-breaks—all of which we must contend with throughout our lives.

Josh McDowell says that trials will either make us bitter or better. If we trust God in all circumstances and hold Him sovereign in our lives, difficulties bring out the best in us. If the pleasures of the world become our ultimate aim, letdowns and disappointments make us bitter.

Some people are "groaners" while others are "praisers." The difference is not the size of the trial but the size of their hearts. If my ultimate goal is to get to heaven and take a lot of people with me, I can appreciate trials because they tend to humble people and make them receptive to the help, forgiveness, and power God offers.

The day my young friend Ricky died in a drowning accident, seven people who knew him accepted Christ as their personal Savior. Martin has had 14 major surgeries on his face to correct a birth defect, yet he called from his hospital bed to praise God for his medical care. Lauren lost a leg to cancer yet continues to excel at our sports camp, blessing and amazing everyone with her fantastic attitude and Christ-given smile.

I'm not trying to tell you that sufferings don't hurt. They do! It usually takes a significant period of time and personal struggle—and perhaps even fear, anger, or doubt—before you get over them. God understands because He has been there! Even Jesus expressed a desire to avoid a painful trial (Mark 14:34-36). But He submitted to God's will and eventually was rewarded with a magnificent triumph. The same future lies ahead for those of us whose sorrows produce "a repentance without regret."

Discussion Starters:

1. How do trials separate genuine Christian faith from counterfeit faith?
2. Think of a trial you are now facing. How might it help make you better rather than bitter and turn you into a "praiser"?
3. How can trials help us appreciate Jesus and identify with Him? (See Hebrews 5:8-9.)

Lifeline:

Home should be a "comforting place" when the trials of life wound a family member.

RECAPTURING THE JOY OF GIVING

"They gave of their own accord, begging us with much urging for the favor of participation in the support of the saints, and this, not as we had expected, but they first gave themselves to the Lord and to us by the will of God."

⟿ 2 Corinthians 8:3-5

Nothing this side of heaven is as fun, as rewarding, or as fulfilling as giving. Just watch children pick out that very special gift for Mom or Dad at Christmas. They almost burst with excitement until the parent opens the gift and says, "Wow! Just what I've always wanted!"

But many of us seem to lose the joy of giving somewhere along the line. One day as 200 hungry teenage boys entered our dining hall for lunch, they found one table set with an abundance of food. Fourteen lucky guys were randomly chosen to sit at that "America" table. The rest of the famished young athletes sat at "Third World" tables—a few of which had beans, rice, and water, and others of which had nothing at all.

The "America" table was lavished with steaks, fried chicken, vegetables, and all sorts of desserts. The "Americans" were free to roam, and I watched with amazement. Four boys filled their plates to overflowing and ate like pigs without regard for their friends. Nine boys ate their fill but were willing to share leftovers. But one fantastic kid spent the entire meal giving away everything he had—and he had a blast! He had more fun than anyone. And when supper rolled around, you can believe he enjoyed his meal to the max.

Today's passage is Paul's praise for the Christians in Macedonia, who were struggling to get by and yet were willing and able to collect an offering to share with others who might need it more. Just off the coast of Florida 2 million children are starving on the tiny island of Haiti—and that's just one small area of poverty. If more American churches discovered the joy of giving known by those wonderful people in Macedonia, the kids of Haiti, as well as many others around the world, would have no want for food. We might not be able to feed the whole world, but we can do more than we're doing now. This week—today—let's try to do *something*.

Discussion Starters:

1. How can you and your family clean out a closet, a cupboard, or even a savings account to help the poor of this world?
2. How would you expect the recipients (and God) to respond to an act of joyful giving on your part?
3. How can your giving become more satisfying and joyful?

Lifeline:

Cast out a few crumbs and you get back a whole loaf.

FOR A WHILE

"For you know the grace of our Lord Jesus Christ, that though He was rich, yet for your sake He became poor, so that you through His poverty might become rich."

🖝 2 Corinthians 8:9

Not much space remained in my assigned seat because the huge fellow in the next seat overflowed into mine. But it turned out to be one of the most interesting flights of my life. Not only was he rich in size, but he was rich in finances as well . . . very rich. The purpose of his trip was to meet 10 close friends and give each of them a very expensive gift. But after I complimented his generosity, he gave me a piece of wisdom I have found far more valuable than what his friends were to receive the next day. He said, "Aw, it's nothin'. I never saw a hearse followed by a U-Haul trailer."

My new friend was right. You can't take it with you. He reminded me of a favorite saying of my dad: "You can only sleep in one bed at a time. Why build an empire to yourself when it's so much more fun to give it away?"

Paul reminds us of the overwhelming example Jesus provided for us. He was God. He was in heaven with His Father. Yet he gave it all up—for a while—to come to earth and be a human being. Not only that, but He also willingly died a horrible death as a condemned criminal. He challenged us in His Sermon on the Mount, "Do not store up for yourselves treasures on earth, where moth and rust destroy, and where thieves break in and steal. But store up for yourselves treasures in heaven" (Matthew 6:19-20).

Jesus willingly became poor for us. We can choose to do the same for others. Just remember that whatever you give in God's name is never lost. It is "stored up." It's out of your possession—but only for a while. Keep in mind that Jesus certainly didn't *stay* poor. Similarly, at the end of this earthly life we can expect to get back more than we can even imagine. And that time it won't be for a while. It will be forever.

Discussion Starters:

1. Why is it so hard to follow Christ's example of giving?
2. Would you consider yourself more of a giver or a taker? Why?
3. How can you improve your giving skills? Be specific, and consider time, talents, and possessions as well as money.

Lifeline:

Your family members have given a lot for you. What can you give back this week?

GIVE UNTIL YOU GIGGLE

"He who sows sparingly will also reap sparingly, and he who sows bountifully will also reap bountifully. Each one must do just as he has purposed in his heart, not grudgingly or under compulsion, for God loves a cheerful giver."

↪ 2 Corinthians 9:6-7

Fifteen thousand of God's most beautiful kids go to school in and around Port-au-Prince, Haiti, in the 22 schools built by my dear friend Pastor Jean Edmond. The children get a good Christian education, one shirt per year, and a meager meal that they get to eat after they finish their math assignment. Yet this is the happiest bunch of kids you've ever laid your eyes on!

Recently some friends and I decided to take Christmas to Haiti, so we prepared 15,000 gift bags packed with Frisbees, stuffed animals, Bibles, and a few other treats. The bags were filled with things the kids had never even dreamed of. Santa Claus ("Papa Noël" to them) went along for the festive presentation to each school. The kids went nuts!

Something happened that Christmas, however, that will forever redefine my concept of "the fun of giving." In each gift bag was a tiny roll of Lifesavers. Try to imagine how much the children loved their very first taste of a Lifesaver. They smiled from ear to ear!

One little boy stole my heart and changed my life as he took the first Lifesaver out of the pack and ate it. He found it so tasty that he immediately wanted to share the experience. In fact, he tried to give the whole pack back to me. That's right—the whole pack! One for him, the rest for me. And he couldn't have been happier!

It's a great principle, whether you're talking about Lifesavers or anything else we tend to accumulate. One of these days, try the "one for me, the rest for others" principle and see how happy it makes your heart.

Discussion Starters:

1. What does today's passage mean when it says (in my own translation), "Give until you giggle"?
2. Why does it sometimes become harder to give after we've accumulated a lot?
3. What needs do you see around you today? How might you give "the whole pack of Lifesavers," so to speak, to help one or more of the people in need?

Lifeline:

What special giving project are you willing to commit yourself to this year?

NOTE: We are planning additional trips to Haiti. If you would like to send a Christmas gift, write us at: Christian Children's Charity, P.O. Box 222, Branson, MO 65615.

CAPTIVE THOUGHTS

"For though we walk in the flesh, we do not war according to the flesh, for the weapons of our warfare are not of the flesh, but divinely powerful for the destruction of fortresses. We are destroying speculations and every lofty thing raised up against the knowledge of God, and we are taking every thought captive to the obedience of Christ."

⤳ 2 Corinthians 10:3-5

A review of almost any year's top 10 movies, CDs, and TV shows will yield a parade of pornographic scenes, raw lyrics, and profanities woven into addictive soundtracks and seductive stage productions. According to *Preview*, a family movie and television review magazine, one recent top-10 list contained a total of 436 crude, obscene, and/or profane references. Media moguls walk away with hundreds of millions of teenage dollars. In return, they leave an entire generation of kids spiritually and morally confused.

Is it right or wrong to listen to a CD that promotes premarital sex?
Is it right or wrong to go to a movie that takes God's name in vain?
Is it right or wrong to watch a TV show filled with sexual innuendoes, crude humor, and sexual jesting?
Should I continue to berate myself for the mistake I made last year?
Should I continue to harbor bitter thoughts against my dad?

Today's scripture is probably the clearest answer to these and many other questions. It tells us that Satan wages war for the control of our thoughts. Not content to stop with unholy thoughts, Satan also builds mental fortresses to encompass those thoughts so that our entire thinking process is corrupted.

Paul provides the military strategy to defeat Satan's schemes: Take every thought captive to the obedience of Christ. In other words, every thought that crosses our minds should be subject to Him. Certainly profanity, pornography, guilt, bitterness, and similar thoughts are not appropriate. Submit your thought life to the lordship of Jesus. Once your thoughts are "captive to the obedience of Christ," you will experience unprecedented freedom.

Discussion Starters:

1. How do Satan's fortresses become entrenched in our minds?
2. What are some practical ways you can take every thought captive to the obedience of Christ?
3. What divine weapons do you have in your arsenal? Are you using them all?

Lifeline:

Your mind is either your biggest friend or your biggest foe.

GOD'S STAMP OF APPROVAL

"But he who boasts is to boast in the Lord. For it is not he who commends himself that is approved, but he whom the Lord commends."

⌐ 2 Corinthians 10:17-18

When *Newsweek* asked thousands of Americans who would be most likely to get to heaven, Mother Teresa came in second. Billy Graham was third. Michael Jordan was high on the list, as were the president and first lady. But the winner, by a whopping majority, was "me." More people thought themselves more likely to be approved and get to heaven than any other person they could think of.

This may not seem surprising at first. After all, those of us who are Christians can be certain of our salvation. And it makes sense that we should be more sure about ourselves than other people.

But on the other hand, the *Newsweek* poll was a national, random survey. It was conducted among the same group of people as other polls that tell us two-thirds of the male population will have sex before age 18, and more than half will have sex with other people after marriage. Many people don't think there's anything wrong with a president who cheats on his wife. Most don't think twice about attending movies where God's name is repeatedly profaned. And still, a vast majority of them can think of no person of faith more likely to get into heaven than "me."

Let's make one thing clear. Your behavior has nothing to do with whether or not you go to heaven. First comes a commitment to Christ. His salvation is the only key that fits heaven's door. Yet as we show Him our love, our behavior should improve. Sometimes people who receive Christ's offer of salvation go on to live lives that don't honor Him. But they shouldn't.

Paul wanted us to be sure that if we're boasting about going to heaven, it's because we've made a conscious decision to do so and are living as Jesus has taught us to—*not* because we think we've been good enough to get there. Those in the first group will one day hear the voice of God saying, "Well done, good and faithful servant" (Matthew 25:21). Those in the second are in for a big surprise.

Discussion Starters:

1. What makes some people so proud of themselves and arrogant toward God?
2. Why does God humble the proud and give grace to the humble (James 4:6)?
3. What does it mean to be "approved" by God?

Lifeline:

We who have received God's stamp of approval should live like it.

ANGEL OF LIGHT

"Even Satan disguises himself as an angel of light."

⇝ 2 Corinthians 11:14

A letter I just received, like so many others from teens I have befriended through the years, bleeds with rationalization. The person writes, "I know the Bible says sex before marriage is wrong, but my boyfriend and I love each other and it seems so right. Something this beautiful just can't be wrong, can it?"

The beer commercials on TV really do look like fun! Those parties on sandy, tropical beaches with hot cars, hot girls, and fun and laughter really make drinking look great. And "TV love" is just as promising, the way those gorgeous couples fall in love and head off to their steamy bedrooms. Anything that's that simple and that rewarding really makes you want to try it yourself.

If you think heavy drinking or premarital sex is either simple or rewarding in the long run, you're fooling yourself. Or more accurately, you're being fooled.

Believe me, we all think sin looks like fun in its earliest stages. But no one ever set out to become an alcoholic with their first drink. No one ever planned to become a heroin addict when they took a hit off of their first marijuana joint. During the passion of their first heavy kiss, no couple ever expects to deal with pregnancy or sexual disease. Satan is a master at getting you started down a path of sin by making it appear to be all fun. But after you're hooked, you *always* discover that there are consequences—many which are worse than you ever could have expected.

"Hey, smoke this great joint." "Take this cool pill." "Drink from this shiny bottle." "Live it up." "Go for it."

Take Satan up on his offer, and you may have fun tonight. But later you *will* pay. That's why he is the master of deception and your number-one enemy. But all you have to do is stand in the true Light that gives life (John 1:4-9), and the phony "angel of light" will be revealed for what he is—the devil himself.

Discussion Starters:

1. Why does the title "angel of light" fit Satan so perfectly?
2. Can you think of a sin you've faced lately that looked really fun at first, but the more you evaluated it, the more you saw its danger?
3. How can you tell for sure whether something is a sin?

Lifeline:

"How can a young man keep his way pure? By keeping it according to Your word" (Psalm 119:9).

MOUNT PERSPECTIVE

"Five times I received from the Jews thirty-nine lashes. Three times I was beaten with rods, once I was stoned, three times I was shipwrecked, a night and a day I have spent in the deep. I have been on frequent journeys, in dangers from rivers, dangers from robbers, dangers from my countrymen, dangers from the Gentiles, dangers in the city, dangers in the wilderness, dangers on the sea, dangers among false brethren; I have been in labor and hardship, through many sleepless nights, in hunger and thirst, often without food, in cold and exposure."

⌒ 2 Corinthians 11:24-27

If you want to climb "Mount Perspective" to get a better view of just how fortunate you are, read today's passage several times. Then ask yourself: *What have I suffered for God lately? What have I sacrificed for Jesus that really cost me something?*

Jennifer told her boyfriend that their relationship would have to be pure or not at all. She was willing to sacrifice it, if necessary, knowing that God would have something better for her later on.

Robert gave his entire savings account to the starving kids in another country as an offering to God. He didn't think twice when he sensed God telling him it was the thing to do.

Lola got 1,000 of her friends to wear "Pray to Jesus" T-shirts to school. I'm guessing some of those kids got laughed at and ridiculed. But they probably won't lose any sleep over it. Compared to Paul's suffering, a few snide remarks don't really amount to much, do they?

A lot of people in this world are doing some *serious* suffering for Jesus. Many die for what they believe. Others relate to Paul's experience of beatings, imprisonment, and perpetual danger. But they continue to believe, and their bold faith continues to demonstrate to others the reality of God. Those dear saints will receive a crown of life the instant they arrive in heaven as they immediately forget the sorrows and pains they faced on earth. It will all be worth it to them. And if we are willing to be a bit bolder for what we believe, it will surely be worth it to us as well.

Discussion Starters:

1. How do Paul's sufferings encourage you in yours?
2. How do our difficulties make us more like Christ? (See 1 Peter 1:6-7.)
3. To what extent are you willing to suffer for Jesus? Are you truly convinced it will be worth it some day? Why?

Lifeline:

"Consider it all joy . . . when you encounter various trials, knowing that the testing of your faith produces endurance" (James 1:2-3).

THORNS

"Because of the surpassing greatness of the revelations, for this reason, to keep me from exalting myself, there was given me a thorn in the flesh, a messenger of Satan to torment me—to keep me from exalting myself! Concerning this I implored the Lord three times that it might leave me. And He has said to me, 'My grace is sufficient for you, for power is perfected in weakness.' Most gladly, therefore, I will rather boast about my weaknesses, so that the power of Christ may dwell in me."

↪ 2 Corinthians 12:7-9

My daughter Courtney was taking 22 hours one semester in college while working an additional 15 hours a week to pay her way. But 37 hours of work and school (plus homework) is a hefty load.

She was hoping for all A's and B's, but right at the end she was surprised to receive a C in math. She seemed disappointed. I told her, "Courtney, I'd be just as pleased with you if you made *all* C's, because I know you've put your whole heart into this semester." I went on to explain that I don't think God would give me straight A's, even though I work hard to do my best. In fact, I think He sometimes hands out a C here and there so I won't become too proud of myself. None of us are good at *everything*. God has designed us to depend on one another, capitalizing on one another's strengths while minimizing our weaknesses.

If anyone deserved straight A's from God, it was Paul. But God was allowing him to endure some kind of recurring problem that Paul called a "thorn." (People have speculated that it could have been epilepsy, poor vision, or any number of other things.) The point of the thorn, he figured out, was so he would never forget what was allowing him to make all those A's the rest of the time—the grace of God.

I, too, am thankful that God cares enough to see me through my infirmities, failures, and imperfections. In doing so, He gives me a great gift—humility. In response, I can only say, *To God be the glory. Anything good that I've done is because of You.*

Discussion Starters:

1. How is God's power made perfect in our weaknesses?
2. How do the C's (or D's or even F's) in our life "torment" us?
3. Why does God show greater love by allowing us to endure difficulties than if He allowed everything to be perfect?

Lifeline:

Identify your ongoing problems and imperfections. Then, if you can be honest about it, thank God for the humility you are learning.

THE STRENGTH OF WEAKNESS

"Therefore I am well content with weaknesses, with insults, with distresses, with persecutions, with difficulties, for Christ's sake; for when I am weak, then I am strong."

↜ 2 Corinthians 12:10

I was with Congressman Jim Ryun in Washington, D.C., where I was speaking on behalf of America's teenagers at the National Day of Prayer. I told him how heartbroken I had been watching him get tripped and then fall to the track in the Munich Olympics, dashing his hopes for the gold medal. He had been the best miler in the world for 15 years, but he lay sprawled on the ground as a pack of less talented runners passed him by and captured the gold, silver, and bronze medals.

Jim only smiled until he finally said, "You know? That was the greatest moment of my life because it was on that day, as I lay on the track and lost the race, that I truly gave my heart to Christ and began to live the life God wanted me to."

Jim now has a family of solid Christian kids and a wonderful wife, Anne, who loves him for his Christian character as much as any woman alive loves a man. Do you think he would trade that away for a gold medal? Do you think he would choose that medal over the seat in Congress that he earned because of his godly heart? I don't think so.

If we're expecting a smooth track ahead of us, free from any stumbles or trip-ups, we're in for sure disappointment. Look at the words Paul used to describe his Christian life: weaknesses, insults, distresses, persecutions, difficulties. And he could have gone on. But his point was that even though he faced such things, he was still content because God remained his source of strength.

We generally choose our heroes because of their strengths. Yet we have much to learn from the heroic examples of people like Paul and Jim Ryun. It was in his falling that Jim Ryun became a success. It was in his weakness that he became so strong. It was in dying to himself that he was born into eternal life.

Discussion Starters:

1. Why are we actually weak when we think we're really strong? (The answer has something to do with pride and humility.)
2. When has a problem weakened you, allowing God to use it to make you stronger than before?
3. On a scale from 1 (least) to 10 (most), how content are you when you're going through difficult circumstances beyond your control?

Lifeline:

When we are strong, we tend to lean on ourselves. When we are weak, we tend to lean on God.

PREPARING FOR THE FINAL

"Test yourselves to see if you are in the faith; examine yourselves! Or do you not recognize this about yourselves, that Jesus Christ is in you—unless indeed you fail the test? But I trust that you will realize that we ourselves do not fail the test."

↩ 2 Corinthians 13:5-6

Studying medicine with average brainpower and playing football with average talent was brutal when I was in college. The only thing worse than getting battered by a national championship team on Saturday was getting battered by my organic chemistry professor on Monday morning. On any test day, Dr. Jeskey was a master at exposing my lack of discipline for studying. But he was especially good (and I was at my worst) when he would unexpectedly deliver an 8½-by-11-inch missile right to the middle of my desk—a dreaded pop quiz! Oh, I bottomed out on many of them.

Today's scripture is a clear warning that we should prepare for the ultimate "final exam," even though we don't know when it is coming. It will count for 100 percent of our grade, so it's very important we pass. In order to get ready, we should give ourselves a "pop quiz" from time to time. As Paul wrote, "Test yourselves to see if you are in the faith." We must be sure we are ready anytime. (Surprise accidents kill people of all ages every day.)

Below are some basic questions you'll need to be sure about. Look up the Scripture references, give them some thought, and then answer honestly.

1. Have you been born again? (John 3:3)
   Does Jesus live in your heart? (Revelation 3:20)
   Do you have a personal relationship with Him? (John 1:12)
2. Is your faith a real, *living* faith? (James 2:14-26)
   Does your faith produce spiritual fruit? (Galatians 5:22-23)
3. Does your love for Jesus make you *want* to obey Him? (John 14:15)
4. When you commit a sin (which we all do), do you confess it to Jesus, sincerely turn from that sin, and walk in the opposite direction? (1 John 1:9)

You don't have to grade this quiz, but give it some serious thought. You won't ever have to answer questions that are any more important than these.

Discussion Starters:

1. How does this "pop quiz" prepare you for your "final exam"?
2. What is one question you think God will ask on your final exam?
3. How can we know for sure whether or not we will pass that last test?

Lifeline:

If all your "pop quiz" answers are affirmative, you'll do well on the "final exam."

GALATIANS

The area of Galatia included the cities of Antioch, Iconium, Lystra, and Derbe, where Paul had established churches on his famous missionary journeys. Paul's letter to the Galatians shines like a welcome lighthouse to all Christians everywhere. Unlike the myriad of other world religions that attempt to please God and gain holiness by good works, Paul makes it clear that the only way to God is by grace, through faith in God's Son, Jesus, our gift of righteousness.

As an acorn must be present before an oak tree can spring up, so must grace first be present before our good works mean anything. Although we want to please God because of the tremendous gratitude that flows from our hearts, the Galatian letter forever frees us from the worry and frustration of attempting to gain God's love by striving to be perfect.

RADICALLY SAVED

"For you have heard of my former manner of life in Judaism, how I used to persecute the church of God beyond measure and tried to destroy it; and I was advancing in Judaism beyond many of my contemporaries among my countrymen, being more extremely zealous for my ancestral traditions. But . . . God . . . was pleased to reveal His Son in me so that I might preach Him among the Gentiles."

↪ Galatians 1:13-16

The amazing beauty of Disney World in Orlando, Florida, is a tribute to how Walt Disney converted swampland filled with snakes and alligators into an architectural paradise of theme parks, golf courses, and real estate opportunities. It is hard to believe that a new CEO of the Disney empire has built upon that wonderful man's dream by creating a film conglomerate that currently makes more R-rated movies than any other filmmaker on earth.

Whether you're 16 or 60, a preacher or a prostitute, your life changes when you give your heart to Jesus. His Holy Spirit enters your heart like springtime rain upon dry, parched soil. If your commitment to Him is genuine, positive changes will take place throughout your lifetime. A person "truly saved" becomes more and more like Jesus, more and more loving, joyful, peaceful, patient, kind, and self-controlled. Like a masterpiece of art, your life grows more valuable with each year passed as you celebrate the "spiritual birthday" that turned wasteland into a majestic work of God.

Radically saved Christians treasure their "Jesus-sized hearts" and never again return to the lifestyle of a nonbeliever.

Radically saved Christians don't delight themselves in gossip, coarse language, pornography, or sexual sin.

Radically saved Christians don't profane God or enjoy films that do.

As Paul opens his epic epistle to the Galatians, he bears witness to God's ability to radically change his heart. Today your life is bearing witness to others who will look at you and see the heart of Jesus.

Discussion Starters:

1. How does God's willingness to change Paul's life (Galatians 1:11-24) reflect the magnitude of His love?
2. In what ways is becoming a Christian a lifetime commitment? Why is it important to follow Christ forever, in all that you do?
3. What can you do if you discover you are falling back into your old ways of living?

Lifeline:

"You will know them by their fruits. . . . A good tree cannot produce bad fruit, nor can a bad tree produce good fruit" (Matthew 7:16, 18).

CRUCIFIED WITH CHRIST

"I have been crucified with Christ; and it is no longer I who live, but Christ lives in me; and the life which I now live in the flesh I live by faith in the Son of God, who loved me and gave Himself up for me."

↶ Galatians 2:20

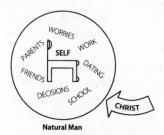

Natural Man

Spiritual Man

My dear friend Bill Bright and his organization, Campus Crusade for Christ, have shown these two pictures to literally hundreds of millions of people around the world. Bill estimates that over 500 million people have been saved as they have come to understand these concepts.

"Natural" man lives for self. The circle represents the man's life; the throne represents the control center (will) of that life. Without the saving power of Christ, all decisions revolve around self, and the person's life ends up a big, confusing mess.

In contrast, "spiritual" man has given his will (heart) to Christ. Jesus is in control. He's not only Savior, but He's Lord as well. He's not just a compartment in your life; He's the center around which everything else revolves. Where there was confusion, there is harmony; where there was bitterness, there is compassion; where there was immorality, there is purity; where there was guilt, there is forgiveness.

The decision to turn everything over to Jesus is not always easy. Paul compared it to being "crucified with Christ." But the new life that Jesus offers is not possible until the "old life" is dead and gone.

A true Christian is not just a better person; he or she is a *new* person.

A true Christian is not just going to heaven; we're living like we're already there!

Discussion Starters:

1. What does it mean to crucify the "old self" with Christ?
2. What does it mean to have Christ "living" in you? How can you allow Him to guide all you do?
3. Is Jesus on the throne in your heart today? How can you tell? If not, what do you need to do to give up your seat?

Lifeline:

If you memorize today's verse, you'll be amazed at how often it comes to mind in the future.

CURSED

"Christ redeemed us from the curse of the Law, having become a curse for us—for it is written, 'Cursed is everyone who hangs on a tree.' "

↶ Galatians 3:13

Eight hundred years before Jesus stepped onto earth in human form, and before His sacrificial death on the cross became an eternal invitation, the prophet Isaiah described in intricate detail what God intended to do and how He would do it.

> But He was pierced through for our transgressions, He was crushed for our iniquities; the chastening for our well-being fell upon Him, and by His scourging we are healed. All of us like sheep have gone astray, each of us has turned to his own way; but the Lord has caused the iniquity of us all to fall on Him. (Isaiah 53:5-6)

I played college football, and as a defensive lineman I endured many crushing Saturday afternoons in stadiums around America. But when I first came to grips with today's passage in Galatians and comprehended that Jesus "became a curse for us," I literally sobbed for an hour like a little boy who'd lost his first girlfriend. I simply couldn't squelch the sadness that welled up in my heart for the injustices inflicted on this dear man.

Paul further explained the "curse" of Jesus in Philippians: "Although He existed in the form of God, [Jesus] did not regard equality with God a thing to be grasped, but emptied Himself, taking the form of a bond-servant, and being made in the likeness of men. Being found in appearance as a man, He humbled Himself by becoming obedient to the point of death, even death on a cross" (Philippians 2:6-8).

Jesus became a curse and died on a cross, all because He loved me and wanted to have a close, personal, intimate relationship with me—just like a father who adopts a beloved child!

His curse became my salvation.

My guilt became His burden.

His purity became my perfection.

Discussion Starters:

1. How do you respond when you consider that God made His Son a curse for you?
2. How would your life be different if Jesus hadn't had the humility and love required to "hang on a tree"?
3. What are some specific things you can do to thank Him for such an overwhelming act of love?

Lifeline:

From now on, when you hear a curse of any sort, let it remind you that Jesus was a curse on your behalf.

DADDY

"But when the fullness of the time came, God sent forth His Son, born of a woman, born under the Law, so that He might redeem those who were under the Law, that we might receive the adoption as sons. Because you are sons, God has sent forth the Spirit of His Son into our hearts, crying, 'Abba! Father!' Therefore you are no longer a slave, but a son; and if a son, then an heir through God."

⌐ Galatians 4:4-7

The day was dark and gloomy as I trudged reluctantly to the local high school football field to see David, a 13-year-old football player who had been to our sports camp just a couple of months before. David's eyes were filled with tears of sorrow over the drowning death of his father, reported only a few hours previously. Behind those eyes I could see he was struggling with questions of doubt and sheer disbelief.

I told David I loved him deeply. As I hugged his sweaty frame, I told him that if he ever needed me, I'd be there for him, like a dad—his second dad. All he had to do was call.

Four years went by, and David's life went slowly downhill. I'd see him occasionally, and our chats were always meaningful, but his world without his dad was empty and he wasn't ready to take me up on my offer. Eventually everything fell apart for him; his life became chaos.

But to my sheer delight, he recently came to my house and began to talk to me like I was his daddy. And he gave his heart to Christ! We spent most of three days together, and my feelings for him were much like those toward my own sons. I was thrilled when he prayed an earnest prayer of repentance, turned from his past, and opened up his heart to let the Savior in to reign.

Like Paul, I know what it's like to be "adopted" and to have my status changed from one of "outsider" to that of "son." I can never repay what God has done for me. But as long as there are good kids like David around, I want to keep trying.

Discussion Starters:

1. "Abba" is a tender expression, sort of like calling God "Daddy." How do you feel about having that privilege?
2. What does it mean to become not only God's child, but also an heir?
3. Who else this week might like to hear about this opportunity?

Lifeline:

From a slave of sin to freedom . . . from an orphan lost in the world to an adopted child in heaven . . . Jesus makes all the difference.

FRUIT

"But the fruit of the Spirit is love, joy, peace, patience, kindness, goodness, faithfulness, gentleness, self-control; against such things there is no law."

⌒ Galatians 5:22-23

The black-tie banquet is an incredible event. We sit in formal attire and glittering jewelry beneath vintage crystal chandeliers. The table is spread with the juiciest filet mignon, lobster, fresh mahi-mahi flown in from the Caribbean, and more. Assorted tropical fruits provide color and wonderful aroma— Hawaiian pineapple, papaya, plump strawberries, mangoes, and . . .

What's this? As a guest reaches for a fresh orange wedge, she is speared by a spiny, prickly pear cactus. Then we begin to notice the slimy, drippy, horse apples . . . too-hot-to-eat Mexican peppers . . . bitter, green persimmons . . . and other inedible, not-yet-ripe fruits.

I'm not describing a literal dinner, but it's a valid illustration of the life of a Christian who first displays "the fruit of the Spirit" and then reverts to "the deeds of the flesh" (Galatians 5:19-21). The old "fruit" is out of place and no longer appealing.

Take a look at the nine qualities listed as "fruit of the Spirit." Once you start to display those things in your life, people take notice. Ask Hally, who was elected homecoming queen of Oklahoma State University after the students were impressed by her godly qualities. Ask Mark Brunnell, who led the Jacksonville Jaguars to the division championship during their first season as an expansion team. His precision passes helped, but they weren't as influential as his Christ-centered, "fruitful" lifestyle that drew the Jaguars together. Ask Michael W. Smith. He's been singing for God so long that he's now more than twice as old as the average age of those who attend his concerts. Yet the fruit of the Spirit continues to exude from his smile, his eyes, and his voice—both on and off the stage.

Without God's Spirit, we're about as appetizing to others as hedge apples, sour grapes, or green persimmons. But when His Spirit controls us, others witness a rich and "fruitful" life devoted to Jesus.

Discussion Starters:

1. Read the list of the "deeds of the flesh" (Galatians 5:19-21). Which of these has God removed from your life?
2. Have you witnessed the "fruit of the Spirit" in another family member? Have you told him or her lately?
3. Which quality from today's passage do you most need the Holy Spirit's help to cultivate in your life?

Lifeline:

Water and fertilizer enable the growth of rich fruit on orchard trees. Prayer, obedience, and God's Word help the fruit of the Spirit grow ripe in the life a believer.

EpHesiAns

During a three-year stay in the magnificent Macedonian city of Ephesus, the apostle Paul established a church that would become an anchor to the Christian faith. Ephesus was influential as a religious, political, and commercial center, and Paul had quite an impact on the Christians at Ephesus.

Paul's epistle to this church takes on special meaning if we remember it was written while Paul was imprisoned in Rome, possibly chained to Caesar's Praetorian guard. This awareness makes the theme of freedom even more clear and significant.

This letter was so cherished by the early church that it was copied countless times and circulated throughout the many churches in Asia Minor. Thousands of new believers found encouragement and instruction from these words of Paul. I think you will, too.

WHO CHOSE WHOM?

"Blessed be the God and Father of our Lord Jesus Christ, who has blessed us with every spiritual blessing in the heavenly places in Christ, just as He chose us in Him before the foundation of the world, that we would be holy and blameless before Him. In love He predestined us to adoption as sons through Jesus Christ to Himself, according to the kind intention of His will."

⌐ Ephesians 1:3-5

Did God choose us, or do we choose Him? It's a question that has been debated in the church for centuries. Sadly, it has divided congregations by the thousands. It has started 10,000 arguments. It has created dissension, factions, pride, and insecurity.

God never intended this kind of response! Today's passage *should* be the most wonderful of all the news in the good news of the gospel, and it *will* be if we comprehend two important scriptural truths. First, God chose you! Second, by the grace of God, you choose Him.

God's message *to the believer* is repeatedly emphasized in Scripture. He chose you. You were handpicked. You were known before you were born. You are His by choice. He created you and was willing to die for you. He couldn't bear the thought of spending eternity without you!

But Scripture is equally clear in stating God's message *to the unbeliever*: "Whosoever will may come." In other words, if you want to follow God, nothing is stopping you! The heart of the gospel is John 3:16: "For God so loved the world, that He gave His only begotten Son, that whoever believes in Him shall not perish, but have eternal life." (The key word that keeps popping up is *whoever*.)

John tells us, "But *as many as received* Him, to them He gave the right to become children of God" (John 1:12, emphasis mine). Peter agrees: "The Lord is not slow about His promise, as some count slowness, but is patient toward you, not wishing for any to perish but for all to come to repentance" (2 Peter 3:9).

How can both be true? Only God knows. But as believers we should be grateful God has chosen us—and motivated us to encourage others to choose Him.

Discussion Starters:

1. How does it feel, knowing that you were chosen by God?
2. How does such knowledge motivate you to tell others about God?
3. Do you tend to get confused trying to understand God's mysterious truths? If so, how do you handle your confusion?

Lifeline:

By grace we have been chosen by God. By faith we are able to choose Him.

LAST ONE CHOSEN

"Remember that you were at that time separate from Christ, excluded from the common-wealth of Israel, and strangers to the covenants of promise, having no hope and without God in the world. But now in Christ Jesus you who formerly were far off have been brought near by the blood of Christ."

⮑ Ephesians 2:12-13

The following is a make-believe story, but see what you think about it.

Mike was a running back on a small college football team. He was very good, but his school never got the exposure needed to get him noticed so he could be drafted into the NFL. He felt great disappointment because he truly believed he had the talent to go professional. No matter. He had to watch the pros on television, just like everyone else.

But with only a couple of weeks left in the season, injuries had left the Denver Broncos short of running backs. To Mike's amazement, he was invited to try out. He made the squad and was even able to play a few downs in the season's final games. And as it so happened, the Broncos went to the Super Bowl—and won.

Later, as the players were being called forward one by one to receive their Super Bowl rings, Mike thought to himself, *I'll never get a ring. I just came on at the end of the season and didn't even play that much.* Yet not only did he get the ring (inscribed with his name), he was also prominent in the team picture. He received full rights as a Super Bowl champion even though he joined the team later than all the other members.

Mike's story is a parable for how God has favored those of us who are not Jewish. Before Christ came, we were not among His chosen people. Yet we are now part of His plan because of the work Jesus did on the cross. He died to give salvation to everyone who believes in Him—Jew or Gentile. We may have been the last ones chosen, but thank God, we're now on the winning team!

Discussion Starters:

1. What did Jesus do to "bring us near" to God? (See Ephesians 2:13.)
2. The passage goes on to describe the importance of unity (2:14-16). Who, within the church, are the people you find hardest to get along with? Why?
3. How can you emulate Jesus in how you include and treat people around you?

Lifeline:

The Lord doesn't care how late in the season you were added. Each and every team member receives full rights and privileges.

IMMEASURABLE LOVE

"And that you, being rooted and grounded in love, may be able to comprehend with all the saints what is the breadth and length and height and depth, and to know the love of Christ which surpasses knowledge, that you may be filled up to all the fullness of God."

⏎ Ephesians 3:17-19

My longtime friend Dr. Horace Wood was 93 years old when he closed his eyes for a nap and woke up in the arms of the Savior whom he had cherished for over 80 years. I never saw a man so much in love with anything or anyone! Every time Dr. Wood began to talk about Jesus, big tears of affection would stream from his eyes. Every night he went to bed listening to some great preacher teaching him more about his first love.

The breadth and length and height and depth of Christ.

I've been a follower of Christ for 25 years, and every year my love for Him and His Word grows sweeter, deeper, and more intimately fulfilling than ever before. In a similar way, my love continues to grow for my wife of 25 years. I liked her the first time I met her. I loved her the first time we kissed. I loved her more when I hid her engagement ring in a box of Cracker Jacks . . . and more when she walked the aisle in gorgeous white wedding lace . . . and more when she delivered our first child. The more I know about her, the more I love her. You can't get to the bottom of love. You can't get to the top of it or reach around it.

God *is* love. The longer you love Him or love someone through Him, the more you realize how little you've seen so far.

In the city on a clear night, you can see about 3,000 stars. In the Ozark Mountains, you can see maybe twice as many. But once I saw the sky from atop a 10,000-foot volcano in Maui, and I could have gazed for a week and never seen all the stars. They go on and on. But even after you get past all the stars in all the galaxies, you'll still find the love of God. And the more of it you comprehend, the more you'll want to know.

Discussion Starters:

1. Why should our love for God grow deeper as the years go by?
2. To what extent have you comprehended the fullness of God's love?
3. How has your ever-deepening love for a person taught you about the ever-deepening love of God?

Lifeline:

Search for deeper love in the people you encounter today.

PRECIOUS TREASURES

"Do not grieve the Holy Spirit of God, by whom you were sealed for the day of redemption. Let all bitterness and wrath and anger and clamor and slander be put away from you, along with all malice. Be kind to one another, tender-hearted, forgiving each other, just as God in Christ also has forgiven you."

↜ Ephesians 4:30-32

The bottom drawer of my dresser contains the most precious treasures I've accumulated in my lifetime. You'll find no gold, precious gems, or rare coins—I'm talking about *priceless* treasures! That's where I keep Jamie's first pair of size one moccasins her grandma made for her, two plaster casts Cooper had to wear as a toddler to correct a slight birth defect, handmade presents I've received from my children, and, best of all, the love letters my wife and my kids have written me through the years.

"Hey, Dad, I love you. You're the best dad in the world."

"Hey, Dad, thanks for always being there for me."

"Daddy, you're my hero."

"Dad, when I grow up, I want to love my kids the way you love us."

The words, though completely undeserved, place diamonds in my hands and gold in my heart. Showing kindness to those you love is not something you should ever overlook. It will put smiles on their faces and songs in their hearts.

If anything on earth can surpass the value of an act of kindness, perhaps it's the gift of forgiveness. Forgiveness is overlooking someone's mistake, saying, "That's okay. I know you didn't mean it." Forgiveness is choosing to not harbor feelings of resentment against someone who may have wronged us. As we come to realize how much God has forgiven us, it becomes easier to shrug off our hurt feelings when someone else offends us.

Besides, look at what Paul says we can expect if we don't choose kindness and forgiveness: bitterness, wrath, anger, clamor, slander, and malice. What kind of life is that?

So as you go through this week, try to remember: Forgiveness opens the treasure drawer; kindness fills it.

Discussion Starters:

1. When those you love check their "treasure drawers," what will they find that you've put there? What else might they like to receive from you?
2. How does forgiveness pave the way for kindness?
3. How does Christ's example make it easier for a believer to be kind and forgiving?

Lifeline:

With the love of Jesus, I can't remember your mistakes . . . and I can't forget your kindness.

FILL IT UP!

"And do not get drunk with wine, for that is dissipation, but be filled with the Spirit, speaking to one another in psalms and hymns and spiritual songs, singing and making melody with your heart to the Lord; always giving thanks for all things in the name of our Lord Jesus Christ to God, even the Father; and be subject to one another in the fear of Christ."

↩ Ephesians 5:18-21

Take the air out of a balloon and it collapses in an instant. Put an empty glass under a gushing faucet and the air dissipates just as quickly.

The moment you become a Christian, Jesus comes into your heart and His Spirit remains in you forever (2 Corinthians 1:22). That "moment of salvation" is when you become God's child and He becomes your Dad. You are baptized (placed) into the body (family) of Christ, and the Holy Spirit makes His home in your heart.

Then why do Christians sin?

Why do Christians hate?

Why do Christians fight?

Why are Christians unhappy?

Just as a balloon with only a tiny puff of air in it will never fly, so a heart filled mostly with self will never be happy. That's why people talk about the importance of being "Spirit-filled."

Being filled with (controlled and empowered by) the Holy Spirit automatically makes you smile. Spirit-filled Christians sing a lot. Spirit-filled Christians forgive others quickly. Spirit-filled Christians have nice things to say about others. Spirit-filled Christian rid their mouths and minds of negative words and harsh thoughts.

Though you receive the Spirit of Christ only once, the *filling* of the Holy Spirit is a recurring need. Just as you can blow up a deflated balloon, so you can ask God to fill you again with His Spirit as you confess your sins and give yourself to Him wholly.

A drunk man is filled with alcohol which controls him in ways he would rather not remember in the morning. But if you're an on-fire Christian filled with the Holy Spirit, God will provide you with positive experiences you'll never forget.

Discussion Starters:

1. How do you describe a heart that is filled with the Spirit of God? Why does God want us to be filled with His Spirit at all times?
2. What is the difference between Jesus as *resident* in your life and Jesus as President in your life?
3. Would you say you are filled with the Spirit today? Are you empty? Or are you somewhere in between? Explain.

Lifeline:

Just as a car must be filled with gasoline, so a Christian must be filled with the Spirit to move forward.

GOD'S FAMILY PORTRAIT

"Children, obey your parents in the Lord, for this is right. . . . Fathers, do not provoke your children to anger, but bring them up in the discipline and instruction of the Lord."

↪ Ephesians 6:1, 4

Just as the best and most valuable paintings were rendered at the hands of masters such as Michelangelo, Picasso, and Rembrandt, so a family is at its best when it is painted by the brush of God. Onto a canvas of affection He adds love in various colors, in perfect proportions and intensities. The result, if no one interferes with His original work of art, is a masterpiece with each relationship interacting perfectly with all the others. Today's Scripture passage tells us how God intends for families to operate.

Dads have the greatest jobs on earth! Our calling is to treat our wives like queens by listening to them, caring for them, serving them, and becoming expert in meeting their needs. Similarly, we are to bring up our children with love and devotion, without creating resentment in their hearts by ignoring them or being cruel in what we say or do.

The happiest wives I know are the ones who trust their husbands to captain the marriage ship. They don't mind asking, "Honey, what do you think?" or "What do you think we should do about this situation?" It is their trust and teamwork within the relationship that helps them become secure on their own and confident in the roles they play.

Children who want to live long and live happily obey their parents. Happiest of all are those who honor their moms and dads by maintaining a positive attitude rather than obeying grudgingly.

The Mona Lisa is enshrined in a gallery of the finest works of art where it can be admired. But even more impressive to many people today is seeing a family that operates the way God intends it to. Ephesians 6:1-4 describes God's "family portrait." If your family lives according to these instructions, others will notice. And more importantly, some day you will all be featured in heaven's gallery.

Discussion Starters:

1. According to today's passage, what should be your role in your family?
2. How can you become more "picture perfect" in that role?
3. Since God's roles for the family are so clear, why do you think so many families experience serious problems?

Lifeline:

An original Picasso on a piece of canvas can be worth tens of millions of dollars. Imagine the value of a vintage family portrait that is hand-painted by the brush of God.

PHILIPPIANS

The book of Philippians is a letter filled with joy. In this epistle, the love, appreciation, warmth, and affection that flood the apostle Paul's heart shine through as clearly as lighted ornaments on a dazzling Christmas tree. How encouraging it must have been for the Philippian Christians to read, "I thank my God in all of my remembrance of you" (1:3). Yet woven throughout this letter of appreciation, Paul includes a number of strong instructions for harmonious virtuous living:

- "Conduct yourselves in a manner worthy of the gospel of Christ" (1:27a).
- "Have this attitude in yourselves which was also in Christ Jesus" (2:5).
- "I have learned to be content in whatever circumstances I am" (4:11).

It is in Philippians that Paul reveals the source of his seemingly endless energy and devotion: "I can do all things through [Christ] who strengthens me" (4:13). And here Paul exposes the roots of his sacrificial lifestyle and his unquenchable hope: "For to me, to live is Christ and to die is gain" (1:21).

I know committed Christians who have memorized this entire book. It would be well worth your while to do so as well. Whether or not you memorize it, be sure to meditate on it the rest of your life. You'll discover that not only is *joy* the theme of this book, but it will also be the by-product of your study. My son Cooper helped write these devotionals.

TO DIE IS GAIN

"For I know that this will turn out for my deliverance through your prayers and the provision of the Spirit of Jesus Christ, according to my earnest expectation and hope, that I will not be put to shame in anything, but that with all boldness, Christ will even now, as always, be exalted in my body, whether by life or by death. For to me, to live is Christ and to die is gain."

↪ Philippians 1:19-21

When we read about the Christian martyrs of the "Bible days," they seem so far from us. Two thousand years ago and halfway around the world are a lot of time and space that diminish the reality of "dying for Jesus." But Peter did it, Paul did it, James did it, and hundreds of thousands have done it since. In fact, more Christians were martyred for their faith in the twentieth century than in any previous century. They died because they truly believed that "to live is Christ and to die is gain."

Do you agree? If you were presented with the choice to either deny Christ or die for your faith, what would you do?

The reality of this verse came shockingly close to home on April 20, 1999, when 17-year-old Cassie Bernall found herself staring down the barrel of a loaded gun. A classmate on a killing rampage at Columbine High School in Littleton, Colorado, asked Cassie if she believed in God. Cassie declared, "Yes, I believe in God." The next thing Cassie saw was the face of Jesus as He welcomed her home to spend eternity in paradise. Two days before Cassie died, almost as if she somehow sensed the impending disaster, she wrote the following words that clearly expressed her living faith in God, who just two years before had come into her heart and saved her soul.

Now I have given up on everything else.

I have found it to be the only way to really know Christ and to experience
The mighty power that brought Him back to life again,

And to find out what it means to suffer and to die with Him.

So, whatever it takes I will be one who lives in the fresh newness of life
Of those who are alive from the dead.

Discussion Starters:

1. What does Cassie's death mean to you?
2. If faced with the same challenge, what do you think you would have done?
3. What are some practical ways you can "die to yourself" and live for Christ today?

Lifeline:

A martyred Christian is a hero, but it is just as heroic to *live* for Jesus.

REWARDS OF LOVE

"Therefore if there is any encouragement in Christ, if there is any consolation of love, if there is any fellowship of the Spirit, if any affection and compassion, make my joy complete by being of the same mind, maintaining the same love, united in spirit, intent on one purpose. Do nothing from selfishness or empty conceit, but with humility of mind regard one another as more important than yourselves; do not merely look out for your own personal interests, but also for the interests of others."

↪ Philippians 2:1-4

For more than 20 years, I've had the indescribable privilege to have been assigned a 50-yard-line seat in a most amazing "arena" where talent, charm, and character have been displayed like no other place on earth.

The players are male and female. The male team dresses in well-tailored tuxedo uniforms; the female team is in exquisite evening gowns. The star of the show wears a pure, dazzling white gown. Her beauty is beyond my ability to describe.

By now, I'm sure you've guessed that the event is a wedding. My "50-yard-line seat" is the spot between the bride and groom where I can place their hands together and invite them to say "I do."

Almost all the weddings at which I've officiated feature a bride and a groom from the staff of our Christian sports camp who met and fell in love there. The number of couples over the past two decades has become too large to keep up with. Even more amazing is that every one of those couples is not only still married, but also very happily married.

Nationally, about half of all marriages end in divorce, and a large percentage of those who stay married aren't truly happy. The difference between those I've closely witnessed and the rest is the daily reality of the few simple verses of Scripture at the top of this page. If you'll study them and apply them diligently in your life between now and your wedding day, you too can expect rewards of love beyond your wildest dreams.

Discussion Starters:
1. Why is putting others' needs before your own so difficult to accomplish?
2. Why does unselfishness bring so much joy to a relationship?
3. What are three specific things you can do, beginning today, to prepare for the selflessness required in a marriage relationship?

Lifeline:
It is in giving that we receive. It is in dying to self that love can truly live.

JUST PLAIN RUBBISH

"I count all things to be loss in view of the surpassing value of knowing Christ Jesus my Lord, for whom I have suffered the loss of all things, and count them but rubbish so that I may gain Christ, and may be found in Him."

↪ Philippians 3:8-9a

What is your favorite title or possession? Is it a tangible item like a car, a girlfriend, a diamond necklace, a letter jacket, a savings account, or your own room? Or is it an elected position like cheerleader, football captain, all-district in basketball, or all-state band? Whatever it is, would you give it up for Jesus? If someone needed it more than you, would you give it to him or her for the sake of Christ?

While you ponder that thought for a minute, let me pose a more practical question. Would you give up your favorite CD if you heard or saw a lyric that was not respectful toward God? How about your favorite TV show? How about a hit new movie at the local theater? What about a relationship that doesn't honor Him? Or a habit? Or a moral value?

Paul has a word for anything that interferes with a truly pure relationship with Christ: *rubbish*. Just as we take out trash before it begins to accumulate and stink, so we need to eliminate anything in our lives that threatens our love and commitment to God—and we need to do so on a regular basis. To be honest, some of us become quite attached to certain pieces of rubbish. But in order to stay focused on the things that are really important, we need to "take out the trash"—all of it.

Jesus made the trip from heaven to earth—and to the cross—to show His love for us. The least we can do is make a trip to the dump and get rid of the rubbish in our lives to show our love for Him.

Discussion Starters:

1. What, if anything, have you given up for Jesus lately?
2. What would you be most reluctant to give up for Jesus? Why?
3. What are some things that aren't necessarily bad on their own yet might be classified as "rubbish" because they interfere with a closer relationship with Jesus?

Lifeline:

Are any of your possessions, positions, or relationships beginning to cause a stink in regard to your spiritual growth? If so, are you willing to "take out the trash"?

CONTENTMENT

"I have learned to be content in whatever circumstances I am. I know how to get along with humble means, and I also know how to live in prosperity; in any and every circumstance I have learned the secret of being filled and going hungry, both of having abundance and suffering need. I can do all things through Him who strengthens me."

↩ Philippians 4:11-13

An old tale is told of a Texas rancher who said, "I don't want much land. I just want everything that joins mine."

During a professional basketball strike, an athlete who had signed a contract for (now get this) over $106 million was heard to say, "The problem with the NBA is the owners are just too greedy."

I know a beautiful young lady who won a huge national beauty pageant. Yet her boyfriend would complain that her features just "weren't perfect enough."

Every year thousands of already thin American girls starve themselves into sickness and even death because they "just can't get skinny enough."

Contentment is a state of mind that can only be found if we are truly relying on God as our source of happiness and fulfillment. Then we can be happy with what we are given. We find peace with the body that God gave us. We discover joy in our circumstances. We are satisfied with our looks. We don't worry so much about our level of wealth or poverty.

Without contentment, you can't get rich enough because there is always somebody with more. You can't become beautiful enough because you're always comparing yourself to others. Someone else always has a hotter car, a faster horse, bigger biceps, more popularity, and so forth.

How can you replace your comparative, competitive tendencies with contentment? To put it simply, you need an attitude of gratitude! Just start being thankful for what you have every day. When you're thankful, you see that there are so many people who have less and who would like nothing better than to be as blessed as you.

What can you be content about today? Start there, and each day keep developing that attitude until you can say, "I will be content in whatever circumstances I face." You should discover that your anxiety level will diminish and your smile will increase as quickly as you can change your mind.

Discussion Starters:

1. In what area of life do you find it hardest to find contentment?
2. Why is discontentment such a joy stealer?
3. How does drawing closer to the heart of God make contentment more real to you personally?

Lifeline:

It's an old saying, but still thought-provoking: "I complained because I had no shoes until I met a man who had no feet."

CoLoSSians

Bob Waliszewski is a youth-culture expert from Focus on the Family. He knows movies, music, and other media like no man on earth. Bob applies his accumulated wisdom to the excellent book of Colossians to help you and me in an area that is very difficult for most Christians—how to live in righteousness.

In Colossians, Paul gives the most descriptive picture of Christ found in any of his letters. Colossians 1:15-20 is a "must" for Scripture memory. It can sweeten your walk with Christ and strengthen your understanding of His purpose like no other place in Scripture.

As we understand Jesus' holiness and "fix our eyes on Him," it is easy to apply Bob Waliszewski's insights. May we learn to eagerly respond to God's greatest compliment to us: "Your body is a temple of the Holy Spirit, . . . therefore glorify God in your body" (1 Corinthians 6:19-20).

WHO'S YOUR HERO?

"[Christ] is the image of the invisible God, the firstborn of all creation. For by Him all things were created, both in the heavens and on earth, visible and invisible, whether thrones or dominions or rulers or authorities—all things have been created through Him and for Him. He is before all things, and in Him all things hold together."

↪ Colossians 1:15-17

It never ceases to amaze me to see who some people idolize . . . and why. In one letters to the editor section of the rock music magazine *Rip*, I ran across the following statements from young music fans:

- "Metallica is my number-one sellout and always will be."
- "I have been a die-hard, obsessed fan of Marilyn Manson for four years now. . . . To show my dedication to [Manson], I just got my seventh tattoo last week. . . . I'd get a hundred more tattoos for my loving Marilyn if I had to."
- "I'm an enormous fan of Garbage. I've seen them in concert twice and, aside from the first time I had sex, those are the best two nights of my life. . . . Shirley Manson is the ultimate rock goddess."

Some sad comments indeed, especially when we realize these statements represent the views of millions of other like-minded young people. Yet with the media defining society's heroes, it's often difficult to break away from the pack and choose worthy ones. We're told whom we should esteem by MTV, on magazine covers, and on the big screen. Never mind that these individuals may be bisexual, alcoholics, drug addicts, witches, or on their fifth marriage.

So how do we know when someone measures up? Paul reminds us that Jesus should be our ultimate hero. Why? To begin with, He's God. He created everything. He has "made peace through the blood of His cross" (Colossians 1:20). And the list could go on and on. His nature, His sacrifice, and His love qualify Him to be mankind's most deserving role model!

Discussion Starters:

1. List your favorite heroes. Why did you include each person? Where would you place Christ on that list?
2. In your opinion, what constitutes a true hero? Besides the reasons listed by Paul in Colossians 1:15-20, what others can you give for why Christ Jesus is the ultimate hero?
3. Name 10 individuals who are frequently idolized in the media. Which, if any, do you feel are worthy of admiration?

Lifeline:

Identify an acquaintance who idolizes someone (a rock star, actor, or sports figure) who openly displays hostility toward God and His kingdom. Write down three things you can do to point your friend to the hero from Nazareth.

NO PLACE TOO DARK

"We proclaim [Christ], admonishing every man and teaching every man with all wisdom, so that we may present every man complete in Christ. For this purpose also I labor, striving according to His power, which mightily works within me."

⤳ Colossians 1:28-29

Toward the end of the book of Colossians, Paul informs his readers that he is currently serving prison time (4:10). Picture yourself in his first-century living conditions. No electric lights. No flush toilets. No gas furnace. No queen-size mattress. It's dingy. Dreary. Smelly. Bug-infested. Cold. To pass the time, there's no telephone, no radio, no prison library, and no TV (which was perhaps a blessing). Sounds miserable, doesn't it? And certainly, in this situation, ministry to others would seem impossible.

Well, not for Paul. His love for Christ and desire to spread the gospel didn't stop at the jailhouse door. Even while in prison, he could write and challenge others to grow in their faith.

Paul desired to present everyone complete in Christ (Colossians 1:28). What a fantastic goal! Yet he went on to say that his work for God wasn't a casual pursuit. It was a struggle. It was labor. But the key was that Paul's source of strength was Christ's energy, "which mightily works within me" (verse 29). As a result, God's energy gave Paul ideas. It opened doors—even in a dingy jail cell.

Have you ever been in a place that seemed too dark to witness for Jesus? Perhaps at your school? In a certain class? Around your family? On a sports team? Looking at Paul's situation reminds us that regardless of what we're going through, regardless of where we find ourselves, Christ can demonstrate His love through us. The call is universal. The rewards are truly great. All it takes is His energy . . . and a willingness to let His love compel us.

Discussion Starters:

1. If Paul had waited for his circumstances to improve, he would have missed some major ministry opportunities. What situations in your life do you consider obstacles to fruitful ministry? Are they really obstacles, or might they be opportunities to adjust your perceptions and increase your faith?
2. Can you think of some new and more fruitful ways to share your faith?
3. What situations has God placed you in that may seem too dark for sharing Christ yet could have great potential if you use Christ's energy?

Lifeline:

Identify a situation you're involved in that has seemed "ministry impossible." Pray to be shown how to present Christ effectively in that situation.

PERSUASIVE ARGUMENTS

"I say this so that no one will delude you with persuasive argument. For even though I am absent in body, nevertheless I am with you in spirit, rejoicing to see your good discipline and the stability of your faith in Christ."

↪ Colossians 2:4-5

I love this quote from comedian Bill Cosby: "The [TV] networks say they don't influence anybody. If that's true, why do they have commercials?"

The apostle Paul realized people—even Christians—could be easily swayed to believe all kinds of strange ideas if they failed to aggressively keep their minds from being polluted. The entertainment industry is notorious for offering a number of "persuasive arguments" that are deceptive, dishonest, and destructive. Here are just a few (either stated directly or implied) from TV programs I've reviewed recently:

- Sex outside of marriage is acceptable.
- Christians are wimps, hypocrites, or dangerous to others.
- On-screen violence and nudity have no negative effect on anyone.
- Homosexuality is a perfectly legitimate lifestyle.

When our media role models laugh at moral standards, they don't just reflect society; they affect the values and integrity of its people. That's why Bill Cosby's quote has a prominent place in my office. Isn't it bizarre that the same television executives who charge $1.3 million for a 30-second Super Bowl spot to influence purchasing can then adamantly deny that their programming sways others' behavior?

Deceptive messages packaged in "persuasive arguments" are easily rejected when we refuse to allow our minds to be bombarded in the first place. The best approach when considering a certain entertainment option is to ask the question "What would Jesus do?" and then take the appropriate action.

Discussion Starters:

1. If Jesus were walking this planet today instead of 2,000 years ago, list three TV shows you think He and His disciples might watch.
2. What are some "persuasive arguments" being promoted on TV and in other media that are actually deceptive and destructive?
3. What do you think are the best ways to guard your heart and mind against alluring, but empty, philosophies?

Lifeline:

Make a card with Psalm 101:3 written on it to place over each family television set as a reminder to think about what you're watching.

CAPTIVE OR FREE?

*"See to it that no one takes you captive through philosophy and empty deception, . . .
according to the elementary principles of the world, rather than according to Christ."*

↪ Colossians 2:8

To justify her allegiance to a controversial rock band, "Heather" wrote a letter to Focus on the Family. She said: "You should realize that the world is not fun and full of life—that the world is full of hate, love, suicide, and murder, and we as Christians—I and millions of depressed teens—turn to music that understands that."

Note the "we as Christians" part. Heather is not some out-of-control Satanist. She's a sophomore in high school who claims to love Jesus. Here's my interpretation of what Heather is really saying: "I'm a Christian and I've been hurt. As a result, I'm often down and in despair. To find some relief, I turn to music that wallows in pain, wallows in messages that promote suicide and angst—messages that I know are far from wholesome. But when I'm depressed, this music seems to offer some consolation."

Can you relate? Have you ever justified a questionable entertainment choice for similar reasons? Have you ever found yourself more interested in pop culture than Christian culture?

Paul was aware of the type of temptation Heather faces. He warned, "See to it that no one takes you captive through philosophy and empty deception."

Unfortunately, Heather shows signs of being a captive. Hollow and deceptive philosophies flow through her headphones and threaten to lead her astray. So far they haven't totally shipwrecked her faith, but they have weakened her witness, lessened her joy, and dampened her love and commitment to her Savior. Rather than finding comfort in the One who truly knows about pain, she has chosen to find "comfort" in the hollow philosophy of musicians who profit from producing troublesome CDs.

Still, it's not too late for Heather to change. It's never too late for anyone. How about you?

Discussion Starters:

1. What philosophies being promoted in pop culture would you classify as "empty" or "deceptive"?
2. How do you prevent potentially destructive entertainment messages from affecting your faith?
3. What are some possible consequences of indulging in entertainment that applauds behaviors, language, and attitudes that are not Christ-honoring?

Lifeline:

Do any of your favorite music groups, TV shows, or movies contain "empty deception"? If so, what should be your response?

SETTING OUR MINDS

"Therefore if you have been raised up with Christ, keep seeking the things above, where Christ is, seated at the right hand of God. Set your mind on the things above, not on the things that are on earth."

~ Colossians 3:1-2

Have you ever found yourself thinking about something twisted or off-color and wished you could turn your brain off? Impossible, isn't it? Even when we're sleeping, the wheels of our minds are turning. Although there is no off button inside your head, it is possible to redirect your thought life. Paul was so convinced of this that in the first two verses of Colossians 3 he tells us what things should take center stage in the theater of our minds.

Unfortunately, it's easy to get sidetracked and set our minds on worldly—even sinful—things. This is especially true when what enters our ears and eyes is contrary to Scripture. So the key to setting our minds on things above is twofold. First, we must be "transformed by the renewing of our minds" (Romans 12:2). This occurs when we diligently meditate upon God's Word. But equally important, we must avoid things that war against our faith. Reading the Bible and watching *Dawson's Creek* or *South Park* just don't mix.

Christians often fail miserably at avoiding harmful entertainment. For instance, church statistician George Barna found that on a percentage basis, more Christians watch MTV than non-Christians. No wonder many teens continue to struggle with thoughts of lust, rebellion, anger, etc.

Philippians 4:8 goes into more detail about improving our thought life. Paul explains that our minds should focus on those things that are pure, lovely, honorable, excellent, and so forth. Today's media *sometimes* meet these standards, but more often they don't. When you catch yourself "setting your mind" on things that are less than pure, remember that your brain doesn't have an off switch—but your CD player does!

Discussion Starters:

1. Have you had any disturbing thoughts lately? If so, are any related to or reinforced by your media diet?
2. What practical steps can you take to renew your mind and set your affections on things above rather than on earthly things?
3. What arguments are you likely to hear from your peers in regard to their choice of movies, music, and TV shows? If they ask why you're concerned about today's media, how would you respond?

Lifeline:

Discuss with a trusted Christian mentor the struggles you face regarding your thought life. Create a plan that will help you more consistently think about things above.

HEART SONGS

"Let the word of Christ richly dwell within you, with all wisdom teaching and admonishing one another with psalms and hymns and spiritual songs, singing with thankfulness in your hearts to God."

⌐ Colossians 3:16

Something about melody helps us remember things. My son memorized all 50 states alphabetically using a tune his second-grade teacher taught him. The other night my daughter "performed" a rap song she had learned that contained a number of phonics rules. Her teacher did her quite a favor when she set the language basics to music rather than just listing them on paper and commanding, "Memorize!"

But long before my children's teachers discovered how music helps us retain information, Paul asked us to consider getting God's Word in our hearts by this method. Although many of us would never consider singing publicly, all of us can sing as Paul suggests: with thankfulness in our hearts to God. We can sing "in our hearts" while walking down the hall at school, on a crowded bus, or in the numerous lines we find ourselves waiting in. The opportunities are endless.

But what kind of songs qualify? Paul says we should sing psalms, hymns, and spiritual songs. Perhaps you already know a number of choruses that feature verses from the Psalms. But have you tried writing some of your own? Remember that no one has to hear them. You're singing them "in your heart." When it comes to "spiritual songs," there are umpteen thousand to choose from—no matter what style of music you enjoy most. Choose from ska, country, rap, alternative, R&B, swing, and everything in-between. The key is to ask, "As I listen to and re-sing this song in my heart, does it edify my spirit?" If so, the Bible says the Word of God will dwell in you more deeply—a promise that's music to my ears.

Discussion Starters:

1. Write down as many Bible verses as you can think of that you learned because of a scriptural song. Do you think you would know these scriptures if you hadn't learned them through song?
2. When does singing "spiritual songs" mean the most to you?
3. If you were sad right now, what would be a good "spiritual song" to sing? What if you were elated? Lonely? Hurt? Confused?

Lifeline:

Identify a Bible verse that you've always wanted to commit to memory. Use the verse as "lyrics" and set it to a tune you already know (or make one up). Sing through the song a few times until it sticks in your mind. If this exercise goes well, try doing this every day for the next 30 days.

LABORING IN PRAYER

"Devote yourselves to prayer, keeping alert in it with an attitude of thanksgiving."

⌐ Colossians 4:2

Did you know that falling TV sets kill about four children every year? That sad and obscure fact was cited in the September 1998 issue of the *Journal of Pediatrics*. The observation got me wondering how many other people are "dead" today because of TV—not because of falling television sets but because of faulty media messages. Consider this statement:

"I personally worry more about television than other forms of media, because it's so pervasive, and it's a primary baby-sitter and value-transmitter for many children. . . . The constant barrage of violence and explicit sexuality reinforces the loosening of human bonds, undermining the evolution of a mature person. For many people, it is affecting not just what they think about but also how they think."

This concern was expressed by Hillary Rodham Clinton and serves to underscore a widespread concern about TV—not just among evangelicals. Even television mogul Ted Turner echoed similar thoughts regarding the tube:

"As a parent with five children, I don't need experts to tell me that the amount of violence on television today can be harmful to children. . . . Television violence is *the single most significant factor* contributing to violence in America" (emphasis added).

Besides guarding our own hearts, we need to influence the entire media culture. There are a number of ways, but none is more important than prayer. The apostle Paul says, "Devote yourselves to prayer, keeping alert in it with an attitude of thanksgiving." Later in the chapter, he compliments a fellow believer by saying he is "laboring earnestly for you in his prayers" (4:12). Do you ever "labor earnestly in prayer" for our nation? For Hollywood? For individual actors, actresses, musicians, and industry insiders? God assures us that we can make a difference. But not until we first hit our knees.

Discussion Starters:

1. How often do you "labor earnestly in prayer" for influential media personalities? Why do you think many Christians never pray for these individuals?
2. What are the keys to seeing our prayers create change in the culture?
3. What scriptural promises assure us that God not only hears us when we pray but also that He will answer?

Lifeline:

Make a list of 31 popular media personalities, and begin to pray for one person each day for the next month. Be specific. Ask the Lord to bring the person to His Son and give him or her a burden for purity, wisdom, and wholesomeness.

A LITTLE SALTY CONVERSATION

"Conduct yourselves with wisdom toward outsiders, making the most of the opportunity. Let your speech always be with grace, as though seasoned with salt, so that you will know how you should respond to each person."

⌒ Colossians 4:5-6

Have you ever wondered what you should do in a situation where someone is talking about a certain movie, TV show, or popular CD that you personally find offensive? Most of us can relate to the uncomfortable feeling of wanting to express our views, but knowing that they could come across as judgmental.

But have you ever considered that these conversations—if done right—could lead to an opportunity to share your faith? The apostle Paul saw the need to encourage the church at Colosse to make the most of *every* opportunity.

Most people love to talk about entertainment: "Did you see *Death Factor* IV yet?" Or "Have you heard Blood Kill's new CD?" Some people respond to such questions by getting preachy—which turns people off. Paul suggests another option: "Let your speech always be with grace."

I suggest we fire up a quick prayer for guidance and wisdom during such times as we look for ways to "salt" the conversation rather than squelch it. I might say something like "I used to love movies like that, but I find I'm having a lot more fun these days since I've quit going. Although entertaining to some degree, they just didn't set well with me in the long run."

This type of response concentrates on what has happened to *me*. It's part of a testimony and is something people just can't argue with. This approach allows you to talk to people without blasting them for making poor entertainment choices. You haven't dumped out the whole saltshaker, but you've salted the conversation.

If they want to hear more, they might ask, "What do you mean you're having more fun? What are you up to?" And their questions may just lead them to the ultimate answer—Jesus Christ. During the next week, let's all look for openings where we can "make the most of every opportunity." May I pass you the salt?

Discussion Starters:

1. Why do many Christians dread witnessing? Could it be possible they go about it all wrong?
2. What are some ways you can "salt" a conversation spiritually?
3. In addition to using the subject of entertainment as an opportunity to witness, what other commonly held conversations can become witnessing opportunities? (Sports talk? Politics? Homework? Hobbies?)

Lifeline:

Write out a paragraph you might use to respond to a friend asking you to go to an R-rated slasher film.

1 & 2 Thessalonians

Paul established a church in the European (Macedonian) port city of Thessalonica on his second missionary journey. The gospel was received there with joy and tremendous appreciation. Paul's encouragement echoes throughout these two Thessalonian epistles as he surrounds his message of instruction with words of affirmation and empowerment.

"You show great love for people."

"You're pursuing purity with all your heart."

"Overall, you're doing great! Keep it up!"

Another feature of the Thessalonian epistles is Paul's focus on *eschatology* (teachings about the second coming of Jesus). Apparently there was a lot of sorrow in this church over fellow believers who had died, so Paul went to great effort to reassure those grieving saints of the return of Christ, the rapture of the church, and our eternal home with Him after we die.

Finally, it's almost humorous to read Paul's rapid-fire spray of one-line instructions as he closes his first letter. He had so much wisdom and encouragement to pass along that he just couldn't quit writing until he had expressed everything that was on his heart.

I am pleased to be joined in the writing of these devotions by son Cooper, who contributed the poems.

IMITATORS OF GOD

"Our gospel did not come to you in word only, but also in power and in the Holy Spirit and with full conviction; just as you know what kind of men we proved to be among you for your sake. You also became imitators of us and of the Lord, having received the word in much tribulation with the joy of the Holy Spirit."

⟿ 1 Thessalonians 1:5-6

Josh had been in trouble ever since he was kicked out of elementary school for carrying a concealed weapon in fifth grade. In high school, recurring fights and extensive drug use had left his heart cold and hard. Although he had a religious background, he had ceased to believe in God. He preferred his biology teacher's Darwinian explanation that people somehow evolved by chance over a long period of time.

Josh had a friend named Brett who for three years had been a fellow drug user and dealer. Brett stopped at my house one day after a friend had almost died in a heroin overdose. That day Brett gave his heart to Christ with sincerity. I challenged him to give up drugs for 21 days, because psychologists tell us it takes 21 to establish a habit. Brett accepted the challenge, and he said no during those 21 days more times than he could count. He also decided to break up with his "drop-dead gorgeous" blonde girlfriend because their relationship had been sexual. Brett was truly a new person, and Josh saw a complete change in his friend.

Josh asked Brett to take him to my house. We talked about evolution for a while, and I cleared up some misconceptions he had been taught. Then Josh said he wanted to give his heart to Christ. I asked him why he wanted to make such a life-changing decision, and he answered with one word: "Brett."

Paul reminds us that what we believe isn't just a bunch of words. The gospel of Jesus Christ has *power*. If you don't believe me, just ask Josh and Brett.

Discussion Starters:

1. Why is a lifestyle dedicated to Christ the most powerful witnessing tool that we have?
2. How consistently do your friends see you living out your faith in Jesus?
3. Does your lifestyle lead your unsaved friends to Christ? What changes could you make that might cause your Christian witness to be more effective?

Lifeline:

Other people see you (and your witness for God), whether you notice them or not! Without saying a word, your actions speak volumes.

OUR GLORY AND JOY

"For who is our hope or joy or crown of exultation? Is it not even you, in the presence of our Lord Jesus at His coming? For you are our glory and joy."

⇝ 1 Thessalonians 2:19-20

Every great company has a vision statement—a lofty, long-range goal that the company is constantly working toward. Everything the company sets out to do is driven by that statement. Lots of good ideas come along, but only those that fit the company's vision statement are pursued.

Individuals can also have clearly defined vision statements. Many of the world's great inventors, ministers, writers, executives, and leaders have carefully thought through what they want to achieve, and they work toward that vision each day with care, passion, and purpose. Such men and women usually get more accomplished in this life, by far, than people who give little consideration to where they are headed.

Paul's vision statement is identified clearly in today's passage. This amazingly selfless, passionate, gospel-spreading apostle was motivated daily to excel at his work by his expectation that someday he would meet Christ face-to-face. In addition, on that day Paul wanted to see men and women from all over the world whom he had led to Christ and nurtured in their faith. Those people, standing by his side in the presence of the Lord and receiving their reward of eternal life in the kingdom of heaven, were Paul's constant source of "glory and joy."

As we read and respond to Paul's writings in 1 Thessalonians (and his other epistles), it's exciting to think that even *we* can benefit from his steadfast vision. Even more exciting is to consider who might benefit from *ours*.

Discussion Starters:

1. Do you have a vision statement? If not, what would you want to include in it?
2. What people would you consider your "glory and joy"?
3. Who are some of the people you want to see standing before Jesus when you meet Him for your eternal reward?

Lifeline:

If perishable things are your glory and joy, you'll be disappointed. If people's souls are your glory and joy, you'll be motivated.

GROWING HOSTILITY

"For indeed when we were with you, we kept telling you in advance that we were going to suffer affliction; and so it came to pass, as you know."

↪ 1 Thessalonians 3:4

For those of us who live in the United States, active persecution of our Christian beliefs has never been much of a problem. But the times are changing; it seems our nation is turning against Christians! Here are some recent actions taken against Christians, as presented in Allan Bloom's book *The Closing of the American Mind* (New York: Simon & Schuster, 1987; pp. 52-54):

- A federal court, referring to a local school district, said that "nothing can be more dangerous . . . than an adolescent seeing the football captain, the student body president or the leading actress in a dramatic production participating in communal prayer meetings in the captive audience setting of a school."
- A child in Kentucky was told she could not submit her chosen drawing for an independent school project. She had drawn a cross.
- An Arizona teacher disciplined a second grader in class for typing the word Jesus on her school computer during a computer lab.
- In Virginia, the Department of Motor Vehicles refused a pastor's request to display "4GOD-SO" on his license plate.
- Six students in Illinois were detained in squad cars and threatened with mace because they prayed around their school's flagpole.

I believe we are only beginning to see the tip of the iceberg. If Jesus doesn't return first, you and I will see increased hostility toward Christians and our beliefs.

If you take a pro-life stance, you are labeled "a narrow-minded anti-abortionist."

If you believe in marriages only between a male and a female, you are scorned as "a homophobic bigot."

If you believe devoutly in Jesus, you're called "an uneducated freak."

Media mogul Ted Turner has stated that "Christianity is for losers."

Paul warned the Thessalonians that afflictions were coming for devoted Christians. I believe that Christians in America can expect the same.

Discussion Starters:

1. In Paul's day, what effect did persecution have on the cause of Christ?
2. Why does suffering tend to strengthen the convictions of Christians?
3. If faced with persecution for your beliefs, how do you think you would respond? How can you be better prepared to respond with boldness?

Lifeline:

Hot fire tempers a band of steel, strengthens it, and allows it to hold a sharp edge. The hot fire of persecution puts the edge on a Christian's lifestyle.

BEYOND MORALITY

"For this is the will of God, your sanctification; that is, that you abstain from sexual immorality; that each of you know how to possess his own vessel in sanctification and honor, not in lustful passion. . . . For God has not called us for the purpose of impurity, but in sanctification."

↜ 1 Thessalonians 4:3-5, 7

I received three letters from Jana that arrived in approximate one-year intervals. The first arrived during the spring of her ninth-grade year.

> Dear Joe,
> I'm so afraid of losing my boyfriend. Even though we're having sex and I know it's wrong, I can't stop for fear that I'll lose him.

Seven months later, during her sophomore year, I received Jana's second letter.

> Dear Joe,
> My boyfriend and I broke up, but now I have another problem. I went to spend the night at my girlfriend's house and we started drinking. A boy I'd never met before was there who had been drinking, too. He started messing around with me and before I realized what I was doing, we had sex. The next day when I came to my senses, I confronted him on what he'd done. He called me awful names and said he never wanted to see me again.

A year later, Jana wrote me another letter:

> Dear Joe,
> I've finally realized what I've been doing the past two years was so wrong. Please tell other kids how badly I've hurt my family and myself. Why do I have to learn things the hard way? Why did I have to go through all of this to learn what God had been telling me all along?

Paul uses the word *sanctification* in reference to Christians. *Sanctified* simply means we are "set apart"—*from* sin, and *to* God. So when it comes to things like sex, our standards must be set higher than others'. It's the only way to avoid personal pain and potential danger.

If you don't believe Paul, just ask Jana.

Discussion Starters:

1. Why does God speak so clearly and so repeatedly about sexual purity?
2. Read 1 Thessalonians 4:6. What does it mean to "defraud" someone of the opposite sex?
3. First Thessalonians 4:8 says, "He who rejects this is not rejecting man but the God who gives His Holy Spirit to you." What does that mean?

Lifeline:

Beyond virginity is *purity*. It heals broken hearts. It establishes shame-free boundaries. It builds incredible marriages.

SONS OF THE DAY

"For you yourselves know full well that the day of the Lord will come just like a thief in the night. . . . But you, brethren, are not in darkness, that the day would overtake you like a thief; for you are all sons of light and sons of day."

↜ 1 Thessalonians 5:2, 4-5

Paul promised the Thessalonians that someday Jesus would return to earth (1 Thessalonians 5:1-11). His followers should be looking forward to the day when He will escort them to an eternal home of joy and safety. Others will be caught completely off guard. For those who don't believe or who aren't prepared, the return of Jesus will be like "a thief in the night."

The book of Revelation confirms what Paul says. Below are a couple of samples:

"No one will be able to buy or to sell, except the one who has the mark, either the name of the beast or the number of his name" (Revelation 13:17). With current computer chip technology, one person (the Antichrist, a.k.a. "the beast") could "mark" every human on earth with laser tattoos and control all economic transactions.

"The number of the armies of the horsemen was two hundred million. . . . [The Euphrates] was dried up, so that the way would be prepared for the kings from the east" (Revelation 9:16; 16:12). Red China is heavily involved in the military affairs of Iraq and Iran, and it is thirsty for the vast Middle East oil reserves. Israel and the United States stand squarely in the way of a military takeover. China now boasts an army of 200 million.

Dozens of other prophecies about the return of Christ and the rapture of the church are being fulfilled before our eyes. Many are quite alarming. But let's not overlook one final word from Paul to the Thessalonians: "Since we are of the day, let us be sober. . . . For God has not destined us for wrath, but for obtaining salvation through our Lord Jesus Christ" (1 Thessalonians 5:8-9).

Jesus could return *today*—a scary thought for some people. But for us who are "sons of day," no news could be better.

Discussion Starters:

1. How does a "child of the day" behave differently than a "child of the night"?
2. If you *knew* Jesus were coming back tomorrow, would you do anything differently? If so, what?
3. How can you encourage your friends or family members to be ready for Jesus' return?

Lifeline:

Make plans as if Jesus won't return for 100 years, but live as if He's coming back today.

GIVE THANKS

"We ought always to give thanks to God for you, brethren, as is only fitting, because your faith is greatly enlarged, and the love of each one of you toward one another grows ever greater."
— 2 Thessalonians 1:3

Today I was broken
and I was made new
in Your image
and by your power
I am redeemed.

Yesterday is but a memory
and seems as though a dream
for I lived not until this day...

As the east is to the west
so are all my sins.
They're gone and out of my life;
it is not a fad or a change of style
but a change of heart and my soul.

As many times as I fall
you will always be there,
and each tear that is shed of mine
is as if it were one of your own,
for you loved me even when I was lost. . . .

Each time I go astray
I pray that you will lead me home,
for it is with you that my soul belongs
and in your presence is where I strive to be;
in your favor is where I desire to live.

Love me today Lord;
that is my prayer,
for I am so empty without you,
and in your presence
my joy overflows.

Discussion Starters:

1. What are a dozen things or people for which you can "give thanks to God" today?
2. How does it make you feel to respond to God's good gifts by giving Him the glory?
3. How do you think God reacts when we offer thanksgiving?

Lifeline:

God has been so good that our joy should overflow in thanksgiving.

DELUDING INFLUENCES

"Then that lawless one will be revealed whom the Lord will slay with the breath of His mouth and bring to an end by the appearance of His coming. . . . For this reason God will send upon them a deluding influence so that they will believe what is false, in order that they all may be judged who did not believe the truth, but took pleasure in wickedness."

        ~ 2 Thessalonians 2:8, 11-12

A trucking company placed the following ad in a local newspaper:

> Wanted: Conscientious and experienced truck driver to transport dynamite across narrow mountain roads.
> Pay is very good.

Three brave drivers interviewed for the job. The foreman asked each of them, "When you turn a tight corner on a mountain road, how close to the edge can you drive without slipping off?" The first driver responded, "No problem! I can get within a foot of the drop-off." The second applicant said, "I've had years of experience, so I can hang the outside edge of my tire over the edge and keep her on the road." The third man said, "I'm sorry, sir. You're asking the wrong person. I respect the load and the danger and would never get close enough to the edge to find out."

Guess who got the job?

A committed Christian stays far from the edge of the cliff of sin. The lukewarm Christian "dances with the devil," dabbling with sin here and there, not respecting the danger.

Just a couple of beers.

Just a little petting.

Just a PG-13 movie—not too much sex or profanity.

Just a couple hours more sleep on Sunday morning.

Just that new CD and then back to giving offerings to God.

Just a date or two with the nonbeliever.

Just a couple of drags on the joint.

Just a couple of pornographic scenes off the Web.

The trouble is, "just a little" of Satan's deluding influence goes a long way. I think that's why the Antichrist ("the lawless one") will rise to power so easily—many "Christian wannabes" won't even recognize him because our tolerance of sin is deadening our spiritual awareness.

When the Lord returns, truth will once more prevail. All delusions will be shattered. And the groans of disappointment will be everywhere.

Discussion Starters:

1. What can you learn about the Antichrist from 2 Thessalonians 2?
2. What are some of Satan's "deluding influences" you are aware of?
3. How can you prevent being deluded—both now and in the future?

Lifeline:

The "angel of light" camouflages sin. Walking in *the* Light reveals sin.

STEADFAST

"But the Lord is faithful, and He will strengthen and protect you from the evil one. We have confidence in the Lord concerning you, that you are doing and will continue to do what we command. May the Lord direct your hearts into the love of God and into the steadfastness of Christ."

⮜ 2 Thessalonians 3:3-5

Solid.
Immovable.
Dependable.
Loyal.
Steadfast.

If you were to outline your hand on a piece of paper (like we did in kindergarten) and write one adjective on each digit to describe your feelings about the nature of God and His Word, what would the adjectives be? If the tables were turned, how do you think God would describe *your* commitment to Him?

Last week a sharp 17-year-old friend of mine made the extremely difficult decision to break up with his girlfriend. He knew she wasn't where she needed to be spiritually, and their relationship wasn't leading toward a godly future. My friend is *steadfast*. He has also walked away from countless parties where alcohol and drugs were present, and he has led some of his friends to Christ by his solid example.

In the rural country around where I live, words are few and character is measured by the work you do and the way you walk your talk. One of the biggest compliments you can receive is when an old cowboy tells someone, "I could turn my back on him and never give it a second thought." The comment reflects a trust in the person's steadfastness.

Jesus handpicked a group of disciples He knew He could entrust to tell the world about Him. Although they had failed in the past, as far as the 11 that were left after the Resurrection, He knew He "could turn His back on them" and they wouldn't let Him down. What great selection skills He had!

Jesus is still calling disciples. Why do you think He has chosen *you*?

Discussion Starters:

1. What two or three adjectives do you think God would use to evaluate you today? How do you *want* Him to describe you?
2. How can a young Christian become steadfast and dependable?
3. Why are steadfast people so respected?

Lifeline:

As you reflect on each of your hard decisions and choices this week, evaluate yourself with an adjective that depicts your character.

1 & 2 Timothy

My favorite human relationship in all of Scripture is between Paul and his "true child," young Timothy. Though they weren't related by flesh and blood, they shared a marvelous father-son friendship in their faith. Because of Timothy's undaunted faith in Jesus and his loyalty and love for Paul, he was chosen to carry the baton of leadership to many newly established churches while Paul was imprisoned and awaiting death.

Paul saw much potential in Timothy and wanted his young disciple to be knowledgeable and prepared for the challenge of faithfully upholding the gospel during a time when others were beginning to dilute and distort it. It would be Timothy's assignment (and privilege) to carry the faith onward.

Paul's encouragement and exhortation to Timothy are scattered throughout his two letters:

"My beloved son."

"I thank God for you and pray for you night and day."

What a "father" Paul was to Timothy! He desired to give Timothy protection, passion, and instruction so Timothy would succeed on his own after Paul's death. Next to Jesus, it was Timothy on Paul's heart most as he breathed his last breath before being martyred for his faith.

These highly personal letters are filled with strong, clear instructions to be diligent, not be ashamed, retain the standard, be strong, suffer hardship, remember Jesus, avoid gossip, flee youthful lusts, cling to Scripture, be sober, and preach the Word. Once again, I'm pleased to have the help of my son Cooper in preparing these devotionals.

FIGHT THE GOOD FIGHT

"This command I entrust to you, Timothy, my son, in accordance with the prophecies previously made concerning you, that by them you fight the good fight, keeping faith and a good conscience, which some have rejected and suffered shipwreck in regard to their faith."

⇌ 1 Timothy 1:18-19

Each of my last two years in college, our undersized Southern Methodist University team played the number-one and number-two teams in the nation, the University of Texas and the University of Arkansas. Texas had a 38-game winning streak; we didn't beat Arkansas for 13 straight years.

We never won the championship, but we did receive a much bigger prize—we learned to train hard and fight as a team, even in the face of insurmountable odds. Each of those Saturday afternoon games was 60 minutes of all-out war. We fought for every yard of Astroturf and Bermuda grass. My body still aches (literally) from the punishing hits I took from our NFL-bound opponents.

Following Christ is precisely that kind of challenge. In a spiritual sense, it is World War III. When a great movie comes out that is sexually explicit, or you're in love with a promiscuous partner, or you get "caught up in the moment," it is a *fight* to stay pure. You're battling not only your natural desires to sin, but also a personal and evil enemy behind those tendencies. So fight the good fight! Acknowledge that your body is a temple of the Holy Spirit and "go to war" to keep out all substances that would deface or weaken that temple. Fight the good fight!

Few challenges on earth are more difficult than establishing and maintaining Christian character and a godly lifestyle in the wake of our nation's amoral plunge into the jaws of hell. Fight the good fight!

Is the cause worth the sacrificial effort and battle scars? You bet it is! I've read about the victory party, and it will be abundantly more rewarding than any price you paid to be there.

Discussion Starters:

1. Do you feel that it's fair to have to "fight" for what you believe? Is it is worth it? Why?
2. Describe a spiritual battle you are in right now. How are doing? Are you determined to win?
3. Who are some people who might encourage you, as Paul did Timothy, to "fight the good fight"?

Lifeline:

The goal of your life should be love from a pure heart and a good conscience and a sincere faith (1 Timothy 1:5).

BIG FAMILIES

"This is good and acceptable in the sight of God our Savior, who desires all men to be saved and to come to the knowledge of the truth. For there is one God, and one mediator also between God and men, the man Christ Jesus, who gave Himself as a ransom for all, the testimony given at the proper time."

↩ 1 Timothy 2:3-6

"Tomahawk" Tom Hund was 6'11" when he played basketball for Kansas State University. Tom was a counselor at our sports camp and had a tremendous love for kids. His huge Kansas smile and his warm, gentle ways gave him a personality more contagious than the chicken pox! Everybody at camp loved him.

As crazy as it sounds, his 6'11" frame wasn't the most remarkable thing about Tom. We all knew that Tomahawk Tom Hund was one of 23 brothers and sisters. That's right, 23. In sports camp talk, that was a complete offense and a complete defense in football (plus a sub), or four basketball teams plus three managers!

As many as 20 of Tom's siblings lived in his home at one time. Four to a bed was the standard in their small Kansas farmhouse. They would all get up early, do the farm chores, and then pile on their own school bus and whisk off to school.

I love big families! So does God! God wants a big family *so* much that He sent His Son to earth to pass out invitations and adoption papers.

God wants *you* in His family. He wants the girl who sits next to you in geometry class. He wants the kid who plays third clarinet in your band. He wants the big defensive end on your football team. In fact, he wants your entire school.

God's desire is that *all* men and women be in His family. It's not hard to join. All they have to do is hear the call, lay down their pride, and receive Jesus Christ as their personal Savior and Lord. Nothing to sign.

God is the most loving Father imaginable. He already has a *lot* of kids. But He won't be satisfied until He gets us all!

Discussion Starters:

1. In what ways does today's Bible passage motivate you to tell your friends about Jesus?
2. How does this teaching affect your perspective about God's nature?
3. What if God weren't so generous? What could you expect?

Lifeline:

"[God] is patient toward you, not wishing for any to perish but for all to come to repentance" (2 Peter 3:9).

GO FORTH

"By common confession, great is the mystery of godliness: He who was revealed in the flesh, was vindicated in the Spirit, seen by angels, proclaimed among the nations, believed on in the world, taken up in glory."

        1 Timothy 3:16

It was the greatest
of commands ever given
for we who were left,
the ones that witnessed
the ascension.

To live each day for Him
as if it were to be our last;
none will know the day or hour
when the Lamb becomes the Lion
and takes us away.

We cry out
and in our arrogance
await His return,
wanting to be on His right hand,
yet we aren't worthy
to be in His presence.

The Lamb was slain
and we must preach
no matter violent nor hostile crowds;
we strive on
in the name of Him.

A moment that is without
an utterance of Him
is one that has been wasted,
a chance past
and an opportunity lost.

So we must take
the cup that has been passed
from the Creator to us,
acting on His last words
and GO FORTH!

Discussion Starters:

1. What do you find "mysterious" about the godliness Paul refers to in today's passage?
2. The third chapter of 1 Timothy describes guidelines for Christian leadership. Read the chapter and determine what, if anything, you need to work on if you seek to follow God more faithfully.
3. Where can you "go forth" this week to make a difference for God?

Lifeline:

The risk we take for Christ is small compared to the price He paid for us.

FAITH TRAINING

"For bodily discipline is only of little profit, but godliness is profitable for all things, since it holds promise for the present life and also for the life to come."

$\hookrightarrow$ 1 Timothy 4:8

Olympic weights, health clubs, tae bo, step-aerobics, crunches, "Abs of Steel," Jazzercise, Gold's Gym, diet plans, swimming workouts, jogging workouts, biking workouts . . . America is in a health and fitness craze. Each year tens of billions of dollars and tens of billions of hours are spent on health, training, and diet regimens. But the results aren't all positive. Most boys grow up thinking their biceps are too small, and one in four girls suffers from some kind of eating disorder.

Fitness and healthy diets are certainly good things. But what would happen to America . . . to your home . . . to yourself . . . if we started training our souls as devotedly as we train our bodies? Can you envision Biblecise, Souls of Steel, Bible Club, God's Gym, memory workouts, and spiritual growth plans?

Pardon the tongue-in-cheek images, but the concept is straight from Scripture, as Paul points out to Timothy in today's verse. Psalm 1 also says it well: "How blessed is the man who[se] . . . delight is in the law of the Lord, and in His law he meditates day and night" (vv. 1-2).

To meditate on God's Word, you have to memorize the Word.

To memorize the Word, you have to study it.

To study the Word, you have to read it.

To read the Word, you have to open your Bible . . . often.

To open your Bible, you have to have a heart that is excited about loving God, knowing God, and living a life with Him at its center.

So start simply, with a few stretching exercises. Stand up and stretch your legs. Jog over to where you keep your Bible. Do a deep knee bend until you're within reach. Stretch your arm out and lift the "weight" of God's Word. Do a few repetitions of page turning until you find a section that appeals to you. Then you're ready for the *real* workout: stretching your heart, soul, and mind as you read and apply God's Word in your quest for spiritual fitness. The more often you do these exercises, the stronger you'll become.

Discussion Starters:

1. Why is spiritual discipline more profitable than bodily discipline?
2. How would you evaluate your current level of spiritual fitness?
3. What kind of a "faith workout" schedule would you like to maintain in the immediate future?

Lifeline:

Lord, give me a heart that *wants* to know You more.

RESPECT

It is a virtue
and a blessing
to all who are around;
it spurs on wisdom
and is its friend.

Without it
we are but sinners
and are not in God's will,
for He writes
so it shall be done.

In our ignorance
we fear not
and in our hatred
we receive not,
for we are without respect.

All who surround
are in awe of those
who have this gift,
and throughout the world
they have no enemies.

Once it is given
it is returned in full,
and with its benefits
it carries
a lifelong friendship.

As a smile warms the room,
so does respect
in a hostile environment
and will heap coals on the head
of the aggressor.

As He did
the one who was raised,
so should we,
for we should strive to be
in His shadow of mercy.

Love one another
and respect each other,
for it is pleasing
in His eyes
as we are in His image.

Discussion Starters:

1. How can you better respect the older people you know?
2. How does respect for other people show respect for God?
3. How would your life and behavior be affected if you treated every stranger as if he or she were as close to you as your closest family members? How would it change any tendencies toward name-calling? Swearing? Lust? Etc.

Lifeline:

Respect: The more you give to others, the more you receive in return.

THE ROOT OF ALL SORTS OF EVIL

"But godliness actually is a means of great gain when accompanied by contentment. For we have brought nothing into the world, so we cannot take anything out of it either. If we have food and covering, with these we shall be content. But those who want to get rich fall into temptation and a snare and many foolish and harmful desires which plunge men into ruin and destruction. For the love of money is a root of all sorts of evil, and some by longing for it have wandered away from the faith and pierced themselves with many griefs."

⟿ 1 Timothy 6:6-10

A better stereo system.

Bigger allowance. Bigger paychecks.

A newer car. A faster car.

The United States is a financial black hole that has enough resources to feed much of the starving world. Yet how many of us are content with what we have? Perhaps we should revise our national motto to "More. Gimme more. I want mo-o-o-ore."

What happened to "enough already"?

Other devotions in this book have told you about the 15,000 kids in Haiti that our camps support. They each have one shirt and one pair of shoes. They live on one bowl of beans and rice per day. That's all they've ever known, and they are thrilled to get it.

Yet in some ways the Haitian children are much more content and happy than the youth of America. I've never seen the Haitian kids shoot each other, threaten a teacher, or call their parents degrading names. On the other hand, the American kids I know who are most content are those who really love God and would give the shirt off their back to someone in need. I believe many young people are less materialistic than preceding generations, and that's encouraging!

At the bottom line is a continual struggle between contentment and greed. The love of money leads to the accumulation of material things, which can lead to idolatry. Anything you own that you wouldn't immediately give to someone who needs it worse is probably becoming an idol. And the more you accumulate, the more you realize you can never have enough.

That's why Scripture puts such a high value on contentment. It *is* the one commodity you can't get enough of.

Discussion Starters:

1. How do material things become idols?
2. How susceptible are you to "the love of money"? Can you see how it might lead to certain "evils"?
3. How do we get out of the cycle of desiring, accumulating, and then desiring still more?

Lifeline:

Material things always leave you wanting more, but contentment satisfies.

BOLD

"God has not given us a spirit of timidity, but of power and love and discipline. Therefore do not be ashamed of the testimony of our Lord or of me His prisoner, but join with me in suffering for the gospel according to the power of God."

↩ 2 Timothy 1:7-8

Be bold in His name
for He commands us so,
and it is for Him
that we live and strive.
There are none who may stand
    in His way;
in this we can have all confidence.

Our Savior is above all
and calls us to do His will;
it is for this reason
that we can let none stand
in the way of His teaching
for whatever the cause.

There is not any who can oppose
or successfully question His power;
it is as He says without flaws,
and for us it is all we need
to back us in our struggle.

He is in our corner
and with Him we are assured
nothing less than a victory,
for He will vanquish our foes
for all eternity.

The job we have is simple:
It is to do what we are told
and to back it
with all that we are worth
no matter the odds we face.

Our timidity is a weakness
and is a cop-out
for what we know we must do.
We mustn't hide behind
our fear or any other emotion.

Strength is not possessed
in numbers of people
or numbers of followers
but in our Lord
and our Redeemer, Jesus Christ.

Discussion Starters:

1. If you're shy by nature, how can you be more bold when God gives you opportunities to speak up or take a stand for Him?
2. When you're at school or work, are you ever "ashamed of the testimony of our Lord"—even a little bit? If so, how do you deal with your feelings?
3. How do you feel after you gather your courage and take a bold stand for God?

Lifeline:

Bold actions are most effective when they spring from a humble heart.

PLEASING THE COACH

"Suffer hardship with me, as a good soldier of Christ Jesus. No soldier in active service entangles himself in the affairs of everyday life, so that he may please the one who enlisted him as a soldier. Also if anyone competes as an athlete, he does not win the prize unless he competes according to the rules."

↜ 2 Timothy 2:3-5

The high school football team I coached was, to be kind, mediocre. We trained hard, we played hard, and we had fun. In fact, we did most everything a team is supposed to do . . . except win.

We had a sophomore named Robert who didn't know squat about the game of football. He was slow and inexperienced, but he had a huge heart for the team and a desire to play. One Friday night, the opposing team's running back was streaking down the sideline right in front of our bench, ball in hand and 10 yards ahead of our pursuing defense.

Suddenly a flash of red shot past me, completely leveling the kid with the ball! And just as quickly, it disappeared. It all happened so fast, the referees didn't even see it.

The opposing coach was livid, as well he should have been. But Robert, who was sick of sitting on the sidelines watching his teammates play and lose, had taken matters into his own hands. He had jumped off the bench, wiped out the guy carrying the ball, and quickly resumed his place on the sidelines. It was over 20 years ago and I'm still laughing.

Everybody wants to play. Nobody wants to sit on the bench!

You can learn a lot about God on a football field. When a coach asks you to play for him, you'd run through a brick wall to please the guy. It sure beats sitting around watching other people who are active in the game.

God wants players, too. Those willing to purify their hearts and live clean lives for Jesus get to play in the greatest, most competitive, most exciting game ever—the struggle for men's and women's souls.

The greatest Coach ever has invited you to be on His starting team. But learn from Paul's instructions—and Robert's mistake. Learn to play by the rules!

Discussion Starters:

1. Can you recall a time when a coach or teacher pointed out how valuable or gifted you were? How did it feel?
2. How does it feel to "please the one who enlisted you" as a Christian?
3. Read 2 Timothy 2. What specific things can you to do to be consistently useful to your heavenly Coach?

Lifeline:

If you ever feel useless, make yourself useful to the Master.

GOD-BREATHED

"All Scripture is inspired by God and profitable for teaching, for reproof, for correction, for training in righteousness; so that the man of God may be adequate, equipped for every good work."

⟿ 2 Timothy 3:16-17

Have you ever wondered what it would be like to hear God talk? Imagine it for a moment. What would He say? How would His voice sound?

Let's say there were some things He really wanted you to know. Maybe He wanted to give you some clear instructions about a problem you were facing, some assurance of His love for you, or a warning that you were about to get hurt. Would you respond, or would you "blow it off"? Would you hurry or take your time? Would you want Him to write His message in the sky like the vapor trail of an airplane, or would you be willing to go out of your way to hear from Him?

I have a strong suspicion that if God literally spoke to you, you would cup your hands to your ears and try to hear every word. If He wrote you a personal love letter, you'd rip it open with passion and absorb every page.

Well, guess what? That's exactly what He did. Every page of the Bible is part of God's message to be piped into your ears and your heart.

All Scripture is God's voice to you, from "In the beginning . . ." (the first phrase of Genesis) to "Amen" (the last word of Revelation). When Paul tells Timothy that Scripture is "inspired by God," the literal translation means "God-breathed." The Bible contains the thoughts, breath, and voice of God.

Does that get you excited or what? I carry God's voice with me everywhere I go. When I have a spare moment, I yank it out of my back pocket to see what He has to say. So can you!

I stand in awe that God would write a love letter to you and me, and deliver it with love straight to our hearts.

Discussion Starters:

1. How is the Bible God's love letter to you, personally?
2. What was the last thing you read from God that made a big difference in your life?
3. What benefits of Bible reading might you be missing out on? (Review today's passage.)

Lifeline:

"Either this book [the Bible] will keep you from sin, or sin will keep you from this book."

FINISH STRONG

"I have fought the good fight, I have finished the course, I have kept the faith; in the future there is laid up for me the crown of righteousness, which the Lord, the righteous Judge, will award to me on that day; and not only to me, but also to all who have loved His appearing."

↪ 2 Timothy 4:7-8

Richard was a talented young man at Kanakuk Kamp, and the fastest kid there. I had never seen anybody faster. Nobody could beat him . . . that is, until the summer Sam came to camp. Sam was one step faster out of the blocks. He covered the first 10 yards of a race like a bolt of lightning.

We would race in three-person teams, with a total of six runners as teams competed against one another. Whenever Richard and Sam were in the same race, Sam would always come in first, and Richard, of course, would be . . . *sixth!* Not second. Not third. Every single time, Richard got sixth place.

Know what happened? You guessed it. Whenever Sam took the lead, Richard would quit running. He couldn't stand the idea of second place, so he never crossed the finish line.

My first year in coaching, I was fortunate to coach at Texas A & M University. Our slogan during spring training was "Finish strong." Every race, every drill, every play, you could hear Coach Stallings or one of the other coaches shouting, "Finish strong!" There was no place for any "Richards" at Texas A & M.

Life is so much like a sports competition. Like a football player, we sometimes get knocked flat. Like a basketball player, we may hear a lot of trash talk and get belittled. Like a track event, other people get ahead of us no matter how hard we try to stay out front. We get discouraged. We want to quit running.

But the runner who keeps his eyes on the prize and his legs pumping to the finish line wins the most important race *every time*. All we have to do is finish strong. God guarantees the victory.

Discussion Starters:

1. How was Paul able to finish strong? How do his words encourage you today?
2. Why do we tend to quit sometimes when we see others outdoing us? How do you keep the "Sams" in your life from making you feel discouraged?
3. How do you think it would feel to be able to say, at the end of your life, "I have finished the course, I have kept the faith"? What can you do *now* to start preparing to make that statement?

Lifeline:

Fight the good fight. Finish the race. Keep the faith!

Titus

I have a friend who refuses to believe in Jesus because of the hypocrisy he sees in Christians, and I doubt that he's the only one. I believe most people who encounter Christians want to know if our faith is genuine. They want to know if we have integrity and conviction that influence our day-to-day activities.

Charles Swindoll has said that the letter to Titus teaches us to pay as much attention to our behavior as we do to our beliefs. In this short book (which many of us seem to skip over), Paul encourages Titus to support his words with actions as he models the gospel. Paul's challenge to Titus serves as a reminder for us to "walk the talk" as we interact with others.

Brett Causey is a 23-year-old friend from Clinton, Mississippi, who grew up playing football, baseball, and basketball. Brett was honored by his classmates as student body president and captain of his football and baseball teams. He was also endowed with numerous postseason honors. He says that Jesus is everything to him and that following Christ is the most incredible challenge he's ever undertaken.

Brett and his big heart for God are going to come through in the following pages. I hope you get as big a kick out of his writings as I do.

ARE YOU EMPTY?

"For there are many rebellious men, empty talkers and deceivers . . . who must be silenced because they are upsetting whole families, teaching things they should not teach for the sake of sordid gain."

↫ Titus 1:10-11

Mike stood on the top rung of a ladder with a paintbrush in his hand, where he had been since 6:00 A.M. He could hear the laughter and shouts of the other kids as they swam and played basketball, and he was mad because he had to paint all day. He had arrived the previous week at the Baptist Children's Village, a residential home for children and teens, because his parents didn't want him. Sure, he had messed up and at 14 had already been expelled from school. But it hurt to be rejected by everyone.

As he painted, his frustration and anger became more intense. He didn't know where to turn for help. In his confusion, Mike wrote with his finger the letters "E-M-P-T-Y" in paint on the wall. That one word described his entire life. No one loved him. No one cared. He had been told repeatedly that he would never amount to anything. Everyone expected him to be just like his alcoholic father, who had abandoned him when he was two years old.

There are a lot of "Mikes" in our neighborhoods and cities who have no hope because they have heard only lies about themselves. They think they are worthless because they have never been told differently.

Mike may attempt to fill the emptiness with alcohol or some other substance to distract him from the pain. But maybe—just maybe—someone will love him for who he is and help him discover the truth about his worth as a child of God. It is time we silence the lies by allowing God to love the "Mikes" of this world . . . through us.

Discussion Starters:

1. If you had to describe your life in one or two words, what words would you choose?
2. Have you ever felt separated from God? How did it feel? What did you do to fill that void?
3. Discouragement and lack of love are two ways the evil one fills our hearts with lies. What are some others? How can those lies be replaced with God's truth?

Lifeline:

Make a list of five words that describe your positive qualities. (Focus more on who you really are rather than things you do well.)

NO COMPROMISE

"For the grace of God has appeared, bringing salvation to all men, instructing us to deny ungodliness and worldly desires and to live sensibly, righteously and godly in the present age, looking for the blessed hope and the appearing of the glory of our great God and Savior, Christ Jesus."

↬ Titus 2:11-13

Reggie White is a former defensive end for the Philadelphia Eagles and Green Bay Packers. For 14 seasons, he played in the National Football League, where he terrorized opposing teams' offenses and dominated as one of the best pass rushers of all time. Reggie is a man after God's own heart. He has had the opportunity to stand fearlessly for Christ on the playing field, in the locker room, and before the media. His courage and boldness are rooted in a deep and passionate love for Christ that affects everything he does.

In a recent interview, Reggie was asked about his views on homosexuality. He responded with the truth of the Bible, proclaiming his belief that homosexual behavior is a sin. His comments brought a tidal wave of insults from homosexual activists, certain media personalities, and even a White House spokesperson. As a result, he lost a pending contract with CBS worth millions, as well as every endorsement he had. All he did was share boldly something from God's Word that he believed to be absolute truth.

Reggie could have prevented a lot of heartache, avoided the insults, and gained millions of dollars if he had been willing to compromise. But instead, he stared the enemy in the face and bore the consequences of the controversy. Praise God he didn't remain silent. He spoke the truth.

Discussion Starters:

1. Do you ever feel that you compromise your Christian beliefs? If so, in what ways?
2. Have you ever been silent when you knew you should have spoken? Why were you silent?
3. Do you believe the Bible is absolute truth? What are some of the things you find hardest to believe? What things do you find hardest to defend to others?

Lifeline:

As a family, you must say no to ungodliness and worldly passions. How can you honor God in your home? (Consider the TV programs you watch, music you listen to, etc.)

I GRANT YOU GRACE

"But when the kindness of God our Savior and His love for mankind appeared, He saved us, not on the basis of deeds which we have done in righteousness, but according to His mercy, by the washing of regeneration and renewing by the Holy Spirit, whom He poured out upon us richly through Jesus Christ our Savior, so that being justified by His grace we would be made heirs according to the hope of eternal life."

⮑ Titus 3:4-7

As a young child, Katherine was always the biggest troublemaker in her family. Not many opportunities passed without her managing to get caught doing something worthy of punishment. And although she loved causing trouble, she feared the inevitable discipline that followed. Fortunately, she had parents who loved the Lord and believed in godly discipline.

One day after getting herself into some serious trouble, Katherine trembled as her mom approached. However, instead of the much-deserved spanking that Katherine expected, her mom looked into her teary eyes and said, "Katherine, I grant you grace." Then her mom simply smiled, hugged her, and walked away! In the days that followed, Katherine received many well-deserved punishments for defiant behavior and wrong decisions. However, every once in a while, rather than doling out the punishment, her mom would say, "Katherine, I grant you grace." Each gift of grace brought great surprise and relief to the young girl.

When Katherine was older, her parents were able to recall her many escapades as a way of teaching her about the grace of God. Katherine was pleased to discover that the invitation of God's grace is extended to us, not just occasionally, but during every moment and every event of our lives!

Whenever some people think of God, they envision an angry figure with thunderbolts in His hand and judgment in His mind. But the next time you do something wrong and fear God's anger, I hope you hear clearly His loving voice saying, "I grant you grace."

Discussion Starters:
1. Can you recall a time in your life when you were granted the gift of grace? How did you feel? How did you respond?
2. Paul says that "being justified by [God's] grace we would be made heirs according to the hope of eternal life." What does that tell you about the importance of grace?
3. How good are you at granting grace to others? How can you get better at it?

Lifeline:
You can't do anything good to make God love you more than He already does. And you can't do anything bad to make Him love you less.

PhileMoN

This shortest of Paul's letters is a passionate appeal to Philemon, a slaveholder whose slave Onesimus had stolen some valuables and run away. Paul had witnessed Onesimus's conversion to Christianity and appealed to Philemon to forgive and warmly accept the return of the fugitive slave. Paul's persuasive words illustrate a beautiful picture of the grace and mercy of our God. The book of Philemon is very relevant to us as well, because as Paul appeals on behalf of Onesimus, so Christ intercedes to make it possible for us to find reconciliation with our Master.

My thanks to Brett Causey for writing this devotional.

ACTIVE FAITH

"I thank my God always, making mention of you in my prayers, because I hear of your love and of the faith which you have toward the Lord Jesus and toward all the saints; and I pray that the fellowship of your faith may become effective through the knowledge of every good thing which is in you for Christ's sake."

~ Philemon 4-6

The Sisters of Charity were invited by the president of Mexico to open a home in Mexico City. The people they ministered to were extremely poor, but the requests of the poverty-stricken Mexicans surprised the sisters very much. The first thing they asked for was not clothes, medicine, or food. They only said, "Sisters, talk to us about God!"

Mother Teresa once picked up a small girl who was wandering the streets, lost and hungry. Mother Teresa offered her a piece of bread. The little girl started eating it, crumb by crumb. Mother Teresa told her, "Eat, eat the bread! Aren't you hungry?" The little girl looked up and said, "I am just afraid that when I run out of bread, I'll still be hungry."

We need to ask God to teach us how our faith can become more active. In this letter, Paul asked Philemon to live out his faith by forgiving Onesimus and accepting the slave as he would accept Paul himself. God might give us the opportunity to make faith more active by feeding a hungry little girl, listening to someone who desperately needs a friend, or even beginning a Bible study at school. As we reach out to other hurting people, it's as if we're helping Jesus Himself (Matthew 25:37-40).

Jesus comes to us in the tattered clothes of the poor, in the hunger of those who have no food, in the naked bodies of the ones who have no clothes, and in the lonely hearts of people who have no one to offer them love. We have placed our trust and faith in Jesus because He has given everything for us. But will we share our faith not only in words, but also in how we live? Will our faith become an active faith, reaching out to others because of our love for Jesus?

Discussion Starters:

1. Has anyone ever loved you with the love of God? How did it make you feel?
2. Is your faith active? In what ways? What motivates you?
3. In what ways can your family live out your faith together?

Lifeline:

Remember that the love and forgiveness of Jesus cannot be earned. They are free gifts which we should desire to share with others.

HeBreWs

No one knows for sure who wrote the book of Hebrews, but in this fantastic book the author lays a convincing foundation for the faith of all Christians, assuring us that Jesus is indeed the Messiah, the Anointed One, the Expected One. As such, Jesus is worthy of our trust and faith, and our only hope for our salvation. To support his argument, the author uses 29 direct quotations from the Old Testament and 53 references to other Old Testament passages.

An emphasis is placed on the priesthood of Jesus. Jewish believers would understand this concept of Jesus being the "high priest" who escorts us into the presence of God, where we can "draw near with confidence to the throne of grace" (4:16).

This splendid book also uses numerous superlatives to describe the person and the work of Christ, such as "much better," "more excitement," and even "perfect." In this descriptive style, the author seeks to underline the idea that Jesus is indeed superior to any other person, angel, principality, or being in all creation.

Hebrews is a complex and thought-provoking book, and may be a challenge to comprehend on first reading. But as you return to the study of Hebrews throughout your lifetime, you will be rewarded as you discover more about the breadth and length and height and depth of Christ.

THE RADIANCE OF GOD'S GLORY

"And [Jesus] is the radiance of [God's] glory and the exact representation of His nature, and upholds all things by the word of His power. When He had made purification of sins, He sat down at the right hand of the Majesty on high, having become as much better than the angels, as He has inherited a more excellent name than they."

↝ Hebrews 1:3-4

To tour the Sistine Chapel in Rome is to see into the mind of perhaps the greatest painter of all time—Michelangelo. The ceiling of the chapel depicts the painter's vision of some of the great wonders and people of history: God, creation, Jesus, the early saints of the faith, and so forth. Witnessing this masterpiece lingers in your mind for a lifetime.

To see a 1990s Duke basketball team is to see greatness among college basketball players, proven by their series of Final Four appearances and back-to-back national championships. Mike Krzyzewski, "the Maestro," is perhaps the greatest basketball coach since John Wooden, with the mind of a true genius! A Krzyzewski team flows across the court like a great artist's paint across a canvas.

To hear the Boston Philharmonic orchestra is to set your ears adrift in a musical paradise. You experience a sea of perfectly balanced melody, harmony, and percussion, all flowing like a Hawaiian wave onto the seashore of your mind.

To witness a Maui sunset . . . a star-blazed sky from atop Mount Kilimanjaro . . . Niagara Falls beneath its perpetual multicolored rainbow . . . is to see the brush strokes of the Creator of the universe.

But more importantly, to look at Jesus is to see God. As we look into the eyes of a gentle, compassionate, 33-year-old man willfully hanging on a cross for the sins of a fallen world, we might not recognize the unfailing, almighty God. Yet Jesus, says the author of Hebrews, is the "exact representation of His nature."

It's been said often, but never with more accuracy: "Like Father, like Son."

Discussion Starters:

1. What does it mean that Jesus is "the radiance of God's glory and the exact representation of His nature"?
2. How does knowing Jesus teach us about the heart of God?
3. What are some specific characteristics of Jesus that cause you to marvel at the nature of God?

Lifeline:

Jesus is a true representation of God. How accurate is the representation of Jesus that others see in you?

ULTIMATE HUMILITY

"But we do see Him who was made for a little while lower than the angels, namely, Jesus, because of the suffering of death crowned with glory and honor, so that by the grace of God He might taste death for everyone. For it was fitting for Him, for whom are all things, and through whom are all things, in bringing many sons to glory, to perfect the author of their salvation through sufferings."

↝ Hebrews 2: 9-10

As far as I'm concerned, snowboarding at blazing speed down freshly packed powder on a Colorado mountainside with my 17-year-old son is the ultimate father-son experience.

Upsetting a nationally ranked football team in a postseason bowl game before national television cameras and screaming fans has to be the ultimate sports experience in my memory.

Walking my daughter down the forest-green-carpeted wedding aisle amid white lace, white roses, and glistening candles, and placing her hand in the trustworthy grasp of her "knight in shining armor," is surely the ultimate relational experience we ever shared.

Gazing into my dear wife's sparkling brown eyes above our twenty-fifth anniversary cake and reflecting on a quarter century of mutual respect, admiration, mountains climbed, dreams dreamed, and heartbeats melded together is definitely the ultimate marital experience (so far, at least).

But of all the ultimates, realized or imagined on this earth, none can ever begin to compare to the ultimate humility displayed by Jesus. He is the one to whom belong all things . . . the one in whom are hidden all the treasures of wisdom and knowledge . . . the one who holds all things together by His power . . . the one to whom God subjected everything in all creation . . . and the one to whom every knee shall one day bow. This man Jesus lowered Himself, humbled Himself, and sacrificed Himself for one reason: God would rather die for you than live without you!

That is *ultimate* love. That is *ultimate* selflessness. That is *ultimate* humility.

Discussion Starters:

1. What emotions and thoughts do you feel when you think about the ultimate humility of Jesus?
2. What emotions and thoughts do you feel when you think about the ultimate love of Jesus?
3. How can you make your family stronger by demonstrating similar humility to those whom you love the most?

Lifeline:

"Love one another, just as I have loved you" (John 15:12).

THE GIFT OF ENCOURAGEMENT

"Take care, brethren, that there not be in any one of you an evil, unbelieving heart that falls away from the living God. But encourage one another day after day, as long as it is still called 'Today,' so that none of you will be hardened by the deceitfulness of sin."

↩ Hebrews 3:12-13

My friend Gene Stallings coached college and professional football for 20 years, winning an NFL championship, conference championships, bowl games, and coach of the year honors. But in reflecting on his career, he told me the most amazing football season of his life was the year he and the Dallas Cowboys went to the Super Bowl with 13 rookies on the team. Nobody expected that kind of success from the Cowboys. I asked Coach his secret, and he said bluntly, "We encouraged the players. It was a season when our coaching staff decided we were going to do everything we could do to make the players feel good about themselves."

If encouragement works with well-paid, adult, 300-pound defensive tackles, how much more with 12-year-old boys going through the pains of junior high? Or a mom who works her heart out all day, every day, as a "household executive"? Or a dad who pours out his energy during long weeks at the office to bring home the bacon and keep the bank account from drying up?

Encouragement is the powerful winch that pulls you out of the quicksand of doldrums, depression, or stages of perceived insignificance. It stands you on your tiptoes and puts a smile on your face.

"Atta boy! I'm proud of you, Son!"

"Way to go, Dad!"

"Thanks, Mom!"

"Super job, young lady!"

"Wow, that was amazing!"

"You're awesome!"

"I love you!"

"You make me so happy when you're around!"

"I'm so lucky to have someone like you in my life!"

You get the idea. Now you take it from here. I know you can do it!

Discussion Starters:

1. In what ways does encouragement enhance your life?
2. Whose encouragement do you need in order to walk closer with Christ?
3. How can encouragement keep you from falling into sin?

Lifeline:

It is said that it takes only 20 minutes to teach a pigeon to bowl. Every time he gets near the ball, give him a grain of corn. Every time he touches it, give him two. With a little encouragement, he will learn in no time.

THE TWO-EDGED SWORD

"For the word of God is living and active and sharper than any two-edged sword, and piercing as far as the division of soul and spirit, of both joints and marrow, and able to judge the thoughts and intentions of the heart."

⮑ Hebrews 4:12

My mom is in a class all her own! Never have I known a woman so consistent in her willingness to serve, her encouragement, and her readiness to ask with her big Texas smile, "What can I do for you?" On the other hand, my brother and I used to complain that she had eyes in the back of her head and ears like a deer in the forest. We called her "Sherlock" because she missed no detail, could tell *before* we tried something sneaky, and knew exactly what we were up to.

Mom's goal was simply to do whatever it took to serve her family and to raise good boys. (I know some days she has to wonder how she did!)

Mom was a wonderful model for the God at whom I would someday marvel. His Word points out my shortcomings. He corrects my faults. He strengthens my weaknesses. If I try to rationalize something I'm doing wrong, my daily Bible study quickly sets my wheels back on track. His guidelines are clear and simple: "Just be like My Son and do what He would do."

But that's not *all* God is to me. He is the all-seeing, trouble-preventing God I serve. In addition, He's a heavenly Father who gives me a shoulder to cry on . . . refuge in a storm . . . companionship in times of trouble . . . constant guidance during unsure times . . . confident access in time of need.

With Jesus in my heart, the guidance of His Word is like a Seeing-Eye dog to a blind man. With Jesus as my Lord, I can go straight to God and open my heart to Him in prayer like picking up a direct phone line where there's never a busy signal.

God always tries to keep me from falling on my face. And even when I don't listen, He's always there to pick me up.

Discussion Starters:

1. What do you think is the significance of God's Word being referred to as a *two-edged* sword?
2. What does the phrase "draw near with confidence to the throne of grace" (Hebrews 4:16) mean to you?
3. What aspects of your relationship with God do you wish to develop more fully? Why?

Lifeline:

The guidance of Scripture and the privilege of prayer are like a two-way radio to and from the throne of God.

TRAINING WHEELS

"For though by this time you ought to be teachers, you have need again for someone to teach you the elementary principles of the oracles of God, and you have come to need milk and not solid food. . . . But solid food is for the mature, who because of practice have their senses trained to discern good and evil."

Hebrews 5:12, 14

The unfinished plywood closets in my boyhood home contained all we wore and everything we owned. My two older brothers and I shared a simple tile-floored room. The closets Dad made gave us a little privacy and probably kept us from killing each other.

My favorite spot was a place on the end of my closet decorated with hand-drawn pencil lines, each marked carefully with the month, day, and year that the line was drawn. For these were the sacred lines that marked my growth (and my brothers') in inches from the floor, from the bottoms of our flat feet to the top of our short athletic haircuts.

Every time I would grow an inch or two, I would grab a pencil and run get Mom. She would make the official measurement, and I would subsequently burst out with proud excitement over my increase in stature. Equally exciting were the days I took the training wheels off my bike, and later when I got my driver's license and no longer needed Mom in the car to go to my girlfriend's house.

Stages of growth. They're the greatest! In today's passage, the author of Hebrews challenges his readers (including us) to consider some growth issues: How long have you been a Christian? How much have you grown? Do you still need a bottle? Are you still wearing diapers? Are you crawling on the floor, waving rattles? Do you still need training wheels? Or are you growing taller and forming some spiritual muscles by digging into God's Word daily, witnessing to friends, praying, integrating Christ-centered conversation into your friendships, and becoming a spiritual adult?

The key question at any age is not "How long have you been a Christian?" Much more important is your answer to "How much have you grown?"

Discussion Starters:

1. How do you measure spiritual growth?
2. If you were keeping a spiritual "growth chart," where would your "growth spurts" be?
3. In what ways would you like to "take the training wheels off" and grow spiritually over the next couple of months?

Lifeline:

Are you tired of "milk" and ready for some steak? Are you committed to setting some new records in your spiritual growth chart? Ready, set, grow!

BETTER THINGS

"For ground that drinks the rain which often falls on it and brings forth vegetation useful to those for whose sake it is also tilled, receives a blessing from God; but if it yields thorns and thistles, it is worthless and close to being cursed, and it ends up being burned. But, beloved, we are convinced of better things concerning you, and things that accompany salvation, though we are speaking in this way."

↩ Hebrews 6:7-9

Sometimes it seems as though you're the only Christian in your school. If you go to parties, it seems everyone is drinking but you. You stay home when you don't feel comfortable attending the same movies as everyone else. You don't date much because you are saving your sexual life for your future spouse. And what's the payoff? Discouragement and loneliness.

Is it worth it? *They* are having so much fun! *They* seem unbelievably happy! What are *you* waiting for? Let me tell you.

They experience guilt by the truckload. *They* have hangovers. *They* get AIDS, herpes, and other sexually transmitted diseases. *They* have nothing to look forward to on their honeymoons. *They* get divorced. *They* have little if any self-respect. *They* aren't respected for their integrity. *They* aren't proud of themselves when they wake up in the morning.

You, however, have everything to look forward to. *You* understand purity and respect. *You* experience forgiveness for the mistakes you've made. *You* receive genuine love and can offer it to others. *You* are one in a million. *You* will hear God's voice saying, "Well done."

When you sow thistle seeds, you get thorns and briars within a month (if that's really what you want). When you plant apple seeds, you get green, leafy trees with precious red apples—but it will take eight to 10 years for the fruit to appear.

The next time you look at what *they* are doing and start to feel left out, keep looking to the future. The good choices you make today will surely be rewarded with better things in due time.

Discussion Starters:

1. As others around you are growing "thorns and thistles," how do you feel? Why?
2. What are some of the "better things" you've seen in the lives of people devoted to God?
3. How can you ensure that you don't settle for less as you wait for the better things God has to offer?

Lifeline:

Look carefully around you and you will quickly see the truth of Galatians 6:7: "Do not be deceived, God is not mocked; for whatever a man sows, this he will also reap."

WHAT GOD CAN'T DO

"In the same way God, desiring even more to show to the heirs of the promise the unchange-ableness of His purpose, interposed with an oath, so that by two unchangeable things in which it is impossible for God to lie, we who have taken refuge would have strong encour-agement to take hold of the hope set before us."

↪ Hebrews 6:17-18

As decades go, the 1950s are remembered as the age of rock and roll; the '60s for drugs; the '70s for hard rock; and the '80s for acid and punk rock. I am convinced that the 1990s will forever be known as the decade when the public learned that lying has no consequences.

The highly publicized trials of O. J. Simpson and Bill Clinton both contained testimony and/or results that were brought into question after the final gavel pounded. Political figures dodged direct questions to avoid getting caught in lies (or telling even bigger ones). Sports heroes used agents and attorneys to bend truth to the breaking point.

If our leaders can lie, why are *we* bound to the truth?

To begin with, if you don't have trust in a relationship, you don't have anything! I trust my family members with everything I have. When we've had problems in this area, we've corrected them and moved on. That's why our family is tight.

Second, God is our only true hero. He can build or destroy the universe with a word. He can mold a man out of a lump of clay and a woman from that man's rib. That's why He sets the standards for us to live by. But there is one thing that God *cannot* do. God cannot lie!

When He says your sins are forgiven, you can take it to the bank. When He says you are His child, you can bet your life on it. When He says that He has a wonderful plan for your life, you can count on it.

If you want proof, you can find 8,000 promises in the Bible for *you* as a child of God. All 8,000 are absolutely true. He gave His Son to prove that He is a person of His word.

As we reflect God's nature, we, too, place a high priority on integrity. Telling the truth is our response to the "gospel truth"—the most incredible truth ever told.

Discussion Starters:

1. Why does God hate lying?
2. Why is telling the truth so vital to all good relationships—with family, friends, etc.?
3. Can you think of any recent lies that you need to confess?

Lifeline:

"One of the striking differences between a cat and a lie is that the cat has only nine lives." (Mark Twain)

THE HIGHEST PRIEST

"For it was fitting for us to have such a high priest, holy, innocent, undefiled, separated from sinners and exalted above the heavens; who does not need daily, like those high priests, to offer up sacrifices, first for His own sins and then for the sins of the people, because this He did once for all when He offered up Himself. For the Law appoints men as high priests who are weak, but the word of the oath, which came after the Law, appoints a Son, made perfect forever."

⤚ Hebrews 7:26-28

The role of church leader is indeed a varied one. Some wear coats and ties. Some appear in long, black robes. Some have black shirts with neatly pressed white, round collars. Some are in shirtsleeves. Some prefer flashy colors. They may have Ph.D.'s, doctorates in divinity, or no degree at all. They may be called bishops, cardinals, priests, pastors, preachers, or teachers.

But no matter what their title, position, or attire, they all have one thing in common: They are people. Mere human beings. They were all born, and they will all die. None are divine. None has a "secret entrance" to God that the rest of us don't know about. We all have the same opportunity to approach God directly on the avenue of faith, paved by the sacrificial blood of Jesus—the only, the supreme, the divine, the all-sufficient High Priest.

You might be Protestant, Catholic, evangelical, or charismatic. You might be American, African, Asian, European, or Chinese. No matter. You go to God the same way everyone else does—"in Jesus' name."

You don't have to have a church or a preacher to go directly to God (although such things are helpful in your ongoing spiritual growth). You don't need a prayer book or flowery words. You don't need to pay anyone. All you need is to go to God sincerely and reverently, with faith "in Jesus' name."

Jesus is our high priest. He is our intercessor to God. He is our guide to the throne of God Himself.

Discussion Starters:

1. What is the role of your church leader? Which aspects of your spiritual growth is that person responsible for? Which are *you* responsible for?
2. What are some things that Jesus does for you that the high priest used to do for believers in God?
3. Why is Jesus more sufficient than any other high priest to connect you to God?

Lifeline:

Your preacher, priest, or pastor might get you to church, but only Jesus can get you to God.

THE NEW COVENANT

"Behold, the days are coming, says the Lord, when I will effect a new covenant with the house of Israel and with the house of Judah. . . . I will put My laws into their minds, and I will write them on their hearts. And I will be their God, and they shall be My people. . . . For I will be merciful to their iniquities, and I will remember their sins no more."

↤ Hebrews 8:8, 10, 12

In the Bible, the strongest agreement between two people wasn't a handshake, an oath, or even a written contract. The most unbreakable bonds were formed when two people, two tribes, or two nations made a covenant with each other. Historians tell us that the following guidelines frequently marked the establishment of a covenant.

1. The two parties exchanged coats to signify, "I am taking all your needs upon myself."
2. The two parties exchanged weapons to show, "If you ever have an enemy, he's mine too!"
3. The two covenant partners cut their palms or wrists and shook hands, mixing their blood. This indicated, "My life is yours and your life is mine."
4. The two rubbed dye into their wounds so the scar would always be noticeable—a sign that the covenant was binding forever.
5. The pair would then split an animal in half and walk between the parts, pledging to each other, "If I ever break this covenant, may God do this (or worse) to me." (See Genesis 15:7-21.)
6. The two would share a covenant meal of bread (symbolizing the body) and "the fruit of the vine" (symbolizing blood). This shared meal finalized the covenant. Now the two were one. From that point on, they were committed to living for each other.

When God made a covenant with Abraham, the Jewish nation became His chosen people. But when Jesus died on the cross, He established a new covenant between God and *all* people. His blood was shed. The scars in His hands are signs of His unbreakable agreement. And the Lord's Supper is a recurring reminder of this incredible, divine, eternal act of sacrificial love.

Discussion Starters:

1. What right did Jesus have to make a covenant with God on your behalf?
2. The covenant wasn't finalized until *after* the covenant meal was shared. In what ways does an understanding of covenants affect your view of Communion?
3. Is your covenant with God a "done deal," or is there still something *you* need to do to make it official?

Lifeline:

Jesus has certainly come through with His part of the covenant. What are you doing for Him?

ONCE AND FOR ALL

"And inasmuch as it is appointed for men to die once and after this comes judgment, so Christ also, having been offered once to bear the sins of many, will appear a second time for salvation without reference to sin, to those who eagerly await Him."

⟿ Hebrews 9:27-28

The Jewish religion had a once-a-year ceremony when the high priest would go into the Holy of Holies in the tabernacle or temple—the one time he was allowed to enter this sacred room—for the sole purpose of placing the blood of a goat upon the cover of the Ark of the Covenant (the "mercy seat"). This offering to God for the sins of the people was good for only one year and was effective only for the Hebrew people the high priest represented.

Joseph Smith and Brigham Young taught that the blood of Jesus *partially* sufficed for the forgiveness of sins. But to complete their salvation, Mormons are expected to accept the teachings of Joseph Smith, conform to a lifestyle of strict religious practices, and commit to a lifetime of rigorous devotion to doing good works.

Other world religions offer a diversity of man-made salvation myths, such as returning to earth in different lives until you finally "get it right" and can move on to heaven.

Yet Scripture clearly teaches that Jesus provides a much better way to salvation. For one thing, His way is the *only* way to God. But in addition, His death on the cross was singularly sufficient to pay for sins—one sacrifice, one time, for all nations and all people who ever live.

All you have to do to take advantage of His incredible gift is to have faith, give Him your heart, and let His Spirit dwell within you. That seals it! You're His forever.

You're a child of God.

You're completely forgiven.

You want to please Him.

You want to tell others about Him.

Jesus died once for all. Just once. For *all*. You make one genuine commitment to serve Him as you invite Him to be your Lord and Savior. Just once. And believe me, it's for *good*!

Discussion Starters:

1. Read Hebrews 9:24-28. What verse refutes the New Age idea that you'll come back to earth as someone else in a later life?
2. How does the passage explain Jesus' blood sacrifice for us?
3. How does the passage clarify Jesus' statement that He is the only way to God?

Lifeline:

Jesus sacrificed Himself to provide us unity with God. As we sacrifice ourselves for others, we will experience unity in the family of God.

TWO BEAMS OF THE CROSS

"Let us hold fast the confession of our hope without wavering, for He who promised is faithful; and let us consider how to stimulate one another to love and good deeds, not forsaking our own assembling together, as is the habit of some, but encouraging one another; and all the more as you see the day drawing near."

↪ Hebrews 10:23-25

Years ago Cooper saw a picture of Jesus hanging lifelessly on the cross. He was overwhelmed by emotional trauma and looked up at me with eyes full of tears. He asked hopefully, "Daddy, did God take away the pain?"

"No," I said softly, "God didn't take away the pain." I explained that Jesus' nerves shattered just like yours or mine would. He was a sinless *human* sacrifice, because no other substitute could restore our relationship with God that sin had destroyed.

That's what I think about when I see the vertical beam of the cross. It stands forever pointing skyward, triumphantly, toward God. Work done. Case closed. Sin paid. Sacrifice accomplished. Salvation purchased. Prayers answered.

Then, as I view the horizontal beam of the cross, I see where Jesus' hands were outstretched. I am reminded that you and I, out of hearts exploding with appreciation, have daily opportunities to reach out and demonstrate the love of Jesus to our parents, our kids, our spouses, our friends . . . even our enemies.

The agonizing reality of Jesus' work on the cross should create a tremor in your soul that shakes the stained-glass windows of your heart. The only possible response is an eternal sense of indescribable appreciation. And the only tangible way to show God how thankful you are is to show *others* and give Him the credit.

As the vertical beam of the cross reaches upward toward God's heart, so the horizontal beam reaches outward from the goodness of my heart to yours.

Discussion Starters:

1. Which needs more work in your life: your "upreach" to God, or your outreach to others?
2. How, specifically, can you show appreciation for Jesus' paying the price for your salvation?
3. How can you "stimulate one another to love and good deeds" this week?

Lifeline:

Express your gratitude for Jesus' sacrifice by being an encouragement to everyone around you.

THE ESSENCE OF FAITH

"Now faith is the assurance of things hoped for, the conviction of things not seen."

↜ Hebrews 11:1

By faith you believe in Jesus.

By faith you live for heaven.

By faith you carry your Bible to school.

By faith you attend your school Bible study group each week.

By faith you save sex for marriage.

By faith you say your prayers at night.

By faith you keep your body pure from drugs and alcohol.

By faith you avoid looking at all forms of pornography.

By faith you suffer ridicule and isolation for being a Christian.

By faith you avoid movies with nudity and profanity.

By faith you witness to your friends.

By faith you boldly confess, when asked, "I'm a follower of Christ."

By faith David told his drug buddies, "No more. I'm a Christian now." Then he told his girlfriend, "The next girl I touch will be my wife."

By faith Dora Tenenoff waits faithfully for her missionary husband who was captured in Colombia seven long years ago. For more than 2,500 lonely nights, she has crawled into bed alone—praying, hoping, crying, and believing that someday he will return to her side.

By faith my dad writes my mom a love letter almost every morning. They've been happily married now for 65 years.

By faith my mom gladly cooks his meals, washes his clothes, and even removes his work boots after a long day.

By faith Cooper listens to my advice and calls his mom when he's out later than expected so she won't have to worry about him.

By faith we can look forward to joining those already in God's "hall of fame" (Hebrews 11).

By faith we live forever in heaven.

Discussion Starters:

1. Without referring to today's verse, how would you define *faith*?
2. Complete this sentence five different ways: "By faith I . . . "
3. Read Hebrews 11 to see how other great people of God have demonstrated faith. What are some other contemporary ways you've witnessed people in your family serving God and each other by faith?

Lifeline:

What are you hoping for today? What things do you believe in that you haven't (yet) seen? Have faith!

FAN SUPPORT

"Therefore, since we have so great a cloud of witnesses surrounding us, . . . let us run with endurance the race that is set before us, fixing our eyes on Jesus, the author and perfecter of faith."

~ Hebrews 12:1-2a

Neither my eyes nor my feet will ever forget the walk into the great domed stadium in Houston for my first bowl game. The stadium was filled with screaming fans, many of whom had traveled a great distance to cheer us on as we played the giants of Oklahoma University. It was as if we could feel our fans pulling us across the goal line time after time as we accumulated 28 bloody, sweaty points—one more than "Goliath's" mere 27.

The author of Hebrews wants us to picture our lives as being on a playing field. Your Coach, Jesus Himself, provides the plays He wants you to run as you go to school, play sports, perform music, and go about your day. You have quite a playbook that includes purity, godliness, forgiveness, encouragement, kindness, diligence, and more.

On the other side of the field, Satan is also calling plays to thwart your progress for God. "Take a short cut." "Tell a small lie." "Cheat on that exam." "Go ahead, lust a little." "You can skip Bible study today."

And some days the competition is close. You get confused, tired, and ready to quit. But you're on a playing field surrounded by supportive fans! Look up at the faithful Old Testament characters who anticipated the promised Messiah but didn't get to know Him. They desperately want you to know you can have "something better" (Hebrews 11:37-40). Then look at your friends and family members who love you dearly and want you to succeed in this game of life.

And finally, look at Jesus. Yes, He's your Coach, but He's also your biggest cheerleader. He knows exactly what you're going through. Watch His lips move and hear His voice: "I did it, and so can you."

Discussion Starters:

1. How does it feel to know that caring supporters are aware of your struggles in your "game of life"?
2. The next time you're about to give up, how can you tap into the support of your number-one fan—Jesus Himself? What difference will His encouragement make to you?
3. Review the "cloud of witnesses" in Hebrews 11. Which person might best understand what you're going through? Why?

Lifeline:

Jesus "endured the cross, despising the shame, and has sat down at the right hand of the throne of God" (Hebrews 12:2). After your hardest trials will come your most magnificent victories.

UNDEFILED

"Marriage is to be held in honor among all, and the marriage bed is to be undefiled; for fornicators and adulterers God will judge."

⇝ Hebrews 13:4

All I wanted was a soft drink, but the wrapper around the bottle also carried a promise: *"Find love on Wednesday night on Fox TV."*

Millions of teens and adults look for love on TV *every* night—with or without the reminders of soft drink companies. You can find pretty much whatever you're looking for: him and her, him and him, or her and her. The people are usually young, attractive, partially nude, and unmarried. The "love" is frequently sexual, inconsequential, wild, and free of worry, guilt, or shame.

Meanwhile, in real life, love is much harder to find. The promises on soft drink labels are coming up short. The words and actions that make the TV relationships seem so fulfilling are disappointingly empty. When I hear from real-life people who sacrifice their morals, Christian beliefs, and bodies for what they perceive to be love, their letters are frequently tear-stained. Somebody's not telling the truth! And millions of young people are feeling very real pain because of false promises. Do we really need to watch this stuff? Do we have to keep falling for every sensuous (yet senseless) ploy?

The steady truth of Scripture comes shining through the beguiling fog of falsehood with the reliability of the morning sunrise: "The marriage bed is to be undefiled."

If you're not married, sex with another person is wrong. It's a sin against God. It's a sin against you. It's a sin against him or her. It hurts; it takes away from a honeymoon; it destroys a pure relationship. It's true whether you're heterosexual, bisexual, homosexual, in junior high, in high school, in college, adult, Democrat, Republican, American, European, Antarctican, whatever, whoever, wherever.

God invented sex. He wrote the book on it. He wants your wedding, honeymoon, and marriage to be fantastic, enchanting, and never-ending. So enjoy a good soft drink once in a while and watch TV occasionally. But don't let either sway you from God's firm and loving reminder, "The marriage bed is to be undefiled."

Discussion Starters:

1. To what extent are your friends infatuated by TV "love"?
2. Why are so many people hooked on TV romance? Why do many fall as a result?
3. What is God's provision if and when we sin in these areas? What, then, is *our* responsibility?

Lifeline:

Preparing for a great marriage begins today with a pure mind and a pure heart.

1 Peter

If you read my books or hear me speak, you probably feel like you know Jamie Jo, my oldest daughter, as if she were one of your own best friends. Jamie has loved God since her earliest memory. She has a passion for the lost and a compassion for the poor. She is a wonderful friend maker who sets a beautiful example for the rest of us. Jamie's soft, gentle heart and her love for God come through clearly as she writes the devotionals for 1 Peter.

Peter was Jesus' most outspoken follower. His passion for knowing and following Jesus made him a "rock" in Scripture. His eloquence in this book assures you that these words weren't written by a mere fisherman on the shores of Galilee but by the Holy Spirit Himself as He breathed the words of God into Peter's pen.

REFINED LIKE GOLD

"You have been distressed by various trials, so that the proof of your faith, being more precious than gold which is perishable, even though tested by fire, may be found to result in praise and glory and honor at the revelation of Jesus Christ."

↩ 1 Peter 1:6-7

Gold is one of the most beautiful and precious elements found in the earth. And "in the earth" is a key distinction of gold. When gold is encased in rocks among the dirt, it looks nothing at all like the 24-carat metal we see in mall jewelry stores. It is dirty and impure.

Before gold becomes something you would want to wear around your finger or neck, it must be refined. Refining is a purification process involving heat, the application of acid, and/or other methods. The purpose is to start with gold-bearing ore and remove all the impurities, leaving gold in its purest form. While you might not look twice at a dirty rock containing gold ore, after the gold has been extracted and refined, it makes people "oooh" and "ahhh."

How would you like to make people "oooh" and "ahhh" about your golden character? What if someone thought you were as precious and priceless as gold? Someone does. The very reason Jesus allows us to undergo trials is because He can use them as a refining process to purify us.

Even though we may have accepted Jesus' offer of salvation, our sinful impurities cling to us and aren't easily removed from our lives. But our sufferings make our impurities more evident. As we see them more clearly, we are able to deal with them. As we keep skimming and scraping off all our ungodly qualities, what's left is more pure and beautiful than before.

Refining fires may be intense, but they aren't ultimately destructive. Indeed, the heat is an essential part of the process to transform a glittery piece of rock into valuable jewelry to be treasured for generations. Genuine gold makes it through the heat. So do genuine Christians.

Discussion Starters:

1. Have you been able to identify the purifying purpose of recent trials, or do you need to start looking a bit harder?
2. Do you think anyone can completely avoid trials in life? If not, how can our trials make us better people?
3. Can you think of both a positive and negative example of how you have responded to "heat" in the past? How can you prepare to face future "refining fires"?

Lifeline:

If we endure the refining process with joy, knowing that the heat will never become greater than we can stand, just imagine what precious jewels we can be.

THE LITTLE BIBLE MAN

"As obedient children, do not be conformed to the former lusts which were yours in your ignorance, but like the Holy One who called you, be holy yourselves also in all your behavior; because it is written, 'You shall be holy, for I am holy.'"

⮜ 1 Peter 1:14-16

When I was a kid, I ate dirt out of a potted plant by our staircase. A friend of mine was so jealous when his little brother was born that he shattered the sliding glass door with a baseball bat.

We all did silly things when we were kids, and now we can look back and laugh at the things we did that were immature or even wrong. One of my favorite stories is about my best friend. As a child, he never did anything wrong, although there was a "Little Bible Man" who kept getting him into trouble. For example, one night he wet the bed. When his parents asked him if he had done it, he innocently shook his head and said, "The Little Bible Man did it."

I think we all have our own versions of "Little Bible Man" whom we would like to take the blame for our wrongdoings. (Flip Wilson went to the other extreme to assign blame when he frequently proclaimed, "The devil made me do it!")

Today's passage urges us to be "obedient children" and "not be conformed to the former lusts which were yours in your ignorance." Peter is confirming what the apostle Paul wrote about doing away with "childish things" (1 Corinthians 13:11). So often we act in ignorance and then look for someone to blame. But if we would wait to hear the prompting of God *before* acting, we wouldn't need to lay blame on anyone else.

We need to keep in mind that childish stories are only funny when they're happening to children. Immaturity is amusing only in reference to kids with immature thoughts and actions. As adults, immaturity and childishness will only earn the scorn or pity of others. So it's time to start taking responsibility for ourselves. Let's leave behind the "Little Bible Man" as we become intelligent men and women who live according to the Bible.

Discussion Starters:

1. What were some of the "childish things" of your past? Why is it important to put them away?
2. What's the best way to make the transformation from childishness to holiness?
3. What is one specific example of how you can act out of self-control and maturity today?

Lifeline:

Being children of God, we grow through the study of His Word and our constant communication with Him in prayer. He will then direct our steps out of childhood and into spiritual maturity.

THE RIGHT CORNERSTONE

"And coming to Him as to a living stone which has been rejected by men, but is choice and precious in the sight of God, you also, as living stones, are being built up as a spiritual house for a holy priesthood, to offer up spiritual sacrifices acceptable to God through Jesus Christ. For this is contained in Scripture: 'Behold, I lay in Zion a choice stone, a precious corner stone, and he who believes in Him will not be disappointed.' "

⎈ I Peter 2:4-6

Having recently had a new home built, today's passage has a much more personal meaning for me than ever before. The house isn't a skyscraper or a mansion, but I have come to understand the importance of a building's *foundation*. Whether building the Taj Majal or a small cottage, the right foundation is needed to bear the weight of the walls. The other bricks or stones will be positioned on top of it, so a crooked or cracked foundation can soon bring down an entire building. And in biblical times, the cornerstone was the key part of a structure's foundation.

It would be safe to say that the foundation of a house is the most important single piece, yet most people don't even think about it. It's seldom seen and never decorated. Sometimes a fancy ceremony is held to "lay the cornerstone," but then it's stuck in the ground to lie unseen, quietly and faithfully serving its purpose.

I found myself getting much more excited about the incidentals of my new home, such as finding the perfect wallpaper and the prettiest comforter. I dreamed at night of hanging the right pictures and finding just the right furniture. To be honest, I didn't give one thought to finding the perfect foundation. One part was so important that the security of my house depended on it, and I just kept flipping through paint samples.

But then, we all tend to ignore a lot of "foundations" in life. Where would a football team be without its linemen to "bear the weight" of its opponents? Where would a business be without the office staff and maintenance crew? Yet we give attention to the "colorful" people who seem to tower above those bland foundations.

More importantly, who is the foundation of your life? You're soon going to be dealing with a lot of "heavy" issues. Can your foundation bear the weight? If not, Peter suggests One who can.

Discussion Starters:

1. Why is a good foundation important?
2. Who or what is the "foundation" on which you are building your life?
3. What is the proof that you have chosen the right foundation?

Lifeline:

With a solid foundation, no storm (trial) will ever destroy us.

OBEDIENT CHILDREN

"Submit yourselves for the Lord's sake to every human institution, whether to a king as the one in authority, or to governors as sent by him for the punishment of evildoers and the praise of those who do right."

$\longleftarrow$ 1 Peter 2:13-14

I was raised in a godly home with parents who honored God and His Word. But can I tell you a secret? It sometimes grated on my human nature, and I occasionally harbored feelings of anger and rebellion in my soul.

For example, I wasn't allowed to do everything other kids did. I didn't get to go to certain movies. Potential parties and public gatherings were checked out before I could attend. Boys who asked me out were critiqued and inspected before they were given my parents' seal of approval.

As a result, I felt that my peers ridiculed me and I was discriminated against. I kept my pain and loneliness deep inside, and I was very unhappy much of the time. I resisted memorizing Bible verses, which my parents urged me and my siblings to do each day.

Yet I loved my parents and respected their teachings, so I complied with their wishes. Now, as I look back, I had a happy life. I was rewarded with God's gift of a wonderful husband who loves me as the girl he always desired in a wife. In fact, I recently thanked my dad publicly for the way he raised us kids. We reap blessings in our lives every day because of the path we walked while growing up.

As a teenager I was usually obedient, though many times reluctantly so. I hope you can learn early in life that obedience—whether to governments or parents—is God's design for His children. The sooner we can learn *willing* obedience, the sooner our lives will take a turn for the better.

Discussion Starters:

1. What are a couple of areas where you resist being obedient to someone in authority?
2. How do you respond when you pursue something you know is wrong and later regret it?
3. What advice can you offer someone who is struggling to be obedient to God's Word?

Lifeline:

Look for signs of rebellion in your life and eliminate them. Try to appreciate the advice of authority figures, and find ways to use it to make yourself a better person.

THE DEPTH OF BEAUTY

"Your adornment must not be merely external—braiding the hair, and wearing gold jewelry, or putting on dresses; but let it be the hidden person of the heart, with the imperishable quality of a gentle and quiet spirit, which is precious in the sight of God."

↪ 1 Peter 3:3-4

Several years ago a large number of people in the United States and Canada, eager to see live news coverage of the wedding of Princess Diana, stumbled out of bed at an incredibly early hour. They were rewarded for their efforts by perhaps the most magnificent wedding in recent history. The church was filled with those fortunate enough to be invited, while outside stood an enormous crowd of "commoners." The overhead camera showed the train of Diana's elaborate gown flowing down the entire length of the chapel aisle. The formal organ music and expensive arrays of flowers added to the pomp of the ceremony.

Yet my dad frequently tells a story about an even more beautiful bride and her wedding. (In fact, he tells it on page 119.) He was performing the marriage ceremony at an outdoor church where a tiny group of friends and relatives sat on rock pews with their feet in gravel. But when the bride appeared, the guests could have been in Westminster Abbey for all they knew. In a white dress that cost less than $100, she was the most glamorous and strikingly beautiful bride in the history of weddings. In the simplicity of her wedding, she was radiant! Her eyes glowed from a deep love for her husband. Her smile radiated from her gentle heart. No expensive dress or fancy church could have made her any more beautiful.

Peter challenges women to quit worrying so much about external beauty—hair, jewelry, clothes, etc. It's inner beauty that matters. You've heard it said that beauty is only skin deep. That's only partially true. If you're a young woman devoted to God, your beauty goes all the way down to your spirit.

Discussion Starters:

1. Peter was addressing wives specifically (1 Peter 3:1). Do you think the truth of today's passage applies only to women? Why or why not?
2. Why do you think the Bible places so much emphasis on inner beauty rather than on the clothes you wear or how you fix yourself up?
3. What are five ways you can demonstrate a "gentle and quiet spirit" today?

Lifeline:

How do you know if you're truly beautiful? Spend some time with a blind person and see what he or she thinks!

THE OSTRICH RESPONSE

"To sum up, all of you be harmonious, sympathetic, brotherly, kindhearted, and humble in spirit; not returning evil for evil or insult for insult, but giving a blessing instead; for you were called for the very purpose that you might inherit a blessing."

⟿ 1 Peter 3:8-9

Give yourself a little test. For each of the following qualities or actions, rate yourself from 1 to 10. "One" means you *never* get it right and need a lot of help. "Ten" means you always act in that manner.

QUALITY/ACTION	MY SCORE
Being harmonious (getting along with others)	
Being sympathetic	
Being brotherly (friendly, protective, etc.)	
Being kindhearted	
Being humble in spirit (not always insisting on your way)	
Ignoring evil acts others do to you	
Letting insults bounce off you	
"Blessing" others (wishing the best for them, as God would do)	

Did you make an 80? When I read today's verses, I want to be like an ostrich and hide my head in the ground so God won't see me!

Did you ever wish you could bite your tongue after blurting out something dumb, bitter, or hurtful, when it's too late to take it back? Do you ever insist on having the last word in an argument? Does something deep within drive you to get even when someone hurts, offends, or insults you?

If we don't quickly deal with personal resentment, it soon becomes a habit—an ongoing attitude! And few things are as unattractive as a person who is always vengeful and never gracious or kind. The unpleasant emotions can even affect us physically, leaving us with a hard and sour countenance. And worst of all, we continue to hurt God and lose friends.

It's time to take our heads out of the sand and take a good look at the things God has given us. Then perhaps we can learn to tolerate the shortcomings of others and treat them as we wish to be treated.

Discussion Starters:

1. What evil or insult are you currently finding hardest to forgive? What are you willing to do to improve the situation?
2. Which of the qualities listed in today's passage do you most need to work on? How do you know?
3. What are the dangers of ignoring Peter's instructions? What are the advantages of obeying them?

Lifeline:

When people repeatedly annoy you, take the advice of my great-grandmother and "Kill 'em with kindness."

BRANCHING OUT

"For the time already past is sufficient for you to have carried out the desire of the Gentiles, having pursued a course of sensuality, lusts, drunkenness, carousing, drinking parties and abominable idolatries. In all this, they are surprised that you do not run with them into the same excesses of dissipation, and they malign you; but they will give account to Him who is ready to judge the living and the dead."

⌒ 1 Peter 4:3-5

When you become a Christian, you probably expect a lot of good changes—forgiveness, freedom, a fresh start, eternity in heaven, and more! So everything is great, right?

To be honest, not *all* the changes in your life will be pleasant ones. For one thing, you are likely to feel stress from being pulled toward your new Christian commitments while still caring what your non-Christian friends say and think about you. They may begin to "malign" you because "you do not run with them into the same [bad habits]." And it's no fun to be accused of not being fun anymore!

First and foremost, you must pursue your relationship with God. It is there where you will find strength. Then, when you are maturing and growing spiritually stronger, you can deal with your non-believing friends.

I like a story told by Dr. Howard Hendricks, professor of theology at Dallas Seminary, in his book. A woman had moved and was complaining that her new neighbors were all nonbelievers. In response, Dr. Hendricks said, "Oh, that's wonderful! You are blessed." The woman was taken aback, but he explained that she and her husband had a wonderful opportunity to show their neighbors the love and joy of Jesus as they settled into their new home.

Being with other Christians helps us stay on the straight and narrow, and we should appreciate their support. But remember that it is our mission to branch out and bring unbelievers to Christ. Some will respond to our efforts. Others may reject or ridicule. All we can do is emulate Christ with our speech and actions, and make a positive difference wherever we can.

Discussion Starters:

1. How can you become a better example of Jesus Christ for those who watch you?
2. How can you share the gospel in your everyday environment?
3. How can you keep yourself strong and in touch with Christ?

Lifeline:

"Be anxious for nothing, but in everything by prayer and supplication with thanksgiving let your requests be made known to God. And the peace of God, which surpasses all comprehension, will guard your hearts and your minds in Christ Jesus" (Philippians 4:6-7).

HAPPILY HOSPITABLE

"Be hospitable to one another without complaint. As each one has received a special gift, employ it in serving one another as good stewards of the manifold grace of God. Whoever speaks, is to do so as one who is speaking the utterances of God; whoever serves is to do so as one who is serving by the strength which God supplies; so that in all things God may be glorified through Jesus Christ, to whom belongs the glory and dominion forever and ever."

⟿ 1 Peter 4:9-11

My grandmother is the most hospitable lady I have ever met, heard of, or even read about. My lifelong dream is to be as hospitable and unselfish as she is. I love going to visit her. Whether you are a grandchild, a friend, or even a complete stranger, she gives you the treatment of an honored guest.

Recently Gran'ma had been working hard all day and had settled into her chair to put her feet up and read a good book. Just then the doorbell rang and in came four grade-schoolers bringing her flowers and cookies. As exhausted as she was, Gran'ma got right up as if she had been expecting their visit for weeks and set out four glasses of lemonade and cookies. The children made themselves at home around her kitchen table. Gran'ma talked with them about their days and about school and their families. They were so happy to be "at home" in my grandmother's house that they ended up staying about an hour, just talking and eating. Then they thanked her and left, leaving their crumbs and dirty dishes behind. Gran'ma happily cleaned up after them and began cooking dinner for her husband. Her afternoon of relaxing and reading had been disturbed, but she was the only one who knew.

In Gran'ma I see that hospitality is not only a God-given gift, but also a talent that she works to develop. She serves with "the strength which God supplies," just as Peter instructs. Everyone who knows her firmly believes that my grandmother is the most accommodating hostess in history. I strongly agree.

Discussion Starters:

1. Why do you think God gives people different spiritual gifts, such as hospitality, compassion, and leadership?
2. What is a gift that God has given you? In what ways are you using it?
3. Who is someone who impresses you with his or her hospitality? What can you do this week to let that person know how much you appreciate him or her?

Lifeline:

If we serve each other using God's strength, then we will be serving each other constantly.

LOOK AT ME!

"Therefore humble yourselves under the mighty hand of God, that He may exalt you at the proper time, casting all your anxiety on Him, because He cares for you."

⌐ 1 Peter 5:6-7

Have you ever heard the expression "You gotta blow your own horn because no one is going to do it for you"? Do you agree?

Aren't there times when you just want to stand on top of your desk at school and yell, "Look at me! I'm a beautiful, talented, hardworking person who deserves better than you guys are treating me"? Don't you want to jump up on the bench and scream, "Hey, Coach! Look at me! I'm better than most of those guys out there! Why do I have to sit on this bench and shine the pine the whole game?" Do you ever just want to smack someone and say, "Quit acting like I'm invisible. Look at me"?

Most of us have such inclinations. Yet when we see other people who "toot their own horns," we don't usually like what we see.

Humility is one of the hardest attributes of God to acquire. Some people shout their accomplishments from the rooftops, probably to cover their inner insecurities. Others seem to have it all together, content in the knowledge that God loves them and without any pressing need for a "day in the sun." Still other quiet people continue to feel that inner "Look at me!" impulse, yet they live with the frustration of never seeming to get noticed. Sometimes I think it may be easier for people who excel at everything—sports, grades, popularity, etc.—to be humble. They can show a little humility now and then and still be in the limelight. Humility may come harder for "average" people.

Sometimes the best we can do is realize that *God* notices. He sees our beauty, talents, desires, and potential. After all, He put all those things within us, and we should continue to use them for Him. If people don't notice now, they will someday. And until then, we can dump all our anxiety and frustration on Him.

When you find it difficult to be humble, remember that Jesus has set an example for us.

Discussion Starters:

1. Do you lean more toward "blowing your own horn" or being humble? Why?
2. How can Jesus' example of humility motivate you to be more humble?
3. How can you show humility the next time you're confronted with the criticism and rejection of others, or when they ignore you completely?

Lifeline:

Don't forget that it is those who are gentle who "will inherit the earth" (Matthew 5:5).

STALKING LIONS

"Be of sober spirit, be on the alert. Your adversary, the devil, prowls around like a roaring lion, seeking someone to devour. But resist him, firm in your faith, knowing that the same experiences of suffering are being accomplished by your brethren who are in the world."

↢ 1 Peter 5:8-9

Lions are marvelous creatures—huge, graceful, patient, and smart! I saw a TV special on how lions hunt, and I was truly amazed. Think how hungry you get right before lunch, and multiply that several times before you even approach a lion's appetite. Personally, I'm not usually willing to wait in a long drive-through line, much less stalk, chase, and kill my hamburger. But that is exactly what lions do.

The TV special showed a group of lions waiting for the right moment to attack a herd of zebras. Two lions stayed near the herd on one side of a nearby river, while three more waited patiently on the other side. They just lay there in the grass for hours. The zebras were completely unaware of any danger as they ate their grass in peace.

When the pair of lions determined the time was finally right, they attacked. Just as planned, the zebras panicked and rushed to cross the river. The lions on the other side of the river easily spotted the weakest zebra in the herd and zeroed in on it. I also learned from the television special that zebras are one of the toughest animals for lions to kill. To begin with, they are fast. And when cornered, they can bite an approaching attacker as they deliver a mean kick to any coming from behind.

Even though the unfortunate zebra put up a valiant fight, the lions had caught him unprepared and unaware of danger. Their patience paid off and they ate their fill.

Peter chooses his imagery well when he compares the devil to a lion. Satan is sneaky, mean, patient . . . and always hungry. As Christians, we must never let down our guard. The danger is *always* out there. But like sheep, if we stay close to the flock and remain responsive to our Shepherd, that lion will never get us.

Discussion Starters:

1. Can you think of an instance when a friend let down his or her guard and suffered the consequences of an attack by the "hungry lion" known as Satan?
2. When have you recently been most susceptible to attack?
3. Specifically, how can you best protect yourself from future attacks? (Reread today's passage.)

Lifeline:

"Greater is He who is in you than he who is in the world" (1 John 4:4).

2 PeTeR

Peter wrote his second letter shortly before he was killed because of his faith in Jesus. He urgently encourages us to be ready and alert so we will not fall into the snare of indifference and false teaching at a time when we desperately need to walk in the light of Jesus. Peter reminds us of the promise and hope of eternity that we have, thanks to the death and resurrection of Jesus. With this reminder, we are warned to return to the true gospel, which comes only through Jesus Christ.

My thanks once again to Brett Causey for writing these devotionals.

EVERYTHING YOU NEED?

"Grace and peace be multiplied to you in the knowledge of God and of Jesus our Lord; seeing that His divine power has granted to us everything pertaining to life and godliness, through the true knowledge of Him who called us by His own glory and excellence."

↬ 2 Peter 1:2-3

In the climax of *Rocky IV,* Rocky Balboa fights a Russian boxer to avenge the death of Apollo Creed. Their boxing match takes place in Moscow. Rocky not only faces an incredibly powerful opponent, but he also is surrounded by a hostile crowd. An entire country is pulling against him. The two fighters slug each other until they are both bruised, bleeding, cut, and exhausted. Can you relate? I can! Sometimes I feel like I cannot take another step because I hurt so much. I feel like the whole world is against me.

God's Word never promises that when we take up the cross of Christ, our problems will disappear. On the contrary, I believe the opposite is true. When you lift up a light in a dark world, the darkness opposes it. Scripture clearly expresses that God has an enemy who will do anything to turn us from the truth. Even though the enemy comes against us, One who is greater always stands with us in our trials and sufferings.

As Peter anticipated his execution, do you think he was fearful or felt alone? Probably so, yet he wrote a powerful message to us. He assures us that we have everything we need to serve, live, love, and grow in Jesus in order to become the people we were created to be. His joy and love for Jesus didn't waver during tough times. When his life might have seemed bleakest, he discovered that Jesus was all he needed.

Whenever your circumstances seem overwhelming, remember that Jesus has transformed you into a new creation. Refuse to give up. Trust that you have been given everything you need because you have been given Jesus!

Discussion Starters:

1. What situations are you involved in where it seems as though the whole world is against you? What will it take for you to trust Jesus to deliver you from such situations?
2. How can you prevent your joy and trust in Jesus from wavering when you encounter difficult times?
3. Do you believe in a God who knows you personally and who makes miracles a reality? If so, how should you respond to Him?

Lifeline:

Reflect on an experience in the past that appeared to be hopeless but in which the Lord Jesus rescued you or delivered you—perhaps in an amazing way.

A NEW DEFINITION OF "EVERYTHING"

"The Lord knows how to rescue the godly from temptation, and to keep the unrighteous under punishment for the day of judgment."

⮌ 2 Peter 2:9

I recently heard Mrs. Sun Ok Lee speak at the Voice of the Martyrs National Missions Conference. She is a frail, small Korean woman. Only a few years ago, she was imprisoned in a North Korean labor camp where she witnessed the executions of many people, including Christians. She said that before she knew Christ, she first heard hymns from the singing of the imprisoned Christians. Mrs. Lee could not understand why these Christians refused to deny the man they called Jesus. They were promised physical freedom for themselves and their families if they would turn from their faith and join the Communist party. When they refused to become slaves to communism, many of them were put to death.

Mrs. Lee was released from prison and fled to South Korea, where she received the Lord Jesus Christ as her personal Savior. With tears streaming down her face, she told us that now she understands why the Christians in prison chose to be executed rather than turn their backs on Jesus. She had realized that to be a Christian, we must be willing to give up everything to follow Him. Her testimony brings a whole new meaning to the concept of "everything."

I thank God for the strength and courage of those Korean believers because we are faced with the same decision as they were. No, our lives may not be in jeopardy, but our eternal souls are. Are we willing to compromise our faith to gain popularity, money, or success?

What are *you* being offered that replaces Jesus as the most important thing in your life? And are you brave enough to make the right choice?

Discussion Starters:

1. Do you know anyone who has suffered for his or her faith in God? If so, how can you support that person?
2. We serve a God who causes "all things to work together for good to those who love [Him], to those who are called according to His purpose" (Romans 8:28). How might the unpleasant circumstances of your life be used by Him?
3. What are three things in your life that threaten to hinder your relationship with God? (Sports? Boyfriend or girlfriend? Work? Car?)

Lifeline:

Commit to pray every day this week for wisdom about the three things you have just listed.

WHEN TIME RUNS OUT

"With the Lord one day is like a thousand years, and a thousand years like one day. The Lord is not slow about His promise, as some count slowness, but is patient toward you, not wishing for any to perish but for all to come to repentance. But the day of the Lord will come like a thief."

⟿ 2 Peter 3:8-10

In the 1996 AFC championship game, the Indianapolis Colts played the Pittsburgh Steelers to determine who would be in the Super Bowl against the NFC champion Dallas Cowboys. The game was well played and evenly matched. With only a few seconds remaining, the Colts were down by four points and had only enough time left for one play. Jim Harbaugh took the snap and dropped back to pass as five wide receivers sprinted toward the end zone almost 60 yards away. The final seconds ticked off the clock as he threw the ball. The ball hit one of the receivers directly in the hands but bounced out. As the receiver fell to the ground, he made another grab at the ball, but it again slipped through his fingers. No more time. The game was over. The Colts lost and the Steelers advanced to the Super Bowl.

In football the game is over when the clock ticks down to zero. In our Christian lives, the race is over when Jesus comes back. What an awesome day that will be for those of us who have trusted Him with our hearts. We will rejoice as we begin eternity with our Lord. Others may wish for more time, but it will be too late. Many will be devastated and utterly heartbroken because they had the opportunity to accept Jesus but chose not to believe.

God desires to have a relationship with you, but He will never force you into one. You must choose to believe in Him. The ball is in your hands. He eagerly awaits your decision. But choose quickly. The clock is ticking.

Discussion Starters:

1. The Bible refers to a "book of life" in which Jesus has recorded the names of all those who have placed their faith in Him (Revelation 3:5; 20:12, 15). Is your name written in His book of life? How do you know?
2. What, if anything, are you doing to strengthen your personal relationship with God?
3. What do you hope to accomplish with your life before the clock runs out?

Lifeline:

If you knew this would be the last day God was going to give you before calling you home to heaven, what would you do? What is keeping you from doing those very things today?

Epistles of John

John, Jesus' disciple, is usually credited with writing five New Testament books: the Gospel that bears his name, the book of Revelation, and these three letters that follow the epistles of Peter. John frequently identified himself in third person as "the disciple whom Jesus loved," and he has much to say about the undeniable importance of love in his three short letters.

In his first letter he makes it clear that "the one who does not love does not know God, for God is love" (1 John 4:8). In his second letter, John connects love with truth and warns of deceivers attempting to mislead God's people. John's third letter is addressed to three men: Gaius, whom John encouraged and affirmed; Diotrephes, whom he criticized and confronted; and Demetrius, whom he praised. It embraces love and truth as well, but also emphasizes the value of grace and compassion.

In this next group of devotions, you'll see more of the great heart for God possessed by my young friend Brett Causey.

THE CHOICE IS YOURS

"This is the message we have heard from Him and announce to you, that God is Light, and in Him there is no darkness at all. If we say that we have fellowship with Him and yet walk in the darkness, we lie and do not practice the truth; but if we walk in the Light as He Himself is in the Light, we have fellowship with one another, and the blood of Jesus His Son cleanses us from all sin."

↩ 1 John 1:5-7

Two years ago, I set off on a backpacking trip with my friend Bill. The trip began with a long and uneventful 11-hour drive. Although it was well after dark when we arrived, and both of us were inexperienced hikers, we decided to strap on our head lamps and hike the four miles up to where we were planning to camp the first night. We made it to our destination, but during the night an unexpected storm blew in with strong winds and pelting rains. The temperature dropped to about 25 degrees. The next morning we decided to end our trip early and head down the mountain. But because we had hiked up in the dark, we failed to recognize the right trail. We took a wrong turn and spent the next two days wandering almost 35 miles in the freezing rain—all because we had made a decision to hike in the dark.

Each day you and I can choose to live with the guidance and direction of our Creator and Savior. Yet when we make our own plans, attempt to be in control, and disregard what He has for us, we choose to walk in darkness.

If we are not seeking the good and perfect plan God has for us (Jeremiah 29:11), we can easily start walking down a dark and destructive path. Jesus died a miserable death on the cross and arose from the dead so you and I may have the abundant life God offers. He is the Son of God who lights our paths. Let's choose to walk in the Light of our Father.

Discussion Starters:

1. Why is it important to seek God's plan for your life for the decisions you make each day?
2. Read Psalm 18:28. In what ways are you walking in darkness?
3. How can we help each other walk in the light of Christ?

Lifeline:

What hard decisions are you facing today? What can your other family members do to help you make the best choices?

THE ULTIMATE EXAMPLE

"The one who says he abides in Him ought himself to walk in the same manner as He walked."

⟿ 1 John 2:6

David was one of the better soccer players in the state of Alabama. He was also a Christian, a leader in his youth group, and active for God at his high school. Other students watched him because he didn't compromise his faith in Jesus.

David did have a bad temper, however, which surfaced while he played soccer. Because of his skill, opposing players often double- and triple-teamed him. In one game he was knocked down again and again, causing him to become increasingly frustrated and angry. David finally was knocked down one time too many and responded by punching out one of the other team's players. He received a red card, ejecting him from that game—and the next one. Later David was upset because he had let a lot of people down. Most importantly, he realized he had let Jesus down, so he decided to come up with a plan to control his temper.

During soccer games, he had the habit of wiping the sweat from his face with the collar of his shirt. He decided to put the letters WWJD inside his collar so that every time he wiped his face he would ask himself, *What would Jesus do*? As he was reminded to keep his focus on Jesus and reflect on how He would respond, David was better able to control his temper.

We often see WWJD on shirts and bracelets, but it is still easy to forget the power of Jesus' name and the example He has provided for us. That's why I like the alternative: WDJD, which stands for "What did Jesus do?" It's a reminder that Jesus gave up everything because He loves us. His was the ultimate example because He lived a perfect life. Jesus endured pain, suffering, insults, betrayals by His best friends, the crown of thorns, the nails, the cross . . . all because He loves us.

Discussion Starters:

1. What do you find the most difficult thing(s) to give up in order to follow Jesus? (Money? Activities? Friends?)
2. What can you do to focus more on His example for how to live your life?
3. What are some consequences you might experience if you don't stay focused on Jesus?

Lifeline:

How can your family be a better example of how Jesus might live in your community?

LET'S NOT KID OURSELVES

"We know love by this, that He laid down His life for us; and we ought to lay down our lives for the brethren. But whoever has the world's goods, and sees his brother in need and closes his heart against him, how does the love of God abide in him? Little children, let us not love with word or with tongue, but in deed and truth."

↜ 1 John 3:16-18

Some people are easy to love. We like to hang around people who are kind and friendly. But how about those who are more difficult to love—the ones who may be rude, shy, sick, or poor? God doesn't tell us to show love just to those who are easy to love; He commands us to love everyone.

I guarantee we would all be in a big heap of trouble if Jesus loved only those who are easy to love. Let's not kid ourselves; we don't make it easy for Jesus to love us. In fact, if He hadn't died on the cross, most of us would never be convinced that He could love us. And even then, many of us still don't believe it.

Jesus has an incredible passion for the people we tend to overlook. Remember how He gave sight to the blind? Can you see His hand on the festering skin of the leper? Do you hear the compassion in His voice as He talked with the woman at the well? Yes, Jesus loves the people we never see because we choose not to see them. We're usually too busy trying to show love to those who are easy to love.

Mother Teresa said, "Because we cannot see Christ, we cannot express our love to Him; but our neighbors we can always see, and we can do for them what, if we saw Him, we would like to do for Christ."

And this is how we should love.

Discussion Starters:

1. Who are the three people you have the hardest time loving?
2. Do you really believe it is possible to love Jesus by loving others? How would you rate your love for Jesus, on a scale from 1 to 10 (1 = lousy, 10 = terrific), based solely on how you treat other people?
3. Can you think of a time when one person's love made a significant difference in your life? Can you think of someone who needs to experience the love of Jesus expressed through you?

Lifeline:

How we live our lives is the most accurate reflection of what we believe. Today, create a game plan for how your family can do something nice for one of your neighbors.

FREEDOM

"Beloved, let us love one another, for love is from God; and everyone who loves is born of God and knows God. The one who does not love does not know God, for God is love. By this the love of God was manifested in us, that God has sent His only begotten Son into the world so that we might live through Him. In this is love, not that we loved God, but that He loved us and sent His Son to be the propitiation for our sins."

↪ 1 John 4:7-10

I was 17 years old when God really challenged me. At that point I knew a lot *about* God, but He wanted me to know *Him*. That's when I established a personal relationship with Jesus Christ. For the first time in my life I experienced love with no strings attached. His love for me didn't change according to how I performed on the baseball field or whether I made an A or a D in biology. He loves me because I am His, and He created me.

My high school years were definitely the most painful and toughest of my life. When I was a sophomore, my dad moved out. Yet it is during such times that God meets us right where we are. That's when God offered me His unconditional love and I chose to accept it.

During those years, I saw God's sacrificial love reflected in my mother's actions. After my parents divorced, my mom gave up many things she might have enjoyed so she could provide for my sisters and me. She gave without expecting much in return. Her sacrificial heart showed me God's love.

John 3:16 speaks powerfully of love so strong that God sacrificed His own Son so you and I can have the gift of eternity with Him. It was God's love that drew Peter from his fishing nets and Matthew from his position of prosperity and power to follow Jesus. After they met Him and experienced His love for others, their lives changed drastically. So can yours.

Discussion Starters:

1. Do you believe God loves you unconditionally, or do you believe His love depends on your behavior? Give some specific examples.
2. Has your life changed because of a personal encounter with Jesus? If so, in what ways?
3. How can you demonstrate sacrificial love in your family? In your friendships? In your school activities?

Lifeline:

The heart is the key to the Christian life. The truth of the gospel is intended to free us to love God and others with our whole hearts. Are you willing to offer your whole heart back to God?

SWEET VICTORY

"For whatever is born of God overcomes the world; and this is the victory that has overcome the world—our faith. Who is the one who overcomes the world, but he who believes that Jesus is the Son of God?"

⟿ 1 John 5:4-5

It was the biggest football game of the year for both the Auburn Tigers and the Alabama Crimson Tide. The score was Alabama 17 and Auburn 15, with only 15 seconds remaining in the 1997 Iron Bowl. The ball was resting on the 23-yard line as Jaret Holmes, the Auburn kicker, trotted out to try for his fourth field goal of the game. With 93,000 fans going crazy, Jaret calmly booted a 40-yarder to win the game, 18-17. It was a sweet victory. Jaret later shared that this kick was one of the most incredible moments of his life.

Jaret Holmes had reason to celebrate. I remember him working hard in high school to recover from knee surgery. I can recall his many sessions of weightlifting and running wind sprints, the long hours of sweat and exhaustion. He eventually overcame his potentially career-ending injury, so his celebration was especially sweet.

Jaret is a Christian whose football talents have given him many opportunities to talk with others about Jesus. After speaking at a kicking camp, a couple of guys were very interested in knowing more about Jesus. Jaret was excited to share what Jesus had done in his life and to see God work in the lives of others. He said that all the field goals he had ever made could not compare to sharing Jesus with those two guys.

Romans 10:9 tells us that if we confess with our mouths that Jesus is Lord and believe in our hearts that God raised Him from the dead, we will be saved. If you choose to accept Jesus into your heart, you are going to heaven, where there will be no more tears, pain, or suffering. All the field goals and accomplishments of a lifetime cannot compare to seeing our Maker face-to-face. No victory will ever be sweeter.

Discussion Starters:

1. Have you ever suffered an injury or been through an intense personal struggle? If so, how did it feel when you finally overcame the problem?
2. The Bible says that we will all stand before God to be judged. Are you confident you will go to heaven? Why or why not?
3. In addition to believing in Jesus, how else should you prepare for judgment day? (See 2 Corinthians 5:10.)

Lifeline:

Suppose a fellow student reads the verses at the top of this page and asks, "How does believing in Jesus help you to overcome the world?" How would you respond?

HIDE AND SEEK

"Now I ask you . . . not as though I were writing to you a new commandment, but the one which we have had from the beginning, that we love one another. And this is love, that we walk according to His commandments."

↜ 2 John 5-6

I heard a true story of a medical missionary team that traveled to a remote village in Africa. The missionaries performed a simple operation and restored the sight of a man who had been blind since birth. After one day of celebration, the man disappeared. A week later the missionaries saw him returning, holding one end of a rope. Holding on to the other end were 30 blind men.

What an example of walking in love! The man was given sight and he immediately wanted to share the gift with those who couldn't see. It should also be our model for evangelism. You and I have received the greatest gift ever given. Are we driven by enthusiasm to share it with others? If we had the cure for AIDS, we would call a big press conference and tell the world. The love and forgiveness of Jesus is the "cure" to sin and death. Why aren't we more excited to spread the good news?

As a child, you probably played hide-and-seek. One person who was "it" counted while everyone else ran to find a good place to hide. After a period of time the counter would shout, "Home free!" meaning it was safe for any remaining hiders to come in without being penalized. This game is a perfect picture of how we can share our faith. Like Adam and Eve, many people tend to hide from God. They may be hiding in your schools, on your sports teams, in your neighborhood, and even in your own home. It's our job to look for these people and share with them the good news of Jesus. And the good news is that God has called "Home free!" He wants us to come to Him without fear of penalty. Everyone needs to hear about a God who passionately loves them.

Who's going to share Jesus with those sitting in class, on your school bus, or at the grocery store? That's right. *You're* "it."

Discussion Starters:

1. Do you really believe that everyone needs Christ? Why?
2. Who are five people you talk to every day that to your knowledge don't have a personal relationship with Jesus?
3. In what practical ways can you show others God's love so they will want to know your motivation?

Lifeline:

You may be the clearest reflection of Christ that your friends ever see.

DELIGHTING IN JESUS

"For I was very glad when brethren came and testified to your truth, that is, how you are walking in truth. I have no greater joy than this, to hear of my children walking in the truth."

↝ 3 John 3-4

While attending a class at the Focus on the Family Institute, I stayed with a host family who clearly demonstrated the love of Jesus in the way they loved each other and me, their guest. Dwight and Laura Cloud confirmed my belief that the greatest gift two parents can give their children is to love each other.

While visiting Dwight at his office at Focus on the Family, he told me there was something I had to hear. He called home and got his youngest son, Cole, on the phone. Dwight handed me the receiver and Cole said, "Mr. Brett, I gave my heart to Jesus." Then Caleb, the older brother, picked up the phone and told me that he and a friend were talking about God, and Cole overheard them. Cole, being only three years old, didn't think he was old enough to be saved. Caleb replied that he wasn't too young—that if he told God he loved Him and asked to be saved, he *would* be. So right then and there, two five-year-olds prayed with a three-year-old, and Cole gave his heart to Jesus.

Psalm 37:4 says, "Delight yourself in the Lord; and He will give you the desires of your heart." Dwight and Laura delight in Jesus and have committed their hearts and family to Him. They would be the first to tell you they are not a perfect family. They encounter overwhelming struggles, challenges, and temptations as they attempt to live as godly parents and spouses. They experience the same frustrations as you and your family do, yet they deeply desire to remain in His will. I really believe that God is proud of His children Dwight and Laura Cloud for attempting to raise kids His way. I know I am.

Discussion Starters:

1. In what ways do you delight in Jesus? How does "walking in truth" show your love for Him?
2. What are the "desires of your heart" today?
3. Read Matthew 18:1-6. What is the importance of having childlike faith?

Lifeline:

How are you preparing your heart to be a godly friend to others? In what ways are you trying to be like Jesus?

JuDe

Jude, half brother to Jesus and brother to James, became a believer as an adult after the resurrection of Jesus. Jude's letter is a spiritual diagnosis of Christ's church. He presents an uncompromising warning and an unbending statement of faith. Jude encourages and challenges us to "contend earnestly for the faith" and to know the faith we profess so we can live out the true gospel. We are warned of many deceivers who will try to cause us to compromise our trust in Jesus. These godless men may even infiltrate our church bodies to create deceit and doubt. As you read Jude's powerful message, think about your own church. What is your church body's spiritual diagnosis?

You'll enjoy Brett Causey's insights again in this section.

SHAME FOR HIS NAME

"For certain persons have crept in unnoticed, those who were long beforehand marked out for this condemnation, ungodly persons who turn the grace of our God into licentiousness and deny our only Master and Lord, Jesus Christ."

⏎ Jude 4

Jude wrote about people who will call Christians names and hurl insults at our God and us. They will try every possible way to plant doubts in our minds. These people serve only themselves by pursuing lust, sex outside of marriage, and other evil desires. If you stand up unashamedly for your faith, consequences are inevitable.

You might be called names. You might be the last one chosen. Maybe you will be sitting at home on Saturday night while everyone else is out partying. You may not be asked to a school dance. Or perhaps you're an excellent employee yet never get a promotion at work.

When we place our faith in Jesus, our priorities shift from those of the world to His. Yes, choosing His way may be costly if we lose friends. But if we decide *not* to choose Jesus, the cost is higher—the loss of our souls.

We serve a God who will never forsake us. He does not abandon us to do battle by ourselves. He fights the war with us. He is our champion! We know He is who He says He is because of the change in our hearts and lives. When the world comes against us and we suffer because we're Christians, we need to remember that our faith cost Jesus His very life. Do not let Jesus' death be in vain! It is time for us to stand boldly for Christ!

Discussion Starters:

1. Have you ever been ashamed to admit you were a Christian? If so, why? How could you act more boldly to demonstrate your love for Jesus?
2. Are you counting on Jesus' death on the cross for your salvation? Are you expecting Him to stand up for you on judgment day? If so, what are you currently doing to stand up for Him?
3. If a stranger observed you for a week, would he or she be quick to witness your faith in Christ? Why or why not?

Lifeline:

Read Jude 12-13. This is a description of people without God. Contrast the passage with verses 20-23, a description of people who depend on God. Which description do you desire to be true of you? How can you make sure it is true of you?

DiGGiNG DeePeR

As you round third base in your progress through this book and begin the home stretch, I'd like to take you on a quest that will help sink your roots several feet deeper into the rich soil of Scripture and all it can do in your life.

In psychological circles it is said that it takes 21 days to establish a habit, either for better or worse. The remainder of this book will be devoted to creating the best habit you will ever develop—reading and applying God's Word in practical ways. You'll find 21 final devotionals to start you on your quest. But I suggest you spend *two* days on each devotional, thereby doubling the 21-day "habit forming" time and making sure the habit sticks.

I've selected 21 crucial truths I believe God wants every teenager to know the most. Set aside time each day to complete each devotional. Perhaps you can read the Scripture passages on the first day, and just spend some time thinking about them and letting them soak in. On the second day, you can answer the questions that are provided. That way you won't feel rushed on either day. It's important to first be clear about what the Bible is saying, and only then try to see how it might apply specifically to you.

Up till now, I hope you have been sharing your devotionals verbally, especially within the context of your family. If not, the practice can be a huge leap into an adventure-filled daily walk with God. But from this point on, you will be combining various cross-referenced scriptures and then recording your insights on paper. This habit, once established, can take you into a more insightful spiritual realm that may be new to you.

So get ready to embark on a discipline I hope will continue until you meet Jesus face-to-face. Here are a few guidelines to get you started.

1. Whether you complete your devotionals alone or with someone you love, have another person hold you accountable for finishing the 42-day experiment. (I suggest that a parent and a teenage son or daughter work together.)

2. Study each passage carefully. Try to determine, "What is God saying?" Look hard for insights and tidbits of wisdom. If you don't understand a passage as it is printed in this book, read the account from your Bible. You can see what has been happening, fill in any portions that have been abbreviated, and put the verse or passage in a more understandable context.

3. Compare and contrast the Old Testament passage and the New Testament passage. See how they relate to each other.

4. Answer the observation questions with as much thought and detail as possible.

5. Look for personal insights that the printed questions don't touch on. Write down your thoughts. Dig deep! Search for truth like you're digging for nuggets in a rich gold mine.

6. Next, and most importantly, write down ways that the scripture affects you personally! Ask and answer questions such as "Knowing this, what changes do I need to make in my life?" and "What would God have me *do* now that I've seen these truths more clearly?"

7. Prayer is the dessert after feeding your soul on God's Word! The A-C-T-S prayer guide is a great technique for being more comprehensive and specific in your prayers.

Adoration is telling God why and how much you love Him.

Confession is identifying your sins and telling God you're sorry. It should be followed by heartfelt *repentance*, which means, "about-face, heading in the opposite direction."

Thanksgiving is simply expressing appreciation for all God has done in your life.

Supplication is prayer on behalf of others, taking their needs and concerns before God's throne of grace.

My precious wife, Debbie-Jo, joined me in preparing the following material.

Days 1 and 2: Understanding God's Word

OLD TESTAMENT VIEWPOINT
"How can a young man keep his way pure? By keeping it according to Your word. With all my heart I have sought You; do not let me wander from Your commandments. Your word I have treasured in my heart, that I may not sin against You. Blessed are You, O Lord; teach me Your statutes. With my lips I have told of all the ordinances of Your mouth. I have rejoiced in the way of Your testimonies, as much as in all riches. I will meditate on Your precepts and regard Your ways. I shall delight in Your statutes; I shall not forget Your word. . . . Your word is a lamp to my feet and a light to my path" (Psalm 119:9-16, 105).

NEW TESTAMENT VIEWPOINT
"Like newborn babies, long for the pure milk of the word, so that by it you may grow in respect to salvation" (1 Peter 2:2).

"For the word of God is living and active and sharper than any two-edged sword, and piercing as far as the division of soul and spirit, of both joints and marrow, and able to judge the thoughts and intentions of the heart" (Hebrews 4:12).

"But prove yourselves doers of the word, and not merely hearers who delude themselves" (James 1:22).

"Therefore everyone who hears these words of Mine and acts on them, may be compared to a wise man who built his house on the rock" (Matthew 7:24).

"So Jesus was saying to those Jews who had believed Him, 'If you abide in My word, then you are truly disciples of Mine; and you will know the truth, and the truth will make you free' " (John 8:31-32).

OBSERVATION: What is God saying?
1. Describe the importance of God's Word in the life of a believer.
2. What are three attitudes a true believer should have toward the Word?
3. What are three responses a true believer should have to the Word?
4. What four metaphors are used in these passages in reference to the Word?

PERSONAL OBSERVATIONS: What else of significance do you see God saying in these passages?

APPLICATION: How do these passages relate to me today? What changes should they bring to my life?

MY PRAYERS:
Adoration: Father, today I praise You for . . .
Confession: Father, I admit that it was wrong for me to . . .
Thanksgiving: Father, today I'm thankful for . . .
Supplication: Father, the people and things I wish to pray for today are . . .

Days 3 and 4: Understanding God's Creation

OLD TESTAMENT VIEWPOINT

"In the beginning God created the heavens and the earth. . . . Then God said, 'Let there be light'; and there was light. . . . And there was evening and there was morning, one day. . . . God made the expanse, and . . . called the expanse heaven. And there was evening and there was morning, a second day. . . . Then God said, 'Let the earth sprout vegetation' . . . and it was so. . . . There was evening and there was morning, a third day. . . . God made the two great lights. . . . He made the stars also. . . . There was evening and there was morning, a fourth day. Then God said, 'Let the waters teem with swarms of living creatures, and let birds fly above the earth in the open expanse of the heavens.' . . . There was evening and there was morning, a fifth day. . . . God made the beasts of the earth after their kind, and the cattle after their kind, and everything that creeps on the ground after its kind; and God saw that it was good. Then God said, 'Let Us make man in Our image, according to Our likeness.' . . . God created man in His own image, in the image of God He created him; male and female He created them. . . . God saw all that He had made, and behold, it was very good. And there was evening and there was morning, the sixth day. . . . By the seventh day God completed His work which He had done, and He rested on the seventh day from all His work which He had done" (selected portions of Genesis 1:1—2:2).

OBSERVATION: What is God saying?

1. What did God create on each day of Creation?
   Day 1:
   Day 2:
   Day 3:
   Day 4:
   Day 5:
   Day 6:
2. Reread Genesis 1:11, 16, 25-26; 2:1-2, looking closely at God's order of creation. How might this conflict with those who say both the Bible and evolution are true?
3. What was God's evaluation of His work after completing each "day"?

PERSONAL OBSERVATIONS: What else of significance do you see God saying in these passages?

APPLICATION: How do these passages relate to me today? What changes should they bring to my life?

MY PRAYERS:
Adoration: Father, today I praise You for . . .
Confession: Father, I admit that it was wrong for me to . . .
Thanksgiving: Father, today I'm thankful for . . .
Supplication: Father, the people and things I wish to pray for today are . . .

Days 5 and 6: Understanding God's Holiness

OLD TESTAMENT VIEWPOINT

"Who is like You among the gods, O Lord? Who is like You, majestic in holiness, awesome in praises, working wonders?" (Exodus 15:11).

"For God is the King of all the earth; sing praises with a skillful psalm. God reigns over the nations, God sits on His holy throne" (Psalm 47:7-8).

NEW TESTAMENT VIEWPOINT

"And the four living creatures . . . do not cease to say, 'Holy, Holy, Holy, is the Lord God, the Almighty, who was and who is and who is to come.' And . . . the twenty-four elders will fall down before Him who sits on the throne, and will worship Him who lives forever and ever, and will cast their crowns before the throne, saying, 'Worthy are You, our Lord and our God, to receive glory and honor and power; for You created all things, and because of Your will they existed, and were created' " (Revelation 4:8-11).

"And they sang the song of Moses, the bond-servant of God, and the song of the Lamb, saying, 'Great and marvelous are Your works, O Lord God, the Almighty; righteous and true are Your ways, King of the nations! Who will not fear, O Lord, and glorify Your name? For You alone are holy; for all the nations will come and worship before You, for Your righteous acts have been revealed' " (Revelation 15:3-4).

OBSERVATION: What is God saying?

1. How do we worship a holy God in practical ways through our daily lives?
2. If you had a top-of-the-line Lamborghini, a 10-carat diamond, or an hour to spend with Michael Jordan, to what extent would you treasure such things? How much higher and more valuable is God than any car, gem, or athlete?
3. What, then, should be our attitude toward God?
4. How do we offend the holiness of God by spending time and money on music or entertainment that profanes His name?

PERSONAL OBSERVATIONS: What else of significance do you see God saying in these passages?

APPLICATION: How do these passages relate to me today? What changes should they bring to my life?

MY PRAYERS:

Adoration: Father, today I praise You for . . .
Confession: Father, I admit that it was wrong for me to . . .
Thanksgiving: Father, today I'm thankful for . . .
Supplication: Father, the people and things I wish to pray for today are . . .

Days 7 and 8: Understanding God's Sovereignty

OLD TESTAMENT VIEWPOINT

"In the beginning God created the heavens and the earth" (Genesis 1:1).

"The Lord has established His throne in the heavens, and His sovereignty rules over all" (Psalm 103:19).

"Then the sovereignty, the dominion and the greatness of all the kingdoms under the whole heaven will be given to the people of the saints of the Highest One; His kingdom will be an everlasting kingdom, and all the dominions will serve and obey Him" (Daniel 7:27).

NEW TESTAMENT VIEWPOINT

"And He got up and rebuked the wind and said to the sea, 'Hush, be still.' And the wind died down and it became perfectly calm" (Mark 4:39).

"While He was still speaking, they came from the house of the synagogue official, saying, 'Your daughter has died; why trouble the Teacher anymore?' But Jesus, overhearing what was being spoken, said to the synagogue official, 'Do not be afraid any longer, only believe.' . . . Taking the child by the hand, He said to her, 'Talitha kum!' (which translated means, 'Little girl, I say to you, get up!')" (Mark 5:35-36, 41).

"God highly exalted Him, and bestowed on Him the name which is above every name, so that at the name of Jesus every knee will bow, of those who are in heaven and on earth and under the earth, and that every tongue will confess that Jesus Christ is Lord, to the glory of God the Father" (Philippians 2:9-11).

OBSERVATION: What is God saying?

1. Sovereignty is defined as supreme status, dominion, or power. How is God's sovereignty described in the Old Testament passages?
2. In the New Testament passages, Jesus demonstrated God's sovereignty by showing power over what three things?
3. What does Jesus' resurrection tell you about God's sovereignty?
4. What position of sovereignty does God award Jesus in eternity?

PERSONAL OBSERVATIONS: What else of significance do you see God saying in these passages?

APPLICATION: How do these passages relate to me today? What changes should they bring to my life?

MY PRAYERS:

Adoration: Father, today I praise You for . . .
Confession: Father, I admit that it was wrong for me to . . .
Thanksgiving: Father, today I'm thankful for . . .
Supplication: Father, the people and things I wish to pray for today are . . .

Days 9 and 10: Understanding God's Adversary

OLD TESTAMENT VIEWPOINT

"Now the serpent was more crafty than any beast of the field which the Lord God had made. And he said to the woman, 'Indeed, has God said, "You shall not eat from any tree of the garden"? . . . You surely will not die!' . . . Then the Lord God said to the woman, 'What is this you have done?' And the woman said, 'The serpent deceived me, and I ate' " (Genesis 3:1, 4, 13).

"You were in Eden, the garden of God. . . . You were the anointed cherub who covers, and I placed you there. . . . Your heart was lifted up because of your beauty; you corrupted your wisdom by reason of your splendor. I cast you to the ground; . . . You have become terrified, and you will cease to be forever" (portions of Ezekiel 28:13-19).

NEW TESTAMENT VIEWPOINT

"You are of your father the devil, and you want to do the desires of your father. He was a murderer from the beginning, and does not stand in the truth because there is no truth in him. Whenever he speaks a lie, he speaks from his own nature, for he is a liar and the father of lies" (John 8:44).

"Even Satan disguises himself as an angel of light" (2 Corinthians 11:14).

"Be of sober spirit, be on the alert. Your adversary, the devil, prowls around like a roaring lion, seeking someone to devour" (1 Peter 5:8).

"And the devil who deceived them was thrown into the lake of fire and brimstone, where the beast and the false prophet are also; and they will be tormented day and night forever and ever" (Revelation 20:10).

OBSERVATION: What is God saying?

1. Describe Satan as God originally created him.
2. What caused Satan's downfall?
3. What names does Scripture use for Satan? What metaphors are used?
4. How does Satan work to influence people? What is his goal in regard to us?
5. What is Satan's ultimate destiny? How can you avoid the same destiny?

PERSONAL OBSERVATIONS: What else of significance do you see God saying in these passages?

APPLICATION: How do these passages relate to me today? What changes should they bring to my life?

MY PRAYERS:

Adoration: Father, today I praise You for . . .
Confession: Father, I admit that it was wrong for me to . . .
Thanksgiving: Father, today I'm thankful for . . .
Supplication: Father, the people and things I wish to pray for today are . . .

Days 11 and 12: Understanding God's View of Sin

OLD TESTAMENT VIEWPOINT

"Moses said to the people, 'Do not be afraid; for God has come in order to test you, and in order that the fear of Him may remain with you, so that you may not sin' " (Exodus 20:20).

"But if you will not do so, behold, you have sinned against the Lord, and be sure your sin will find you out" (Numbers 32:23).

"Hate evil, you who love the Lord, who preserves the souls of His godly ones; He delivers them from the hand of the wicked" (Psalm 97:10).

" 'Also let none of you devise evil in your heart against another, and do not love perjury; for all these are what I hate,' declares the Lord" (Zechariah 8:17).

NEW TESTAMENT VIEWPOINT

"If we say that we have fellowship with Him and yet walk in the darkness, we lie and do not practice the truth; but if we walk in the Light as He Himself is in the Light, we have fellowship with one another, and the blood of Jesus His Son cleanses us from all sin. If we say that we have no sin, we are deceiving ourselves and the truth is not in us. If we confess our sins, He is faithful and righteous to forgive us our sins and to cleanse us from all unrighteousness. If we say that we have not sinned, we make Him a liar and His word is not in us" (1 John 1:6-10).

"No one who is born of God practices sin, because His seed abides in him; and he cannot sin, because he is born of God" (1 John 3:9).

OBSERVATION: What is God saying?

1. Describe and define sin according to Scripture.
2. How does sin affect our human relationships? How does it affect our relationship with God?
3. What sins do you currently struggle with most often?
4. What personal sin(s) do you tend to rationalize?
5. What is God's remedy for our sin problem? What is our responsibility in His solution?

PERSONAL OBSERVATIONS: What else of significance do you see God saying in these passages?

APPLICATION: How do these passages relate to me today? What changes should they bring to my life?

MY PRAYERS:

Adoration: Father, today I praise You for . . .
Confession: Father, I admit that it was wrong for me to . . .
Thanksgiving: Father, today I'm thankful for . . .
Supplication: Father, the people and things I wish to pray for today are . . .

Days 13 and 14:
Understanding God's Heart on Prayer

OLD TESTAMENT VIEWPOINT

"If My people who are called by My name humble themselves and pray and seek My face and turn from their wicked ways, then I will hear from heaven, will forgive their sin and will heal their land" (2 Chronicles 7:14).

"Delight yourself in the Lord; and He will give you the desires of your heart" (Psalm 37:4).

"The sacrifice of the wicked is an abomination to the Lord, but the prayer of the upright is His delight" (Proverbs 15:8).

"Call to Me and I will answer you, and I will tell you great and mighty things, which you do not know" (Jeremiah 33:3).

NEW TESTAMENT VIEWPOINT

"Suppose one of you has a friend, and goes to him at midnight and says to him, 'Friend, lend me three loaves; for a friend of mine has come to me from a journey, and I have nothing to set before him.' . . . I tell you, even though he will not get up and give him anything because he is his friend, yet because of his persistence he will get up and give him as much as he needs. So I say to you, ask, and it will be given to you; seek, and you will find; knock, and it will be opened to you. For everyone who asks, receives; and he who seeks, finds; and to him who knocks, it will be opened" (Luke 11:5-10).

"Whatever you ask in My name, that will I do, so that the Father may be glorified in the Son. If you ask Me anything in My name, I will do it" (John 14:13-14).

OBSERVATION: What is God saying?
1. God can do anything He wants without our help! Why does He allow us, through prayer, to participate in His plans?
2. Why does God ask us to pray before He grants us success?
3. Why do many prayers appear to go unanswered?
4. What does it mean to "delight yourself in the Lord"?
5. Why does Jesus ask you to pray continually about what's on your heart?

PERSONAL OBSERVATIONS: What else of significance do you see God saying in these passages?

APPLICATION: How do these passages relate to me today? What changes should they bring to my life?

MY PRAYERS:
Adoration: Father, today I praise You for . . .
Confession: Father, I admit that it was wrong for me to . . .
Thanksgiving: Father, today I'm thankful for . . .
Supplication: Father, the people and things I wish to pray for today are . . .

Days 15 and 16: Understanding God's Prophecies of Jesus' Incarnation

COMPARE THESE OLD TESTAMENT AND NEW TESTAMENT VIEWPOINTS

"But as for you, Bethlehem Ephrathah . . . from you One will go forth for Me to be ruler in Israel" (Micah 5:2).

"Jesus was born in Bethlehem of Judea in the days of Herod the king" (Matthew 2:1).

"Behold, a virgin will be with child and bear a son, and she will call His name Immanuel" (Isaiah 7:14).

"[Joseph] kept [Mary] a virgin until she gave birth to a Son; and he called His name Jesus" (Matthew 1:25).

"Behold, your king is coming to you; He is just and endowed with salvation, humble, and mounted on a donkey, even on a colt, the foal of a donkey" (Zechariah 9:9).

"They brought it to Jesus, and they threw their coats on the colt and put Jesus on it" (Luke 19:35).

"I said to them, 'If it is good in your sight, give me my wages; but if not, never mind!' So they weighed out thirty shekels of silver as my wages" (Zechariah 11:12).

"[Judas Iscariot] said, 'What are you willing to give me to betray Him to you?' And they weighed out thirty pieces of silver to him" (Matthew 26:15).

"For dogs have surrounded me; a band of evildoers has encompassed me; they pierced my hands and my feet" (Psalm 22:16).

"When they came to the place called The Skull, there they crucified Him and the criminals, one on the right and the other on the left" (Luke 23:33).

OBSERVATION: What is God saying?

1. Above are five of the 300 or more detailed Old Testament prophecies fulfilled by Jesus. Summarize them in your own words.
2. What do fulfilled prophecies tell us about God's Word?
3. Could anyone other than Jesus have fulfilled these messianic prophecies? Explain.

PERSONAL OBSERVATIONS: What else of significance do you see God saying in these passages?

APPLICATION: How do these passages relate to me today? What changes should they bring to my life?

MY PRAYERS:

Adoration: Father, today I praise You for . . .
Confession: Father, I admit that it was wrong for me to . . .
Thanksgiving: Father, today I'm thankful for . . .
Supplication: Father, the people and things I wish to pray for today are . . .

Days 17 and 18: Understanding God's Son

OLD TESTAMENT VIEWPOINT

"For a child will be born to us, a son will be given to us; and the government will rest on His shoulders; and his name will be called Wonderful Counselor, Mighty God, Eternal Father, Prince of Peace. There will be no end to the increase of His government or of peace, on the throne of David and over his kingdom, to establish it and to uphold it with justice and right-eousness from then on and forevermore. The zeal of the Lord of hosts will accomplish this" (Isaiah 9:6-7).

NEW TESTAMENT VIEWPOINT

"[Christ] is the image of the invisible God, the firstborn of all creation. For by Him all things were created, both in the heavens and on earth, visible and invisible, whether thrones or dominions or rulers or authorities—all things have been created through Him and for Him. He is before all things, and in Him all things hold together. He is also head of the body, the church; and He is the beginning, the firstborn from the dead, so that He himself will come to have first place in everything. For it was the Father's good pleasure for all the fullness to dwell in Him, and through Him to reconcile all things to Himself, having made peace through the blood of His cross; through Him, I say, whether things on earth or things in heaven" (Colossians 1:15-20).

OBSERVATION: What is God saying?

1. Isaiah wrote this and many other Messianic prophecies about the "Christ who is come" 800 years before Jesus was born. How did he know so many details about Jesus?
2. What is Isaiah saying in this passage about the Messiah who is to come?
3. "Messiah" comes from the Hebrew word *Messiach*. The same word in Greek is *Christos*, from which we get the word "Christ." These titles all mean "the Anointed One." Consult the Colossians passage and list five things that make Jesus Christ different from all other religious figures who were ever born.
4. How can these passages help you understand the concept of the Trinity of God?

PERSONAL OBSERVATIONS: What else of significance do you see God saying in these passages?

APPLICATION: How do these passages relate to me today? What changes should they bring to my life?

MY PRAYERS:

Adoration: Father, today I praise You for . . .
Confession: Father, I admit that it was wrong for me to . . .
Thanksgiving: Father, today I'm thankful for . . .
Supplication: Father, the people and things I wish to pray for today are . . .

Days 19 and 20: Understanding God's Sacrifice

OLD TESTAMENT VIEWPOINT

"They shall take some of the blood [from an unblemished year-old male lamb] and put it on the two doorposts and on the lintel of the houses. . . . The blood shall be a sign for you on the houses where you live; and when I see the blood I will pass over you, and no plague will befall you to destroy you when I strike the land of Egypt. . . . And when your children say to you, 'What does this rite mean to you?' you shall say, 'It is a Passover sacrifice to the Lord who passed over the houses of the sons of Israel in Egypt when He smote the Egyptians, but spared our homes' " (Exodus 12:7, 13, 26-27).

NEW TESTAMENT VIEWPOINT

"For God so loved the world, that He gave His only begotten Son, that whoever believes in Him shall not perish, but have eternal life" (John 3:16).

"By this will we have been sanctified through the offering of the body of Jesus Christ once for all. . . . He, having offered one sacrifice for sins for all time, sat down at the right hand of God. . . . Therefore, brethren, since we have confidence to enter the holy place by the blood of Jesus, by a new and living way which He inaugurated for us through the veil, that is, His flesh, and since we have a great priest over the house of God, let us draw near with a sincere heart in full assurance of faith, having our hearts sprinkled clean from an evil conscience and our bodies washed with pure water" (Hebrews 10:10, 12, 19-22).

"[You were redeemed] with precious blood, as of a lamb unblemished and spotless, the blood of Christ" (1 Peter 1:19).

OBSERVATION: What is God saying?

1. What was taking place during the occurrence of the first Passover? What future event did this ceremony symbolize?
2. Compare and contrast the Old Testament "Passover lamb" and the New Testament "Lamb of God."
3. Why does sin demand a payment?
4. Why was Jesus' sacrifice acceptable to God and sufficient for our sins?

PERSONAL OBSERVATIONS: What else of significance do you see God saying in these passages?

APPLICATION: How do these passages relate to me today? What changes should they bring to my life?

MY PRAYERS:

Adoration: Father, today I praise You for . . .
Confession: Father, I admit that it was wrong for me to . . .
Thanksgiving: Father, today I'm thankful for . . .
Supplication: Father, the people and things I wish to pray for today are . . .

Days 21 and 22:
Understanding God's Covenant

OLD TESTAMENT VIEWPOINT

" 'Behold, days are coming,' declares the Lord, 'when I will make a new covenant with the house of Israel and with the house of Judah, not like the covenant which I made with their fathers in the day I took them by the hand to bring them out of the land of Egypt, My covenant which they broke, although I was a husband to them,' declares the Lord. 'But this is the covenant which I will make with the house of Israel after those days,' declares the Lord, 'I will put My law within them and on their heart I will write it; and I will be their God, and they shall be My people. . . . . I will forgive their iniquity, and their sin I will remember no more' " (Jeremiah 31:31-34).

NEW TESTAMENT VIEWPOINT

"This cup which is poured out for you is the new covenant in My blood" (Luke 22:20).

"For this reason He is the mediator of a new covenant, so that, since a death has taken place for the redemption of the transgressions that were committed under the first covenant, those who have been called may receive the promise of the eternal inheritance. For where a covenant is, there must of necessity be the death of the one who made it. . . . And according to the Law, one may almost say, all things are cleansed with blood, and without shedding of blood there is no forgiveness" (Hebrews 9:15-16, 22).

OBSERVATION: What is God saying?

1. A covenant is an unbreakable promise made by God. The old covenant was written on tablets of stone. Where is the new covenant written?
2. What was necessary before the new covenant could come to pass?
3. How did Christ fulfill the requirements of the covenant?
4. What do the new covenant and old covenant have in common? How do they differ?

PERSONAL OBSERVATIONS: What else of significance do you see God saying in these passages?

APPLICATION: How do these passages relate to me today? What changes should they bring to my life?

MY PRAYERS:

Adoration: Father, today I praise You for . . .
Confession: Father, I admit that it was wrong for me to . . .
Thanksgiving: Father, today I'm thankful for . . .
Supplication: Father, the people and things I wish to pray for today are . . .

Days 23 and 24: Understanding God's Spirit

OLD TESTAMENT VIEWPOINT

"Behold, a group of prophets met [Saul]; and the Spirit of God came upon him mightily, so that he prophesied among them" (1 Samuel 10:10).

"So the Spirit lifted me up and took me away; and I went embittered in the rage of my spirit, and the hand of the Lord was strong on me" (Ezekiel 3:14).

NEW TESTAMENT VIEWPOINT

"I will ask the Father, and He will give you another Helper, that He may be with you forever; that is the Spirit of truth, whom the world cannot receive, because it does not see Him or know Him, but you know Him because He abides with you and will be in you. . . . But the Helper, the Holy Spirit, whom the Father will send in My name, He will teach you all things, and bring to your remembrance all that I said to you" (John 14:16-17, 26).

"And He . . . will convict the world concerning sin and righteousness and judgment. . . . But when He, the Spirit of truth, comes, He will guide you into all the truth; for He will not speak on His own initiative, but whatever He hears, He will speak; and He will disclose to you what is to come. He will glorify Me, for He will take of Mine and will disclose it to you" (John 16:8, 13-14).

OBSERVATION: What is God saying?

1. Compare and contrast the activity of the Holy Spirit in the Old Testament (before Christ) and the New Testament (after Christ).
2. Joel's prophecy gives an amazing description of the Holy Spirit's future role. When was this prophecy fulfilled? (See Acts 2:1-18.)
3. What are the attributes (characteristics) of the Holy Spirit revealed in the previous passages?
4. The Holy Spirit gives us comfort and courage in times of personal difficulty. When have you experienced His comfort and courage?
5. What two specific works or ministries does the Holy Spirit accomplish in a believer's life?

PERSONAL OBSERVATIONS: What else of significance do you see God saying in these passages?

APPLICATION: How do these passages relate to me today? What changes should they bring to my life?

MY PRAYERS:

Adoration: Father, today I praise You for . . .
Confession: Father, I admit that it was wrong for me to . . .
Thanksgiving: Father, today I'm thankful for . . .
Supplication: Father, the people and things I wish to pray for today are . . .

Days 25 and 26: Understanding God's Salvation

OLD TESTAMENT VIEWPOINT

"After these things the word of the Lord came to Abram in a vision, saying, 'Do not fear, Abram, I am a shield to you; your reward shall be very great.' Abram said, 'O Lord God, what will You give me, since I am childless, and the heir of my house is Eliezer of Damascus?' And Abram said, 'Since You have given no offspring to me, one born in my house is my heir.' Then behold, the word of the Lord came to him, saying, 'This man will not be your heir; but one who will come forth from your own body, he shall be your heir.' And He took him outside and said, 'Now look toward the heavens, and count the stars, if you are able to count them.' And He said to him, 'So shall your descendants be.' Then he believed in the Lord; and He reckoned it to him as righteousness" (Genesis 15:1-6).

NEW TESTAMENT VIEWPOINT

"If you confess with your mouth Jesus as Lord, and believe in your heart that God raised Him from the dead, you will be saved; for with the heart a person believes, resulting in righteousness, and with the mouth he confesses, resulting in salvation. For the Scripture says, 'Whoever believes in Him will not be disappointed.' . . . So faith comes from hearing, and hearing by the word of Christ" (Romans 10:9-11, 17).

"For by grace you have been saved through faith; and that not of yourselves, it is the gift of God; not as a result of works, so that no one may boast" (Ephesians 2:8-9).

OBSERVATION: What is God saying?

1. How does a person obtain salvation (eternal life)?
2. What amount of works can earn salvation? Why?
3. Who gets the glory for our salvation? Why?
4. What do you think of God's plan? (Can you think of a better one?)
5. How do you verify what you believe in your heart?
6. How does genuine faith differ from intellectual belief?
7. Salvation comes when you give your heart to Jesus, and His Spirit comes into you and takes control of your life. Has this happened to you? How can you be sure?

PERSONAL OBSERVATIONS: What else of significance do you see God saying in these passages?

APPLICATION: How do these passages relate to me today? What changes should they bring to my life?

MY PRAYERS:

Adoration: Father, today I praise You for . . .
Confession: Father, I admit that it was wrong for me to . . .
Thanksgiving: Father, today I'm thankful for . . .
Supplication: Father, the people and things I wish to pray for today are . . .

Days 27 and 28: Understanding God's Grace

OLD TESTAMENT VIEWPOINT

"The Lord is compassionate and gracious, slow to anger and abounding in lovingkindness. He will not always strive with us, nor will He keep His anger forever. He has not dealt with us according to our sins, nor rewarded us according to our iniquities. For as high as the heavens are above the earth, so great is His lovingkindness toward those who fear Him. As far as the east is from the west, so far has He removed our transgressions from us. Just as a father has compassion on his children, so the Lord has compassion on those who fear Him" (Psalms 103:8-13).

NEW TESTAMENT VIEWPOINT

"Now Saul, still breathing threats and murder against the disciples of the Lord, went to the high priest, and asked for letters from him to the synagogues at Damascus, so that if he found any belonging to the Way, both men and women, he might bring them bound to Jerusalem. As he was traveling, it happened that he was approaching Damascus, and suddenly a light from heaven flashed around him; and he fell to the ground and heard a voice saying to him, 'Saul, Saul, why are you persecuting Me?' And he said, 'Who are You, Lord?' And He said, 'I am Jesus whom you are persecuting, but get up and enter the city, and it will be told you what you must do.' . . . So Ananias . . . said, 'Brother Saul, the Lord Jesus, who appeared to you on the road by which you were coming, has sent me so that you may regain your sight and be filled with the Holy Spirit' " (Acts 9:1-6, 17).

OBSERVATION: What is God saying?

1. What theme do these two biblical narratives have in common?
2. Loving-kindness is love based upon what the giver (God) has done for the one receiving the love (us). What has God done for us that makes us love Him so?
3. How does God's grace compensate for our sin?
4. Why is it impossible to earn God's love?
5. Paul was very aggressive in persecuting Christians prior to his conversion. How did God respond to his hostility? Why?
6. How are you encouraged by God's grace to Paul?

PERSONAL OBSERVATIONS: What else of significance do you see God saying in these passages?

APPLICATION: How do these passages relate to me today? What changes should they bring to my life?

MY PRAYERS:

Adoration: Father, today I praise You for . . .
Confession: Father, I admit that it was wrong for me to . . .
Thanksgiving: Father, today I'm thankful for . . .
Supplication: Father, the people and things I wish to pray for today are . . .

Days 29 and 30:
Understanding God's Place for Me

NEW TESTAMENT VIEWPOINT

I'm in Christ. *"Therefore if anyone is in Christ, he is a new creature; the old things passed away; behold, new things have come"* (2 Corinthians 5:17).

Jesus is my friend. *"No longer do I call you slaves, for the slave does not know what his master is doing; but I have called you friends, for all things that I have heard from My Father I have made known to you"* (John 15:15).

I am not condemned. *"Therefore there is now no condemnation for those who are in Christ Jesus. For the law of the Spirit of life in Christ Jesus has set you free from the law of sin and of death"* (Romans 8:1-2).

I am Christ's ambassador. *"You will receive power when the Holy Spirit has come upon you; and you shall be My witnesses both in Jerusalem, and in all Judea and Samaria, and even to the remotest part of the earth"* (Acts 1:8).

My body is His temple. *"Do you not know that you are a temple of God and that the Spirit of God dwells in you?"* (1 Corinthians 3:16).

OBSERVATION: What is God saying?

1. From these verses, describe a Christian's relationship with Christ (from God's viewpoint).
2. Give some personal examples of what it means to you to be:
   - Jesus' friend—
   - Forgiven—
   - A temple in which His Spirit lives—
   - An ambassador to represent Jesus on earth—
3. How would your life change if you really believed all these truths and thought about them more often?

PERSONAL OBSERVATIONS: What else of significance do you see God saying in these passages?

APPLICATION: How do these passages relate to me today? What changes should they bring to my life?

MY PRAYERS:

Adoration: Father, today I praise You for . . .

Confession: Father, I admit that it was wrong for me to . . .

Thanksgiving: Father, today I'm thankful for . . .

Supplication: Father, the people and things I wish to pray for today are . . .

Days 31 and 32: Understanding God's Mercy

OLD TESTAMENT VIEWPOINT

"The Lord looked at [Gideon] and said, 'Go in this your strength and deliver Israel from the hand of Midian. Have I not sent you?' He said to Him, 'O Lord, how shall I deliver Israel? Behold, my family is the least in Manasseh, and I am the youngest in my father's house.' But the Lord said to him, 'Surely I will be with you, and you shall defeat Midian as one man.' . . . The Lord said to Gideon, 'I will deliver you with the 300 men who lapped [water] and will give the Midianites into your hands.' . . . When they blew 300 trumpets, the Lord set the sword of one against another even throughout the whole army; and the army fled" (Judges 6:14-16; 7:7, 22).

NEW TESTAMENT VIEWPOINT

"The scribes and the Pharisees brought a woman caught in adultery, and . . . said to [Jesus], 'Teacher, this woman has been caught in adultery, in the very act. Now in the Law Moses commanded us to stone such women; what then do You say?' . . . When they persisted in asking Him, He straightened up, and said to them, 'He who is without sin among you, let him be the first to throw a stone at her.' . . . They began to go out one by one. . . . Straightening up, Jesus said to her, 'Woman, where are they? Did no one condemn you?' She said, 'No one, Lord.' And Jesus said, 'I do not condemn you, either. Go. From now on sin no more' " (John 8:3-11).

OBSERVATION: What is God saying?

1. Mercy is defined as "not receiving a judgment or punishment we deserve." How do you see mercy being demonstrated to the Old Testament Israelites? To the woman caught in adultery?
2. What is significant about Gideon being the "least" and the "youngest"?
3. Gideon began with 32,000 soldiers. Why did God want him reduce the army to 300 against an enormous and powerful enemy?
4. What similarities do you see between God's mercy to Israel and Jesus' mercy to the sinful woman?
5. What do these two accounts tell you about God's heart for you?

PERSONAL OBSERVATIONS: What else of significance do you see God saying in these passages?

APPLICATION: How do these passages relate to me today? What changes should they bring to my life?

MY PRAYERS:

Adoration: Father, today I praise You for . . .
Confession: Father, I admit that it was wrong for me to . . .
Thanksgiving: Father, today I'm thankful for . . .
Supplication: Father, the people and things I wish to pray for today are . . .

Days 33 and 34: Understanding God's Blessings

OLD TESTAMENT VIEWPOINT

"How blessed is the man who does not walk in the counsel of the wicked, nor stand in the path of sinners, nor sit in the seat of scoffers! But his delight is in the law of the Lord, and in His law he meditates day and night. He will be like a tree firmly planted by streams of water, which yields its fruit in its season, and its leaf does not wither; and in whatever he does, he prospers" (Psalm 1:1-3).

NEW TESTAMENT VIEWPOINT

"Blessed are the poor in spirit, for theirs is the kingdom of heaven.
Blessed are those who mourn, for they shall be comforted.
Blessed are the gentle, for they shall inherit the earth.
Blessed are those who hunger and thirst for righteousness, for they shall be satisfied.
Blessed are the merciful, for they shall receive mercy.
Blessed are the pure in heart, for they shall see God.
Blessed are the peacemakers, for they shall be called sons of God.
Blessed are those who have been persecuted for the sake of righteousness, for theirs is the kingdom of heaven" (Matthew 5:3-10).

OBSERVATION: What is God saying?

1. The term *blessed* means "happy, content, satisfied, and fulfilled." What are three choices you could make that might hinder God's blessings in your life?
2. What kinds of people are mentioned to whom God promises to give His blessings?
3. What are three things that delight you?
4. To be "poor in spirit" means to be like a humble beggar coming to God, trusting in Him alone for your joy and fulfillment. Why does God want us to come to Him in need, with our hands open and empty?
5. Hungering and thirsting for food is easy to understand. What does it mean to hunger and thirst for righteousness?

PERSONAL OBSERVATIONS: What else of significance do you see God saying in these passages?

APPLICATION: How do these passages relate to me today? What changes should they bring to my life?

MY PRAYERS:

Adoration: Father, today I praise You for . . .
Confession: Father, I admit that it was wrong for me to . . .
Thanksgiving: Father, today I'm thankful for . . .
Supplication: Father, the people and things I wish to pray for today are . . .

Days 35 and 36:
Understanding God's Eternal Plan

OLD TESTAMENT VIEWPOINT
"Enoch walked with God; and he was not, for God took him" (Genesis 5:24).

"Then the woman said to Elijah, 'Now I know that you are a man of God and that the word of the Lord in your mouth is truth' " (1 Kings 17:24).

NEW TESTAMENT VIEWPOINT
"I am the way, and the truth, and the life; no one comes to the Father but through Me" (John 14:6).

"And [the thief on the cross] was saying, 'Jesus, remember me when You come in Your Kingdom!' And He said to him, 'Truly I say to you, today you shall be with Me in Paradise' " (Luke 23:42-43).

"For the Lord Himself will descend from heaven with a shout, with the voice of the archangel and with the trumpet of God, and the dead in Christ will rise first. Then we who are alive and remain will be caught up together with them in the clouds to meet the Lord in the air, and so we shall always be with the Lord" (1 Thessalonians 4:16-17).

OBSERVATION: What is God saying?
1. How did each of these people express their faith in God?
    - Enoch:
    - Elijah:
    - Thief on the cross:
    - You:
2. According to Scripture, how can we be assured of eternal life in heaven?
3. What does the 1 Thessalonians 4:16-17 passage add to your comprehension of God's eternal plan?
4. What does this statement mean: "Born once, die twice. Born twice, die once"?

PERSONAL OBSERVATIONS: What else of significance do you see God saying in these passages?

APPLICATION: How do these passages relate to me today? What changes should they bring to my life?

MY PRAYERS:
Adoration: Father, today I praise You for . . .
Confession: Father, I admit that it was wrong for me to . . .
Thanksgiving: Father, today I'm thankful for . . .
Supplication: Father, the people and things I wish to pray for today are . . .

Days 37 and 38: Understanding God's Gifts

OLD TESTAMENT VIEWPOINT

"Now the Lord spoke to Moses, saying, 'See, I have called by name Bezalel. . . . I have filled him with the Spirit of God in wisdom, in understanding, in knowledge, and in all kinds of craftsmanship." (Exodus 31:1-6).

NEW TESTAMENT VIEWPOINT

"Since we have gifts that differ according to the grace given to us, each of us is to exercise them accordingly: if prophecy, according to the proportion of his faith; if service, in his serving; or he who teaches, in his teaching; or he who exhorts, in his exhortation; he who gives, with liberality; he who leads, with diligence; he who shows mercy, with cheerfulness" (Romans 12:6-8).

OBSERVATION: What is God saying?

1. We tend to think of "spiritual gifts" as a New Testament concept. But how was God's Spirit manifested in Bezalel? What other Old Testament figures who "received God's Spirit" in regard to a special task?
2. The Greek word *charisma* (interpreted "gift") means "a gift from God that brings you joy." What are some things you do for God that bring you great joy? Might any of these things be "spiritual gifts"?
3. Match the gifts listed in Romans 12 with these definitions:

_____ The ability to discern truth from evil and speak clearly the Word of God

_____ Delight in meeting the needs of others

_____ Research and presentation of biblical truths

_____ Motivating and encouraging fellow believers toward godliness

_____ Joyfully presenting gifts to God and His world

_____ Giving organization and direction to a body of believers

_____ An attitude of sympathy, empathy, and kindness to someone in need

4. Why does God give different gifts to different people in the Body of Christ?

PERSONAL OBSERVATIONS: What else of significance do you see God saying in these passages?

APPLICATION: How do these passages relate to me today? What changes should they bring to my life?

MY PRAYERS:

Adoration: Father, today I praise You for . . .

Confession: Father, I admit that it was wrong for me to . . .

Thanksgiving: Father, today I'm thankful for . . .

Supplication: Father, the people and things I wish to pray for today are . . .

Days 39 and 40:
Understanding God's Expectations

OLD TESTAMENT VIEWPOINT

"My son, keep my words and treasure my commandments within you. Keep my commandments and live, and my teaching as the apple of your eye. Bind them on your fingers; write them on the tablet of your heart" (Proverbs 7:1-3).

"There is a way which seems right to a man, but its end is the way of death. . . . A wise man is cautious and turns away from evil, but a fool is arrogant and careless" (Proverbs 14:12, 16).

NEW TESTAMENT VIEWPOINT

"Go therefore and make disciples of all the nations, baptizing them in the name of the Father and the Son and the Holy Spirit" (Matthew 28:19).

"For this is the will of God, your sanctification; that is, that you abstain from sexual immorality; that each of you know how to possess his own vessel in sanctification and honor, not in lustful passion" (1 Thessalonians 4:3-5).

"By this we know that we have come to know Him, if we keep His commandments. The one who says, 'I have come to know Him,' and does not keep His commandments, is a liar, and the truth is not in him; but whoever keeps His word, in him the love of God has truly been perfected" (1 John 2:3-5).

OBSERVATION: What is God saying?

1. Why does a sincere Christian want to please God with obedience?
2. How does the Holy Spirit enable you to obey God?
3. What would you say to someone who says he or she is a Christian yet willingly continues to sin?
4. According to Matthew 28, what is your main duty as a true believer?

PERSONAL OBSERVATIONS: What else of significance do you see God saying in these passages?

APPLICATION: How do these passages relate to me today? What changes should they bring to my life?

MY PRAYERS:

Adoration: Father, today I praise You for . . .
Confession: Father, I admit that it was wrong for me to . . .
Thanksgiving: Father, today I'm thankful for . . .
Supplication: Father, the people and things I wish to pray for today are . . .

Days 41 and 42: Understanding God's Prophecies of Jesus' Second Coming

OLD TESTAMENT VIEWPOINT

"Now at that time Michael, the great prince who stands guard over the sons of your people, will arise. And there will be a time of distress such as never occurred since there was a nation until that time; and at that time your people, everyone who is found written in the book, will be rescued. Many of those who sleep in the dust of the ground will awake, these to everlasting life, but the others to disgrace and everlasting contempt. . . . But as for you, go your way to the end; then you will enter into rest and rise again for your allotted portion at the end of the age" (Daniel 12:1-2, 13).

NEW TESTAMENT VIEWPOINT

"And I saw heaven opened, and behold, a white horse, and He who sat on it is called Faithful and True, and in righteousness He judges and wages war. His eyes are a flame of fire, and on His head are many diadems; and He has a name written on Him which no one knows except Himself. He is clothed with a robe dipped in blood, and His name is called The Word of God. And the armies which are in heaven, clothed in fine linen, white and clean, were following Him on white horses. From His mouth comes a sharp sword, so that with it He may strike down the nations, and He will rule them with a rod of iron; and He treads the wine press of the fierce wrath of God, the Almighty. And on His robe and on His thigh He has a name written, 'King of Kings, and Lord of Lords' " (Revelation 19:11-16).

"And if anyone's name was not found written in the book of life, he was thrown into the lake of fire" (Revelation 20:15).

OBSERVATION: What is God saying?

1. What names, terms, and symbols are used to describe Jesus in the previous passages?
2. What is significant about "the book of life"?
3. Who do you think comprise the "armies" that follow "the white horse"?
4. Do Bible passages such as these make you feel more frightened or hopeful? Why?

PERSONAL OBSERVATIONS: What else of significance do you see God saying in these passages?

APPLICATION: How do these passages relate to me today? What changes should they bring to my life?

MY PRAYERS:

Adoration: Father, today I praise You for . . .
Confession: Father, I admit that it was wrong for me to . . .
Thanksgiving: Father, today I'm thankful for . . .
Supplication: Father, the people and things I wish to pray for today are . . .

BOOST YOUR FAMILY'S FAITH
More Great Resources From Dr. Joe White and Focus on the Family

LifeTraining

Help your teens (and the rest of the family!) establish a strong, lasting faith in God. This unique devotional from popular author, speaker and camp director Dr. Joe White equips parents and kids with tools to strengthen their spiritual foundation. There's even a section devoted entirely to memorization and 100 Bible verses no Christian should leave home without! Hardcover or paperback.

• • •

The "Life on the Edge Tour"— Coming Soon to a Community Near You!

Does a day and a half with your teens, learning ways to enhance communication, build your faith and strengthen family unity, sound too good to be true? It's not, and it's exactly what you'll experience at Focus on the Family's "Life on the Edge Tour." Featuring such captivating speakers as Dr. Joe White, *Brio* editor Susie Shellenberger, Miles McPherson and many others, it's the weekend conference your family will never forget!

Tune Your Teens Into "Life on the Edge LIVE"!

You give them the best advice. But sometimes counsel is better taken when it comes from an unbiased, outside but trusted source—like Focus on the Family's "Life on the Edge LIVE." Co-hosted by none other than author, family counselor and teen authority Dr. Joe White, this nationally syndicated live call-in radio show gives teens a safe place to talk about the issues on their minds *and* hearts. Listen along with them and spark conversations you never thought possible!

• • •

For more information about the ministry, or if we can be of help to your family, simply write to Focus on the Family, Colorado Springs, CO 80995 or call 1-800-A-FAMILY (1-800-232-6459). Friends in Canada may write Focus on the Family, P.O. Box 9800, Stn. Terminal, Vancouver, B.C. V6B 4G3 or call 1-800-661-9800. Visit our Web site—www.family.org—to learn more about the ministry or to find out if there is a Focus on the Family office in your country.

We are here for you!

Check your local Christian bookstore for these and other Focus on the Family resources.

WELCOME TO THE FAMILY!

Whether you received this book as a gift, borrowed it from a friend, or purchased it yourself, we're glad you read it! It's just one of the many helpful, insightful and encouraging resources produced by Focus on the Family.

In fact, that's what Focus on the Family is all about—providing inspiration, information and biblically based advice to people in all stages of life.

It began in 1977 with the vision of one man, Dr. James Dobson, a licensed psychologist and author of 16 best-selling books on marriage, parenting, and family. Alarmed by the societal, political, and economic pressures that were threatening the existence of the American family, Dr. Dobson founded Focus on the Family with one employee—an assistant—and a once-a-week radio broadcast, aired on only 36 stations.

Now an international organization, Focus on the Family is dedicated to preserving Judeo-Christian values and strengthening the family through more than 70 different ministries, including eight separate daily radio broadcasts; television public service announcements; 11 publications; and a steady series of books and award-winning films and videos for people of all ages and interests.

Recognizing the needs of, as well as the sacrifices and important contribution made by, such diverse groups as educators, physicians, attorneys, crisis pregnancy center staff and single parents, Focus on the Family offers specific outreaches to uphold and minister to these individuals, too. And it's all done for one purpose, and one purpose only: to encourage and strengthen individuals and families through the life-changing message of Jesus Christ.

• • •

For more information about the ministry, or if we can be of help to your family, simply write to Focus on the Family, Colorado Springs, CO 80995 or call 1-800-A-FAMILY (1-800-232-6459). Friends in Canada may write Focus on the Family, P.O. Box 9800, Stn. Terminal, Vancouver, B.C. V6B 4G3 or call 1-800-661-9800. Visit our Web site—www.family.org—to learn more about the ministry or to find out if there is a Focus on the Family office in your country.

We'd love to hear from you!

THE 100 BIBLE MEMORY VERSES EVERY CHRISTIAN TEENAGER NEEDS TO KNOW

(2 each week for 50 weeks)

Your word I have treasured in my heart, that I may not sin against You.

⤷ Psalm 119:11

1.   Mark 8:34
"And He summoned the crowd with His disciples, and said to them, 'If anyone wishes to come after Me, he must deny himself, and take up his cross and follow Me.' "

3.   Mark 8:36-37
"For what does it profit a man to gain the whole world, and forfeit his soul? For what will a man give in exchange for his soul?"

5.   Mark 9:42
"Whoever causes one of these little ones who believe to stumble, it would be better for him if, with a heavy millstone hung around his neck, he had been cast into the sea."

7.   Mark 10:8-9
"And the two shall become one flesh; so they are no longer two, but one flesh. What therefore God has joined together, let no man separate."

9.   Mark 10:45
"For even the Son of Man did not come to be served, but to serve, and to give His life a ransom for many."

11.   Mark 11:25
"Whenever you stand praying, forgive, if you have anything against anyone, so that your Father who is in heaven will also forgive you your transgressions."

13.   Mark 12:31
"The second is this, 'You shall love your neighbor as yourself.' There is no other commandment greater than these."

15.   Mark 14:62
"And Jesus said, 'I am; and you shall see the Son of Man sitting at the right hand of Power, and coming with the clouds of heaven.' "

17.   Mark 16:16
"He who has believed and has been baptized shall be saved; but he who has disbelieved shall be condemned."

19.   Romans 1:17
"For in it the righteousness of God is revealed from faith to faith; as it is written, 'But the righteous man shall live by faith.' "

4.   Mark 8:38

"For whoever is ashamed of Me and My words in this adulterous and sinful generation, the Son of Man will also be ashamed of him when He comes in the glory of His Father with the holy angels."

2.   Mark 8:35

"For whoever wishes to save his life will lose it, but whoever loses his life for My sake and the gospel's will save it."

8.   Mark 10:43-44

"But it is not this way among you, but whoever wishes to become great among you shall be your servant, and whoever wishes to be first among you shall be slave of all."

6.   Mark 10:6-7

"But from the beginning of creation, God made them male and female. For this reason a man shall leave his father and mother."

12.   Mark 12:30

"And you shall love the Lord your God with all your heart, and with all your soul, and with all your mind, and with all your strength."

10.   Mark 11:24

"Therefore I say to you, all things for which you pray and ask, believe that you have received them, and they will be granted you."

16.   Mark 16:15

"And He said to them, 'Go into all the world and preach the gospel to all creation.' "

14.   Mark 14:61

"Again the high priest was questioning Him, and saying to Him, 'Are You the Christ, the Son of the Blessed One?' "

20.   Romans 3:23

"For all have sinned and fall short of the glory of God."

18.   Romans 1:16

"For I am not ashamed of the gospel, for it is the power of God for salvation to everyone who believes, to the Jew first and also to the Greek."

21. Romans 5:1

"Therefore, having been justified by faith, we have peace with God through our Lord Jesus Christ."

23. Romans 5:4

"And perseverance, proven character, and proven character, hope."

25. Romans 5:8

"But God demonstrates His own love toward us, in that while we were yet sinners, Christ died for us."

27. Romans 6:17

"But thanks be to God that though you were slaves of sin, you became obedient from the heart to that form of teaching to which you were committed."

29. Romans 8:1

"Therefore there is now no condemnation for those who are in Christ Jesus."

31. Romans 8:14

"For all who are being led by the Spirit of God, these are sons of God."

33. Romans 8:38

"For I am convinced that neither death, nor life, nor angels, nor principalities, nor things present, nor things to come, nor powers…"

35. Romans 10:9

"That if you confess with your mouth Jesus as Lord, and believe in your heart that God raised Him from the dead, you will be saved."

37. Romans 12:1

"Therefore I urge you, brethren, by the mercies of God, to present your bodies a living and holy sacrifice, acceptable to God, which is your spiritual service of worship."

39. Romans 12:4-5

"For just as we have many members in one body and all the members do not have the same function, so we, who are many, are one body in Christ, and individually members one of another."

41. Romans 13:1

"Every person is to be in subjection to the governing authorities. For there is no authority except from God, and those which exist are established by God."

43. Romans 13:14

"But put on the Lord Jesus Christ, and make no provision for the flesh in regard to its lusts."

45. 1 Corinthians 6:18

"Flee immorality. Every other sin that a man commits is outside the body, but the immoral man sins against his own body."

47. 1 Corinthians 6:20

"For you have been bought with a price; therefore glorify God in your body."

24. Romans 5:5

"And hope does not disappoint, because the love of God has been poured out within our hearts through the Holy Spirit who was given to us."

22. Romans 5:3

"And not only this, but we also exult in our tribulations, knowing that tribulation brings about perseverance."

28. Romans 6:23

"For the wages of sin is death, but the free gift of God is eternal life in Christ Jesus our Lord."

26. Romans 6:1-2

"What shall we say then? Are we to continue in sin so that grace may increase? May it never be! How shall we who died to sin still live in it?"

32. Romans 8:31-32

"What then shall we say to these things? If God is for us, who is against us? He who did not spare His own Son, but delivered Him over for us all, how will He not also with Him freely give us all things?"

30. Romans 8:6

"For the mind set on the flesh is death, but the mind set on the Spirit is life and peace."

36. Romans 10:10

"For with the heart a person believes, resulting in righteousness, and with the mouth he confesses, resulting in salvation."

34. Romans 8:39

"Nor height, nor depth, nor any other created thing, will be able to separate us from the love of God, which is in Christ Jesus our Lord."

40. Romans 12:21

"Do not be overcome by evil, but overcome evil with good."

38. Romans 12:2

"And do not be conformed to this world, but be transformed by the renewing of your mind, so that you may prove what the will of God is, that which is good and acceptable and perfect."

44. 1 Corinthians 2:2

"For I determined to know nothing among you except Jesus Christ, and Him crucified."

42. Romans 13:13

"Let us behave properly as in the day, not in carousing and drunkenness, not in sexual promiscuity and sensuality, not in strife and jealousy."

48. 1 Corinthians 9:24

"Do you not know that those who run in a race all run, but only one receives the prize? Run in such a way that you may win."

46. 1 Corinthians 6:19

"Or do you not know that your body is a temple of the Holy Spirit who is in you, whom you have from God, and that you are not your own?"

49. 1 Corinthians 10:13
"No temptation has overtaken you but such as is common to man; and God is faithful, who will not allow you to be tempted beyond what you are able, but with the temptation will provide the way of escape also, so that you will be able to endure it."

51. 1 Corinthians 13:5
"[Love] does not act unbecomingly; it does not seek its own, is not provoked, does not take into account a wrong suffered."

53. 1 Corinthians 13:7-8a
"[Love] bears all things, believes all things, hopes all things, endures all things. Love never fails."

55. 2 Corinthians 1:4
"[God] comforts us in all our affliction so that we will be able to comfort those who are in any affliction with the comfort with which we ourselves are comforted by God."

57. 2 Corinthians 6:14
"Do not be bound together with unbelievers; for what partnership have righteousness and lawlessness, or what fellowship has light with darkness?"

59. 2 Corinthians 10:5
"We are destroying speculations and every lofty thing raised up against the knowledge of God, and we are taking every thought captive to the obedience of Christ."

61. Galatians 2:20
"I have been crucified with Christ; and it is no longer I who live, but Christ lives in me; and the life which I now live in the flesh I live by faith in the Son of God, who loved me and gave Himself up for me."

63. Ephesians 2:8-9
"For by grace you have been saved through faith; and that not of yourselves, it is the gift of God; not as a result of works, so that no one may boast."

65. Ephesians 4:32
"Be kind to one another, tender-hearted, forgiving each other, just as God in Christ also has forgiven you."

67. Ephesians 5:4
"And there must be no filthiness and silly talk, or coarse jesting, which are not fitting, but rather giving of thanks."

69. Ephesians 6:2-3
"Honor your father and mother (which is the first commandment with a promise), so that it may be well with you, and that you may live long on the earth."

71. Philippians 1:21
"For to me, to live is Christ and to die is gain."

73. Philippians 2:3
"Do nothing from selfishness or empty conceit, but with humility of mind regard one another as more important than yourselves."

75. Philippians 3:13-14
"Brethren, I do not regard myself as having laid hold of it yet; but one thing I do: forgetting what lies behind and reaching forward to what lies ahead, I press on toward the goal for the prize of the upward call of God in Christ Jesus."

52. 1 Corinthians 13:6
"[Love] does not rejoice in unrighteousness, but rejoices with the truth."

50. 1 Corinthians 13:4
"Love is patient, love is kind and is not jealous; love does not brag and is not arrogant."

56. 2 Corinthians 5:21
"He made Him who knew no sin to be sin on our behalf, so that we might become the righteousness of God in Him."

54. 2 Corinthians 1:3
"Blessed be the God and Father of our Lord Jesus Christ, the Father of mercies and God of all comfort."

60. 2 Corinthians 12:9
"And He has said to me, 'My grace is sufficient for you, for power is perfected in weakness.' Most gladly, therefore, I will rather boast about my weaknesses, so that the power of Christ may dwell in me."

58. 2 Corinthians 9:6
"Now this I say, he who sows sparingly will also reap sparingly, and he who sows bountifully will also reap bountifully."

64. Ephesians 2:10
"For we are his workmanship, created in Christ Jesus for good works, which God prepared beforehand so that we would walk in them."

62. Galatians 5:22-23
"But the fruit of the Spirit is love, joy, peace, patience, kindness, goodness, faithfulness, gentleness, self-control; against such things there is no law."

68. Ephesians 6:1
"Children, obey your parents in the Lord, for this is right."

66. Ephesians 5:3
"But immorality or any impurity or greed must not even be named among you, as is proper among saints."

72. Philippians 2:2
"Make my joy complete by being of the same mind, maintaining the same love, united in spirit, intent on one purpose."

70. Ephesians 6:13
"Therefore, take up the full armor of God, so that you will be able to resist in the evil day, and having done everything, to stand firm."

76. Philippians 4:13
"I can do all things through Him who strengthens me."

74. Philippians 2:4
"Do not merely look out for your own personal interests, but also for the interests of others."

77. Colossians 1:15

"He is the image of the invisible God, the firstborn of all creation."

79. Colossians 3:13

"Bearing with one another, and forgiving each other, whoever has a complaint against anyone; just as the Lord forgave you, so also should you."

81. 1 Thessalonians 5:21-22

"But examine everything carefully; hold fast to that which is good; abstain from every form of evil."

83. 1 Timothy 2:3-4

"This is good and acceptable in the sight of God our Savior, who desires all men to be saved and to come to the knowledge of the truth."

85. 2 Timothy 2:22

"Now flee from youthful lusts and pursue righteousness, faith, love and peace, with those who call on the Lord from a pure heart."

87. 2 Timothy 3:17

"So that the man of God may be adequate, equipped for every good work."

89. Hebrews 12:1

"Therefore, since we have so great a cloud of witnesses surrounding us, let us also lay aside every encumbrance and the sin which so easily entangles us, and let us run with endurance the race that is set before us…"

91. Hebrews 13:4

"Marriage is to be held in honor among all, and the marriage bed is to be undefiled; for fornicators and adulterers God will judge."

93. 1 Peter 1:7

"So that the proof of your faith, being more precious than gold which is perishable, even though tested by fire, may be found to result in praise and glory and honor at the revelation of Jesus Christ."

95. 1 Peter 3:15

"But sanctify Christ as Lord in your hearts, always being ready to make a defense to everyone who asks you to give an account for the hope that is in you, yet with gentleness and reverence."

97. 2 Peter 1:6

"And in your knowledge, self-control, and in your self-control, perseverance, and in your perseverance, godliness…"

99. 2 Peter 1:8

"For if these qualities are yours and are increasing, they render you neither useless nor unfruitful in the true knowledge of our Lord Jesus Christ."

80. 1 Thessalonians 4:3
"For this is the will of God, your sanctification; that is, that you abstain from sexual immorality."

78. Colossians 2:9
"For in Him all the fullness of Deity dwells in bodily form."

84. 2 Timothy 1:7
"For God has not given us a spirit of timidity, but of power and love and discipline."

82. 1 Timothy 1:5
"But the goal of our instruction is love from a pure heart and a good conscience and a sincere faith."

88. Hebrews 10:24
"And let us consider how to stimulate one another to love and good deeds."

86. 2 Timothy 3:16
"All Scripture is inspired by God and profitable for teaching, for reproof, for correction, for training in righteousness."

92. 1 Peter 1:6
"In this you greatly rejoice, even though now for a little while, if necessary, you have been distressed by various trials."

90. Hebrews 12:2
"Fixing our eyes on Jesus, the author and perfecter of faith, who for the joy set before Him endured the cross, despising the shame, and has sat down at the right hand of the throne of God."

96. 2 Peter 1:5
"Now for this very reason also, applying all diligence, in your faith supply moral excellence, and in your moral excellence, knowledge..."

94. 1 Peter 2:2
"Like newborn babies, long for the pure milk of the word, so that by it you may grow in respect to salvation."

100. 1 John 1:9
"If we confess our sins, He is faithful and righteous to forgive us our sins and to cleanse us from all unrighteousness."

98. 2 Peter 1:7
"And in your godliness, brotherly kindness, and in your brotherly kindness, love."